PEERS, QUEERS, AND COMMONS

Britain, unlike most European countries, continues to deny gay men full legal equality. Why does the British political establishment refuse to accept equal rights for homosexuals?

In a fascinating and detailed account of the post-war gay movement, *Peers, Queers, and Commons* looks back over four decades of the struggle for dignity and human rights which led to the emergence of Gay Pride. Combining contemporary newspaper reports, articles, letters and cartoons, the book spans the anti-gay witch-hunts of the early 1950s and the Wolfenden Report in 1957, to the ten year battle towards decriminalisation in the 1967 Sexual Offences Act.

This up-to-date account charts the growth of the identifiable gay community in the 1970s. It also presents the first full critical assessment of the effects of Thatcherism in the 1980s. It documents a decade when the gay movement was forced on to the defensive by the twin pressures of the devastating personal threat of AIDS and a right-wing fundamentalist backlash. Its culmination is in an analysis of the notorious battle against Clause 28: a confrontation enlisting the rich diversity and strength of the gay movement, and powerfully demonstating its potential for future campaigning.

PEERS, QUEERS, AND COMMONS

The struggle for gay law reform
from 1950 to the present

Stephen Jeffery-Poulter

London and New York

First published 1991
by Routledge
11 New Fetter Lane, London EC4P 4EE

Simultaneously published in the USA and Canada
by Routledge
a division of Routledge, Chapman and Hall, Inc.
29 West 35th Street, New York, NY 10001

© 1991 Stephen Jeffery-Poulter

Typeset in Baskerville by Michael Mepham, Frome, Somerset
Printed and bound in Great Britain by
Biddles Ltd, Guildford and King's Lynn

British Library Cataloguing in Publication Data
Jeffery-Poulter, Stephen 1957–
Peers, queers, and commons: the struggle for gay law
reform from 1950 to the present
1. Great Britain. Homosexuality. Political aspects
I. Title
305.90664

Library of Congress Cataloging in Publication Data
Jeffery-Poulter, Stephen. 1957–
Peers, queers, and commons: the struggle for gay law
reform from 1950 to the present/ by Stephen
Jeffery-Poulter.
p.   cm.
Includes bibliographical references and index.
1. Homosexuality–Law and
legislation–Great Britain–History
2. Gay liberation movement–Great Britain–History
I. Title.
KD4103.J44   1991
306.76'6'0941 – dc20   90-47743
                                                CIP

ISBN 0–415–05760–4

*This book is dedicated to the fond memory of
Ken Stewart, who died after a full life in 1986. He will
be remembered by many for his generosity of spirit and
a unique gift for friendship.*

In the name of the tens of thousands who wore the badge of homosexuality in the gas chambers and concentration camps, who have no children to remember, and whom your histories forget, we *demand* honour, identity and liberation.

(Gay Liberation Front Pamphlet 1971)

CONTENTS

ACKNOWLEDGEMENTS

First and foremost I must thank Alan Jeffery for his encouragement, advice and unflagging practical support during the five years it has taken to write this book. Freida Stack, my tutor at Southampton University, first gave me the idea of writing a dissertation on gay law reform as part of my degree course in 1980 and was therefore most directly responsible for initiating this project. The definitive study of the 1967 Act by my professor, Peter Richards, in his book *Parliament and Conscience* was an important inspiration, and his interest in the project was much appreciated. For that initial study I was grateful to Antony Grey and Leo Abse for taking the time and trouble to discuss their role in the story; and to Christian Elliott of the Campaign for Homosexual Equality (CHE) for the information he provided about CHE's activities at that time. I was also indebted to the Albany Trust for allowing me access to their unique collection of newspaper cuttings stretching back to the late 1940s (which have since found their way into the Hall Carpenter Archive – and sadly out again). It was this dissertation which persuaded me to write an updated and much expanded history of gay law reform.

Gill Davies, my editor at Routledge, must take all the credit for seeing this project finally into print; her support to a first-time author has been unstinting, and her quick and efficient dealings at every stage of the process I'm certain could not be equalled. Fiona McIntosh played an invaluable role as my unofficial 'editor' over the book's long gestation period, reading the first draft of each chapter and returning it with copious notes, comments and criticism. She not only provided a sounding board for ideas but was a pillar of strength during moments of doubt and confusion. I am also grateful to Charles Laing for his painstaking care in proofreading the manuscript for me, and correcting (time and again) my favourite spelling mistakes. I am indebted to Sue and Peter Sheriff for helping me out of a practical crisis when the wonders of modern technology let me down at a crucial moment. My thanks must also go to Charles Foden (who might best be described as my *oldest* friend) for giving me the benefit of his opinion on my work in the light of more than 70 years unexpurgated experience of the gay world, and for providing me with the idea for the book's introduction. Pratap Rhugani's detailed notes and suggestions were invaluable in tightening and sharpening the final draft.

Once again Antony Grey and Leo Abse very kindly gave of their time to reflect on changes and developments over the last ten years, and in addition I would also like to thank MPs Chris Smith (twice), Robin Squire and Matthew Parris for giving me their opinions on parliamentary prospects for gay law reform and the attitudes of their own parties towards the matter. Professor Peter Campbell of the Conservative Campaign for Homosexual Equality (twice), Paul Cheesman of the Social Democrats for Gay Rights and Brian Stone of the Social and Liberal Democrats for Lesbian and Gay Rights (DELGA) provided me with help and information about the work of their respective organisations and the policies of the political parties in which they operate, for which I am very grateful. Nick Billingham and Peter Ashman of the CHE Law Reform Committee and Nigel Warner of Gay Lobby kindly shared their views and experiences of recent law reform campaigns with me on more than one occasion. And my thanks too to Michael Cashman and Tim Barnett of the Stonewall Group for fitting me into their hectic schedules. Jeff Dudgeon was extremely helpful in giving me details of his extraordinary personal campaign which finally brought gay law reform to Northern Ireland, and I was very pleased to be able to meet him in person for a useful discussion. Jim McManus was also most kind in providing me with background information about the Scottish Homosexual Rights Group and its history and campaigns.

If it hadn't been for the treasure trove of material which was stored for a brief while in the Hall Carpenter Archive at the London Lesbian and Gay Centre (LL&GC), which owes its existence primarily to the efforts of Julian Meldrum and the financial support of the GLC, I would probably have still been researching this book in the year 2000! I am grateful for Julian's help and observations in the early days of my research, and later I received considerable practical assistance from his successor Peter Daniels. However, I must record my considerable concern that the Archive has been split up: the lack of a central repository of cuttings and material on the Clause 28 campaign has severely hampered my research for the final three chapters and limited the range of material to which I had access. I know I only scratched the surface of the fascinating wealth of information which had been gathered together in the Hall Carpenter collection, and which represented a unique and precious record of a history which we are only just beginning to reclaim. I hope that the lesbian and gay community will realise how vital it is to retrieve the material and find a permanent home for it, since no one else is likely to care in the current climate.

Last, but by no means least, I am indebted to the coverage provided by the gay press from the original *Gay News*, through to the *Pink Paper*, *Capital Gay* and *Gay Times*.

Stephen Jeffery-Poulter
London
June 1990

INTRODUCTION
Medieval and monstrously cruel laws

I was walking along Princes Street towards my hotel. The war was still on, and the whole city was blacked out. In such dim lighting as there was, one could just make out the forms of passers-by – and I bumped into a tall figure in a foreign naval uniform. One of us struck a match to light cigarettes. He was a Norwegian sailor, typically Scandinavian in appearance, flaxen-haired and smilingly attractive. He may have had a few drinks, too: he was eager for anything, and perhaps lonely. (Loneliness is as strong an incentive, often, as lust.) I recalled that there was an air-raid shelter under the gardens a few yards from where we were standing. Neither of us could speak the other's language, but he readily came down to the shelter with me. Down there it was completely dark, but another match showed a bench running along one side of the shelter.... In a matter of seconds he had slipped his trousers half-way down, and was sitting on the bench, leaning well back. We embraced and kissed, warmly enough, but my interest was concentrated lower down, on a long, uncircumcised, and tapering, but rock-hard erection; and I was soon on my knees. Too concentrated, and too soon perhaps; for in a few moments the stillness of the shelter was broken by a terrifying sound – the crunching, very near at hand, of boots on the gravelled floor. Instantly the blinding light of a torch shone full on us, and a deep Scottish voice was baying, in a tone of angry disgust: 'Och, ye bastards –°ye dirty pair o' whoors...' No concealment was possible... and I stood up, to confront a young Scottish policeman... with an older special constable lurking behind him.

1

For the young man relating the story the consequences of this untimely interruption were potentially disastrous. The behaviour he was engaged in, although it only involved another consenting adult male and was taking place in circumstances which allowed for a considerable degree of privacy, could have earned him a prison sentence of up to two years. Apart from losing his liberty he would have been forced to resign the parliamentary seat he had so recently won, and would also have wrecked a highly successful career as one of the country's best known journalists.

However, the young Tom Driberg had already learned that his social position was a strong weapon in this type of situation. Regaining his composure he presented the policeman with his official visiting-card which established his identity as a Member of Parliament and the celebrated *Daily Express* gossip columnist 'William Hickey'.

> The policeman scrutinised the card gravely. Then he exploded. 'William Hickey!' he said. 'Good God, man, I've read ye all of my life! Every morning...' After a few more exchanges, he turned to his colleague, the special, and told him to go, saying he could handle the matter himself. My hopes rose a little, but it was not until he shooed away the Norwegian sailor... that I began to feel fairly safe, and suggested that we should continue our talk upstairs in the gardens. So we did. He was seven years my junior, but talked to me 'like a father'. I lied to him as convincingly as I could, swearing that if he would let me off I would never do such a thing again; it worked. In twenty minutes or so, we were good friends, on a writer-and-reader basis.... When we said goodnight, we shook hands, and he even gave a – not too formal – salute.[1]

Tom Driberg's life neatly brings together the most important strands of this book. He was a nationally renowned journalist for a deeply conservative newspaper which prided itself on upholding traditional Christian family values; an able politician who held senior posts in the Labour Party and influenced the policies of the Wilson Government; and yet with the tacit acceptance of many of his colleagues he was able to lead an uncompromising and highly promiscuous homosexual lifestyle. When he was brought before a court early in his career for alleged homosexual activity (which ironically on that occasion he had not actually committed) his employer, Lord Beaverbrook, ensured that the story was kept out of the national press, and his subsequent acquittal meant that his public reputation remained unblemished. Thereafter, the matter of his sexuality seemed irrelevant to his success, which in itself protected him from prosecution and exposure despite his continuing compulsion for making sexual pick-ups in public places which he later admitted were the 'Ruling Passions' of his life. The incident which he describes above provides a particularly appropriate starting point for a study of the changes which have taken place over the last 40 years in the legal and social status of homosexual men in the United Kingdom.

To begin with, it serves to remind us that any consideration of homosexuality and the law is directly concerned with actual sexual activity. Under English and Scottish law it has never been a crime simply to be homosexual – only to indulge in homosexual activity. (Lesbianism, on the other hand, has never even been acknowledged to exist by the law!) Up until the present century this generally meant that homosexuality was only punished when it intruded into the public domain, or as part of a deliberate campaign to improve public morality. This attitude, added to the strong social taboos forbidding any mention of the subject, inevitably forced homosexuals to meet in secret and encouraged the development of a clandestine homosexual underworld where social and sexual contacts could be made. This particularly suited the puritan morality of middle-class Victorian England whose decent citizens were more than happy to sweep all forms of sexuality under the carpet where they could be safely ignored.

The fear and ignorance which this situation bred among the general public inevitably produced the outraged but uncertain response of the policeman in Driberg's story. It was this embarrassed uncertainty which often enabled powerful men with wealth, social position or public standing to avoid exposure by bluff or bribery. These same reactions also underpinned the hypocritical double standards of English public life which permitted a successful man all manner of private vices provided he could prevent a public scandal. Tom Driberg clearly understood and played this system for all it was worth, although as a politician and a journalist he was in a strong position to influence the laws and attitudes which constrained his own sexual appetites. He never became publicly associated with the campaign for homosexual law reform, which would have doubtless benefited greatly from his experience;

3

instead he seemed to be satisfied with indulging his voracious promiscuity under the disapproving noses of the Establishment.

The lot of the homosexual has improved quite dramatically since the 1940s, and in particular since 1967 when certain aspects of homosexual behaviour were decriminalised. As public awareness has grown there was a greater acceptance of homosexuality, and this in turn permitted the emergence of a gay community with its own identity and lifestyle. A public admission of homosexuality is no longer a disgrace, and many openly gay men have successful careers in all sections of private and public enterprise, as well as in local politics and even in Parliament. By the late 1980s over 20,000 gay men and lesbians were to be seen marching through London every year celebrating their Gay Pride and solidarity. In villages, towns and cities all over the country gay couples live openly together and play an active part in the lives of their local communities.

Given the centuries of ingrained prejudice against homosexuality these achievements have been made very quickly, and with relatively little struggle. The lives of a whole generation of homosexual men have been gradually transformed over the last 40 years as British society has become markedly less puritanical towards sexuality in all its manifestations. Gay men, suddenly granted immunity from prosecution, quite naturally exploited this trend towards a more progressive morality to the full in exploring their new-found freedom. Since the basis of their oppression had related to their sexuality it was perhaps inevitable that their liberation focused their attention even more closely on that aspect of their lives. Commercial interests were quick to cash in on this overwhelming sexual need and by the late 1970s a thriving network of clubs, pubs and discos had grown up on the back of a new gay lifestyle based on frenetic promiscuity and unbridled hedonism. But this insular existence only helped to perpetuate the ghetto mentality which had existed before 1967. It was defended on the grounds that the prejudices of heterosexual society still oppressed homosexuals and therefore they could only free themselves from this oppression by the creation of a separate society. Some gay men rejected the selfishness of this 'scene' and tried instead to create alternative social groupings; others avoided specifically 'gay' environments altogether, arguing that their sexuality was an entirely personal matter which could now be expressed legally in private.

Meanwhile, the vast majority of homosexuals have remained trapped in secret double lives by their own guilt, doubts and fears. It is hardly surprising that attempts to build a gay community which appeals to millions of gay men whose only common link is their sexuality have so far met with little success. The combination of selfish sectional interests and continuing heterosexual intolerance has ensured that even today homosexual men have no effective national voice and very little political influence, although they form one of the largest minority groups in this country. This is despite the fact that gay men are still treated by British law as second-class citizens and therefore suffer various forms of discrimination in employment, housing and education. According to the judiciary, the civil service, most sections of the national and local press, and the police force, homosexuality is still regarded as 'contrary to public policy' and cannot therefore be accepted as an equally valid alternative to heterosexuality.

Although opinion polls taken throughout the 1960s and 1970s confirmed that the general public were increasingly viewing homosexuality with greater tolerance and understanding, by the 1980s there were clear signs that this trend was beginning to be reversed. In part this was linked to a growing backlash against permissiveness engineered by the right wing Christian fundamentalist lobby, whose reactionary opinions have been allowed to influence political decisions taken by the Thatcher Government throughout the last decade. But it was undoubtedly the arrival of Aids, conveniently labelled 'the gay plague' by the tabloid press, which has fuelled the increasing public intolerance against the gay community. Lacking even the minimal protection offered to other disadvantaged groups such as women and ethnic minorities by Equal Opportunities and Race Relations legislation, gay men and lesbians have been subjected to an unprecedented barrage of homophobic abuse in most sections of the press which has unashamedly encouraged an increase in fear and hatred of homosexuals among the Great British public. The moral panic which has been created over Aids has been used as an excuse by many sections of the media to give a public platform to organisations and individuals advocating compulsory screening and quarantine for its predominantly homosexual victims, and the return of criminal sanctions to prevent homosexual activity. This undoubtedly created the political climate in which the Thatcher Government was able to include the notorious Section 28 as part of the Local Government Act (1988) to prohibit local authorities from 'intentionally promoting homosexuality' as a 'pretended family relationship'.

It seems that the time is ripe for the gay community to assess how much real progress has been made towards homosexual equality over the last four decades. It is only by examining the errors of the past that realistic plans can be laid for the future, and the relative dangers of this latest threat to gay rights can be assessed. This is what I have attempted to do in the following chapters. Since it is sexual activity between men which has been singled out by the law, which has largely chosen to ignore lesbianism, this book inevitably looks at the law reform issue primarily as it has affected gay men. Whilst lesbians, both individually and *en masse*, have played a vital role in the struggle and I have acknowledged that wherever appropriate, a study of lesbians and the law deserves a separate volume which I do not feel qualified to write.

While homosexuality remained a criminal offence all public manifestations of it were inevitably of direct political relevance, and therefore the early part of the book covers a fairly wide scope. But with the growth and fragmentation of the gay community from the early 1970s onwards this approach would have forced me to take too many interesting diversions and inevitably it would have confused the narrative line and softened the focus of the story. Therefore, from 1967 onwards I have deliberately concentrated on the pursuit of gay law reform in the national political arena. Wherever possible I have used first-hand accounts, reports or letters from published contemporary sources and supplemented these by later written recollections, histories and biographies. As I was too young to remember many of the events in the first half of the book I have had personal discussions with a number of individuals who played key roles in this story to help me piece together an accurate picture, but I have not felt it appropriate to quote their private views verbatim, although their names are listed in the acknowledgment section.

I have tried to give a balanced account of this slice of recent gay history but it is impossible to be totally objective when dealing with such an emotional and complex issue as human sexuality. I believe that the right to express one's sexuality without harm to others is a fundamental human right, and that any decision to allow the law to interfere in the private sexual habits of millions of its otherwise law-abiding citizens is an unjustifiable infringement of civil liberties. In virtually every other country in Western Europe gay men enjoy much greater legal equality and protection from discrimination. With moves towards greater European harmony I believe it is high time that this country adopted the enlightened attitudes of its European Community partners.

Some 50 years ago such considerations of basic liberty were of practical relevance to the generation of young men fighting a war against totalitarian regimes built on prejudice and oppression. As the chaos of total war broke down the barriers of race, class and creed, traditional standards of morality seemed increasingly irrelevant in a dangerous world. Thrown together in an environment of all-male cameraderie which spurned conventional mores it was inevitable that many men found the opportunity to express their homosexual feelings for the first time. Charged with liberating Europe from tyranny it was not surprising that some began to question the barbaric laws which denied their freedom of sexual expression and looked forward to a post-war society which would respect their individual rights. Even as the Allies began preliminary plans for the liberation of Europe moves were already afoot to put pressure on the British Government to re-assess the laws against homosexuality. The following letter which appeared in the *New Statesman* in September 1943, reveals the terms of debate which were to become familar a decade later, as well as the strength of Establishment opposition which would have to be overcome.

The Home Secretary promises us improved conditions for the psychological treatment of prisoners after the war. It may be anticipated that homosexuals will form a large proportion of those on whom he wishes to experiment, in spite of public assertions by experts... that cure is impossible. His time would be far more profitably employed in revising the medieval and monstrously cruel laws which he now administers against these unfortunate people. It is the law which inflicts most of the psychological damage. What the Home Secretary proposes to do is akin to giving a patient a pound of arsenic with one hand, and treating him for chilblains with the other.... Surely it is time that the general public demanded a revision of the law on the lines of the Code Napoleon, accepted by most civilised countries a century ago.[2]

1

A FIT SUBJECT FOR MUSIC HALL HUMOUR: 1950–6

It is not a question of tolerance of things that are evil; it is a question of trying to understand what is going on. Until one can really understand it, how can one effectively deal with it?

Lord Chorley – House of Lords 19/5/54

INTER CHRISTIANOS NON NOMINANDUM

It is a disease which cannot easily be eradicated, being driven deeper underground, perhaps, when it becomes too blatant, but generally the efforts of the police can only result in a certain number of prosecutions and driving more offenders to other places.... The Victorian policy of pretending that unpleasant things do not exist is out of date and ineffective. They do exist, and are likely to become worse unless immediate action is taken.

The 'disease' which was causing so much concern to the citizens of Richmond according to this editorial in the *Thames Valley Times* on 4 May 1949 was, in fact, homosexuality. Despite its insistence that this unpleasant subject should no longer be swept under the carpet, the newspaper could not actually bring itself to mention the dreaded word, and instead merely made reference to 'a kind of "underworld" life'. However, to have broached the subject at all, even in such an oblique manner, was quite unusual at a time when any reference to such behaviour was strictly taboo both in the press and in polite conversation. This attitude was by no means a new one: half a century earlier public revulsion towards homosexuality was so strong that Oscar Wilde had dubbed it 'the love that dare not speak its name'.

The roots of this widespread fear and ignorance lay deeply buried in the Western Christian tradition. The Hebrew Old Testament contained passages condemning sexual activity between men (along with all types of sexual behaviour which did not produce children), and the story of the destruction of the cities of Sodom and Gomorrah was interpreted as a warning to anyone guilty of this terrible sin of the awful punishment which would be visited upon them by a vengeful God. The early Christian Church disapproved strongly of all sexual activity, although it did grudgingly allow sexual intercourse within marriage for the purposes of producing offspring. During the Middle Ages this puritanical attitude reached its peak and in England Ecclesiastical Courts had the power to punish individuals who broke the strict moral laws laid down by the Church. Anal intercourse, usually described as 'buggery' or 'sodomy', was dealt with only by these courts and any person found guilty of this 'crime' could be handed over to the civil authorities to be burnt. In 1533 as part of Henry VIII's reformation of the church in England the powers of the church courts were curtailed and 'the abominable Vice of Buggery committed with mankind or beast' became a criminal offence punishable by the State, and one which carried the death penalty.

This situation persisted for the next three centuries and although Robert Peel, the great reforming Victorian Home Secretary, carried out a major consolidation of the English criminal law in the 1820s involving the abolition of the death penalty for more than a hundred offences, buggery continued to be punishable by death. During the debates on these reforms the Victorian MPs could not bring themselves to use the word buggery and instead referred to it as the crime '*INTER CHRISTIANOS NON NOMINANDUM*' – 'not named amongst Christians'. After 1836 no further executions for buggery or sodomy were carried out and the death penalty for this behaviour was finally abolished in 1861, to be replaced by life imprisonment for the crime itself, and a maximium of ten years penal servitude for those merely attempting to commit it.

Two decades later the Criminal Law Amendment Act of 1885 introduced new, wide-ranging restrictions on homosexual behaviour by extending the scope of the criminal law to cover, for the first time, all forms of sexual activity between men, whether committed in public or in private. The Bill itself had originally made no mention of homosexuality and was intended to 'make further provision for the protection of women and girls, the suppression of brothels and other purposes'. However, a new clause was introduced by backbench MP, Henry Labouchère to provide that:

> Any male person who, in public or private, commits or is a party to the commission of, or procures or attempts to procure the commission by any male person of any act of gross indecency with another male person, shall be guilty of a misdemeanour.

It was late in the evening, the House of Commons was half empty, and the gentlemen who were present were much discomforted by the consideration of such unsavoury subjects. A single reservation about the relevence of Mr Labouchère's amendment to the issues under discussion was brushed aside by the Speaker and without further debate it was accepted as part of the Bill; although not before Sir Henry James had proposed that the penalty for such behaviour should be increased from one year's imprisonment to two.[1]

Such repressive legislation was becoming increasingly common during this period as politicians responded to the fears of the respectable and affluent middle classes that standards of sexual morality were declining and that the innocence of their children was being threatened by a rising tide of vice and prostitution. But even *The Times* had reservations about certain sections of this particular statute, although it did not make clear whether these extended to the Labouchère Amendment.

> There may be some changes lately made in the Bill which exceed the limits of sound policy and prudent legislation; but at this stage in the discussion it is better to accept some questionable provisions than to imperil the passing of the measure.[2]

As soon as the new Act was published correspondence in the press drew attention to the opportunities the Labouchère clause would provide for blackmail and dubbed it 'The Blackmailer's Charter'. More than 60 years later, in 1952, Gordon Westwood observed:

> the Bill that has provided thousands of pounds for hundreds of blackmailers in the last fifty years and inflicted the acutest agony of mind on millions of people was passed

10

without forethought and without discussion, and is still the law of the land today.[3]

A CONSPIRACY OF SILENCE

By the early 1950s anyone reading newspapers which specialised in the 'shock! horror!' school of popular journalism could not have failed to notice the growing number of reports of court cases concerning what was euphemistically termed 'improper behaviour' between males (the term 'homosexual' was noticeable only by its absence). The *News of the World* took a particular interest in this field and hardly a week would pass without an article giving a dry and carefully phrased account of one of these trials. The majority involved the 'seduction' of young boys by older men, many of whom were scoutmasters, teachers or clergymen. Alongside the smaller number of cases of such behaviour between pairs of adult males a new trend of 'chain prosecutions' seemed to be emerging. In one such case ten men, two youths and a boy of 15 appeared before magistrates at Dorking in Surrey charged with various kinds of 'impropriety' and were subsequently committed for trial. Invariably the police would start this type of investigation after the confession of one man had incriminated a second who would then, in turn, be persuaded to name others. Those who were convicted of this type of offence usually faced prison sentences of between one and five years, although gentlemen of otherwise good character often got off with lighter sentences.

In May 1952 the Editor of the *Daily Mirror*, Hugh Cudlipp, decided that the time had come to break this 'conspiracy of silence' and commissioned a series of articles entitled 'EVIL MEN' which appeared in the *Mirror*'s stablemate the *Sunday Pictorial*. Although Cudlipp later claimed that these were 'a sincere attempt to get to the root of a spreading fungus'[4] the total absence of objectivity and the tone of outraged morality smack more of sensationalism than sincerity.

The natural British tendency to pass over anything unpleasant in scornful silence is providing cover for an unnatural sex vice which is getting a dangerous grip on the country.... A number of doctors believe that the problem would best be solved by making homosexuality legal between consenting adults. This solution would be quite intolerable – and inef-

11

fective. Because the chief danger of the perverts is the corrupting influence they have on youth.... Most people know there are such things – 'pansies' – mincing effeminate young men who call themselves queers. But simple, decent folk regard them as freaks and rarities.... If homosexuality were tolerated here, Britain would rapidly become decadent.[5]

The deeply rooted objections to homosexuality expounded here were not grounded in religious dogma, but instead presented primarily in a social and medical context. Homosexuality is described as a sexual 'vice', implying that it is an undesirable habit which has been deliberately chosen; and once the idea of choice has been accepted it follows that other people can be persuaded to indulge in similar behaviour. Since the young are perceived as being the most sexually inexperienced and therefore the most susceptible to persuasion, they will be most at risk of being seduced into this terrible sexual perversion. And so the 'corruption of youth' theory has been firmly set in place – one of the most potent arguments which has continued to undermine all efforts towards homosexual equality throughout the last 40 years and remains as dangerous and insidious today as it was in 1952. Of course, once the nation's youth has been 'infected', then eventually the whole of society becomes riddled with this awful malaise which ultimately either renders it weak to enemy attack, or so rotten that it collapses from within – as did the once-mighty Roman Empire, according to some popular theories.

Nowhere in these articles was any evidence of a statistical or scientific nature produced to back up these assertions; the sources were simply anecdotal. Although it was admitted that there were homosexual men in all walks of life, and many had served with bravery and distinction in the Second World War, popular stereotypes were continually paraded and the prevalence of homosexual prostitution and promiscuity was exposed with prurient disapproval. The final instalment of the series looked at theories about the causes of the condition and revealed that current thinking in the medical profession considered homosexuality to be a form of mental illness. So, not only was homosexuality a sickness of the soul and therefore a sin, but it was now conveniently categorised by modern medicine as a disease of the mind. This therefore made a contemporary solution to the problem much clearer:

What is needed is a new establishment for them, like Broad-moor. It should be a clinic rather than a prison, and these men should be sent there and kept there until they are cured.[6]

Fortunately, for those wanting a calmer and more authoritative overview of the subject Gordon Westwood's book *Society and the Homosexual* had just been published, examining the social and sexual lives of homosexual men and the ways in which the existing state of the law affected them. In reviewing theories regarding the extent and causes of homosexual behaviour the findings of the Kinsey Report of 1948 were given considerable prominence.

more than one man in three has had some experience of homosexuality and of the unmarried men, over half have been involved in such behaviour. Kinsey's investigation showed that the frequency of overt homosexuality was much higher than had ever been realised at every social level, and in every age group, in every walk of life, in town and country, in single and married men.

From this study of 12,000 American men it had emerged that 4 per cent were exclusively homosexual throughout their lives, and that a further 8 per cent were homosexual for at least three years between the ages of 16 and 55. If these percentages also applied to the male population of England and Wales then at least 650,000 men were attracted only to members of their own sex, and a further two million had strong homosexual tendencies! Clearly society could not lock all these men up in prisons or mental hospitals, therefore Westwood went on to make a persuasive and cogent case for reforming the existing law which attempted to do just that.

Any law which is so remote from the real habits of the people that it turns over a quarter of the male population into secret criminals cannot be said to be fitted to the needs and lives of the men it governs.[7]

AN INDICATION OF MORAL DECADENCE?

Although this breaking of the taboo on the subject was an important step foward it was of little practical help to the growing number of men who were victims of what appeared to be a concerted police crack down on homosexuality. The number of offences of 'indecency with males' known to the police in 1952 was 1,686 compared to only 299 cases in the years 1935 to 1939.[8] Included among that number was the brilliant but eccentric mathematician Alan Turing whose wartime work in breaking the Nazi's secret Enigma code had not only earned him an OBE but had also laid the foundations for the invention of the first electronic computer. His uncompromising attitude to his homosexuality was now seen as a security risk and his successful prosecution for indecency resulted in him being required to undertake drug treatment which produced impotence and made him develop breasts. He committed suicide two years later at the age of 41.

Not only did this high level of prosecutions show no signs of diminishing during 1953, but in addition there were a number of cases involving well-known public figures. At the beginning of January Labour MP William Field was arrested in Piccadilly Circus and charged with persistently importuning men for an immoral purpose. At a hearing on 17 January Field pleaded not guilty and disputed the evidence of the two police officers who had arrested him. Field was found guilty on one of two counts and fined £15 with 20 guineas costs. Still proclaiming his innocence he lodged an appeal, but when this was dismissed in October he resigned his parliamentary seat. In the same month a well-known author, Rupert Croft-Cooke, was found guilty of offences concerning two young sailors and sent to prison for nine months. A fortnight later the recently knighted actor, Sir John Gielgud, pleaded guilty to persistently importuning for an immoral purpose in a public lavatory and was fined £10 by a magistrate who advised him to seek the advice of a doctor. However, all these cases were overshadowed by the scandal which had broken on 16 October when Scotland Yard announced that the debonair young aristocrat, Lord Montagu of Beaulieu, and his friend, film director Kenneth Hume, were to be charged with 'serious offences' involving two boy scouts.

On 1 November 1953 the *Sunday Times* became the first of the quality newspapers to comment on the startling rise in the number of cases of this kind. Although its leader article acknowledged that the growing public awareness of homosexuality made it necessary for a lead to be given in considering the issue, it went on to reiterate many of the old prejudices and myths surrounding the subject. It did, however, draw attention to the polarisation of attitudes towards homosexuality which seemed to be taking place in British society.

Public opinion here moves on two contrasted planes. The great majority of ordinary people view male inversion as an abomination which ought to be stamped out.... By contrast, sophisticated circles are apt to treat homosexuals with amused tolerance, to regard such inversion as a mere aberration, to argue that its practitioners are cases for the psychiatrist rather than the courts, if one need bother about them at all.

It was no surprise to find that the paper dismissed the latter view, arguing that every attempt should be made to discourage this 'unnaturalness' and suggesting that it could be curbed through self-control and moral rectitude. This reasoning was based on contemporary psychological theory that homosexuals were of two distinct types: a minority of 'inverts' who were congenitally predisposed to their sexual preference, and the majority of 'perverts' who adopted their homosexual habits as a deliberate preference.

It is not, in the long run, a socially uncontrollable phenomenon. If, for some, perversion is an inherent and deep-rooted psychopathic state, for a far greater number it is a tendency which can be resisted, sublimated, or never awakened.

On the same day the *News of the World* reported that judges around the country were expressing their uneasiness about the increasing number of cases of indecency between men; one had described the trend as 'an indication of moral decadence that is wholly regrettable', while another was of the opinion that 'People must be taught that this sort of conduct cannot be tolerated. It is bad not only for the individual but for the nation.' Many of these senior members of the legal establishment must have been surprised when the jury at the Montagu trial in December not only dismissed the more serious charge against the young Peer but also found themselves unable to reach a verdict on a second charge which had been brought by the Director of Public Prosecutions at a very late stage in the proceedings. A re-trial was ordered, but would be delayed for some months.

It is unlikely that it was pure coincidence that the issue of homosexual law reform was raised openly for the first time in the House of Commons on 3 December 1953 by Conservative MP, Sir Robert Boothby, and Labour's Desmond Donnelly.[9] They both called on the Government to set up a Royal Commission to examine the law relating to homosexual offences and to recommend any changes which might be made 'in the light of modern scientific knowledge and of recent discoveries in the field of psychology and psychiatry'. The Home Secretary informed the House that the problem was under consideration and he was therefore unable to make a statement about it at the present time. This did not prevent him from giving his personal opinions on the subject which played up the twin fears of the threat of homosexual behaviour becoming more widespread and the inevitable corruption of youth:

> homosexuals in general are exhibitionists and proselytisers and are a danger to others, especially the young, and so long as I hold the office of Home Secretary I shall give no countenance to the view that they should not be prevented from being such a danger.

Another MP seemed rather disturbed by this reply and suggested that a more sophisticated approach was needed:

> Is it not a fact that public opinion itself has been at fault for a great many years in treating the question of homosexuality as a fit subject for music hall humour... and that if the public itself can be persuaded to approach this matter in the right way from both the criminal and the medical point of view much good may be done?

But even the most optimistic advocates of change could not have foreseen that it was to be further bizarre developments in the Montagu case which would produce a surge of public revulsion against the excesses of the anti-homosexual witch-hunt.

LAW AND HYPOCRISY

Early in the morning of 9 January 1954 the unfortunate Lord Montagu, still awaiting re-trial, was arrested on new charges relating to improper behaviour which was supposed to have taken place between the Peer and two young airmen in the summer of 1952. Lord Montagu's cousin Michael Pitt-Rivers and his friend Peter Wildeblood, a journalist, were also arrested for similar offences with these men. At the opening of the trial in March the prosecution accused the three defendants of conspiring to incite Corporal Edward McNally and Aircraftsman John Reynolds into committing improper acts and unnatural offences by means of seduction and lavish hospitality.

As the Crown's case continued a number of disturbing and unexplained incidents came to light. Both Montagu's and Pitt-River's London flats had been searched in their absence, and without their knowledge or permission, by detectives who had not obtained search warrants. All three men had been denied access to their solicitors immediately after their arrest and Wildeblood's statement was subsequently ruled inadmissible as evidence on the grounds that it had not been made voluntarily. Lord Montagu's passport was discovered to have been tampered with and dates altered 'in a way prejudicial to his evidence' while it was in the possession of the police. In addition, public disquiet became focused on two fundamental aspects of the case. Firstly it was revealed that the two airmen had been promised immunity from prosecution if they turned Queen's Evidence (the police had, however, made no attempt to prosecute anyone else although both McNally and Reynolds had admitted to having sexual relationships with other men). Secondly the glaring publicity which had surrounded the arrests and the preliminary hearing at Lymington Magistrates Court (where an attempt to have the case heard 'in camera' was rejected), along with the reports of Lord Montagu's previous trial, must have inevitably prejudiced the opinions of the jury against the accused.

On 24 March all three men were found guilty: Montagu was jailed for 12 months, Pitt-Rivers and Wildeblood for 18 months. But as the prosecution's star witnesses McNally and Reynolds were bundled into a police car outside the court the waiting crowd booed and jeered at them, and when the convicted men were removed later their reception, as Peter Wildeblood subsequently recalled, was even more of a surprise.

the crowd began to press round us, shouting. It was some moments before I realised that they were not shouting insults, but words of encouragement. They tried to pat us on the back and told us to 'keep smiling', and when the doors were shut they went on talking through the windows and gave the thumbs-up sign and clapped their hands.[10]

This response was clearly not one that might have been expected from a public that was supposed to disapprove strongly of the crimes in question. In its editorial on 28 March 1954 under the heading 'Law and Hypocrisy' the *Sunday Times* expressed its dissatisfaction about the outcome of the trial:

> The law, it would seem, is not in accord with a large mass of public opinion. That condition always brings evil in its train: contempt for the law, inequity between one offender and another, the risk of corruption of the police.... The case for a reform of the law as to acts committed in private between adults is very strong. The case for an authoritative enquiry into it is overwhelming. An interim report under the auspices of the Moral Welfare Council of the Church of England has recently given that case clear support.

This far-sighted document referred to by the newspaper, emanating as it did from such a distinguished committee of the Church, gave a significant boost to those advocating reform of the law. The Report suggested that homosexual conduct should not be punished by criminal sanctions but left to individual conscience as were other sins like adultery, fornication and lesbianism. By arguing that the law should no longer interfere in the realm of private morality it decisively removed the religious foundations of the existing legislation against homosexual behaviour. It recommended that homosexual and heterosexual behaviour should be treated equally before the law with a common age of consent of 17, and that only homosexual activity in public or involving assault, violence, fraud or duress should be subject to legal sanctions.

The repercussions of the Montagu trail continued to rumble on in all sections of the press. A letter in the *Spectator* on 16 April suggested that the contradictory public reaction to its outcome was a clear sign that people wanted to see a change in the law.

> Laws are the subconscious expression of a country and it is precisely these collective twinges of guilt and perplexity that eventually create the mood for a reformer to uproot the causes. Inversion can never be abolished, harsh laws can. There are three prerequisites to most reforms: the maturing of public opinion, a sort of tribal guilty conscience and a courageous legislator. Judging by newspaper correspondence of the last few months, the first two conditions are here already. Perhaps the third – a spokesman with enough pluck and unselfishness to complete the trio – will soon appear. There are hopeful signs.

Even newspapers at the popular end of the market had begun to question the prevailing policy of repression. An article in the *Sunday People* argued that the Montagu trial had

> exposed the complete failure of our so-called 'civilisation' to find any remedy for sexual perversion to replace cruel and barbaric punishment.... Society must realise that imprisonment is no cure for abnormality.[11]

On the same day the *News of the World* revealed that a number of MPs intended to ask questions about the case in the House of Commons. Included amongst their number was Sir Robert Boothby who seemed to be emerging as one of the main parliamentary advocates of homosexual law reform. In February he had reiterated the case for a Royal Commission to examine existing legislation against homosexuality in a lecture given to the Hardwicke Society. He drew attention to the misery suffered by many homosexuals who lived in fear of the law and at the mercy of the blackmailer and extortionist. He maintained that the law was unevenly applied around the country, and that it only uncovered a tiny proportion of the homosexual acts and was therefore unfair and ineffective. He placed great emphasis on the Church of England Moral Welfare Committee's conclusion that although such behaviour was sinful it should not be treated as a crime. However, he did not underestimate the difficulties faced by the advocates of reform.

> I am well aware that this is not a popular cause.... Nevertheless, I believe that the magnitude of the problem and the amount of avoidable suffering that is being caused demand that it should be faced.[12]

In April, MP Desmond Donnelly made these same points in an adjournment debate which he had tabled to press once again for a commission to look into the laws on homosexuality.[13] Clearly the Government felt it had to do something to contain the growing public controversy surrounding the issue and Mr Donnelly was rewarded by the news that the Home Office would be setting up a departmental committee to undertake a thorough investigation which would 'throw useful light on the scope and nature of these difficult and controversial problems'. The clear hope that this concession would take the heat out of the situation was thwarted by the unexpected news that the Earl Winterton was to initiate a debate in the House of Lords on 19 May to 'try to bring the matter into better perspective'.[14]

In the opening speech of the first full-scale debate on the single issue of homosexuality in the history of the two Houses of Parliament the noble Earl left the the new committee in no doubt as to the conclusions he expected its as-yet unappointed members to reach with regard to this 'filthy, disgusting, unnatural vice'. After dismissing all the arguments for legalising homosexual behaviour on the basis of his 50 years' experience of public life (and the opinions of 'a legal acquaintance'), he felt sure that the committee would recommend that the existing laws be maintained, and he went on to conclude that

> the real remedy for the increase in this horrible vice is a greater awareness of its evil and a much greater condemnation by public opinion of those who are known to practise it.

His most valuable contribution to the discussion was his surprisingly accurate assessment of the Government's motives for setting up the inquiry.

> I know of no better method of putting off legislation than by appointing a committee. It usually does not report for a year or so – sometimes two years, and not until the next Parliament. And whenever the Government in power are faced with anything which looks like political dynamite they appoint a committee.

Speaking on behalf of the Government Lord Lloyd felt obliged to challenge the Earl's interpretation of certain 'facts' and suggested that any further consideration of the issue might be better left until the proposed committee had produced its report. Lord Jowett revealed that 95 per cent of the cases of blackmail that he dealt with during his time as Attorney General had arisen out of homosexuality. Along with many of his fellow peers he accepted that his own revulsion towards the subject should be put aside in order that the issue could be seen clearly.

> we are here face to face with a terrible evil and we have to try and find a solution which is not based on prejudice or on merely a dislike of what is a very evil thing.

The Bishop of Southall could not agree with these sentiments:

Once a people lets its ultimate convictions go, then there can
be no stopping half way, and the whole moral bottom is in
danger of falling out of a society.

The majority of speakers saw homosexual urges as some sort of
terrible affliction or curse which the committee might find some
way of alleviating or curing, and even those who supported reform
emphasised their strong disapproval of such behaviour. Lord
Chorley was one of the few speakers who rejected such uninformed
speculation.

I rather deplore a good deal of the discussion which has
taken place... because it seems to me it has taken place on
an emotional rather than on a scientific level... this very
difficult problem needs to be tackled in the light of cool,
clear scientific knowledge and discussed on the basis of facts
which have been ascertained.

A MATTER OF PUBLIC CONCERN

A couple of months after this debate Sir John Wolfenden, Vice
Chancellor of Reading University, received a message from the
Home Secretary, Sir David Maxwell-Fyfe, inviting him to an in-
formal meeting about a new committee which was being set up. A
few days later Sir John found himself by coincidence travelling to
London on the same overnight sleeper train as the Home Secretary
and sent a note to the Minister suggesting that they met there and
then in order to save time. As Sir John later recalled:

I suspect he had been half undressed when he got my
message. But he nobly put his overcoat over what was left;
and so it happened that my first conversation about the
whole business took place as we sat side by side on his
sleeping berth.[15]

Since the subject of this impromptu discussion was 'vice' it was
perhaps fortunate that the potentially compromising circumstances
of this meeting were not revealed until 1976!

A week later, in the more conventional surroundings of the
Minister's private office, Sir John Wolfenden was formally asked to
head a wide-ranging inquiry into the two issues of homosexuality
and prostitution. In August it was officially announced that Sir John
would be chairing the inquiry, assisted by 15 assorted worthies

including three OBEs, two MPs, a judge and a Marquess. In its
leader on 27 August 1954 *The Times* warned the members of the
committee that they would need

> unusual courage and common sense.... The crucial question
> before the committee is not whether homosexual relations
> are sinful, but whether the law should punish them as
> such.... The answer that the committee has to give, at once
> humane and just, cannot be easy and is bound to be con-
> troversial. But it is socially necessary that it should be given.

Arriving at the Home Office for the first meeting of his committee Sir John was greeted by the doorman: 'Vice, Sir? – Room 101'.
He started the proceedings by making some preliminary observations about the task ahead: the Committee would need to establish
one or two basic principles around which their recommendations
could be framed; these recommendations needed to be presented
clearly and simply so that they could be understood by any ordinary
member of the public; and that every member of the committee
should follow his or her conscience in putting forward proposals,
since whatever final recommendations were put before the public
a significant proportion of the population were bound to disagree
with them! To begin with, the Lord Chief Justice of England was
invited to give his views; he then, in turn, nominated two judges
with strongly opposing opinions to present the cases for and against
law reform. Sir John takes up the story:

> And so it went on, for two crowded years. We read moun-
> tains of memoranda submitted as written evidence; and we
> interviewed dozens of oral witnesses. We did honestly try to
> include all those who thought they had a message for us,
> whether they were aiming to be 'objective' or were explicitly
> 'subjective'.... From time to time facetious gossip column
> writers asked if we were undertaking first hand experience
> in relevant fields. For my part I thought it prudent to avoid
> public lavatories in the West End.[16]

During the first two years of the Committee's deliberations the
number of recorded offences of 'indecency between males' known
to the police jumped to their highest ever levels: 2,034 offences in
1954, and the all time record of 2,322 in 1955 of which 1,065 were
sent to prison. However, no public figures were involved, chain
prosecutions were less common and judges seemed less inclined to

imprison offenders, preferring instead to fine them or bind them over on condition that they sought psychiatric treatment. Although general media interest had dwindled back to the reporting of these court cases the *New Statesman* magazine bravely continued to espouse the case for law reform, and in January 1955 printed an article written by an anonymous 'biological' homosexual who painted a pitiful picture of the living hell which the existing law imposed on him and his fellow 'sufferers' and pleaded for an end to the situation. The reaction from the magazine's readers was swift, vitriolic, and in several cases, anonymous:

It is a long time since I read in the press a notice which is so shocking, and indeed disgusting as the article in your current issue.... The habit under question is one which I have always thought is talked about with bated breath as a thing unspeakable, and rightly so.... Who could assess the harm which might... be done by such an article getting into the hands of the adolescent or the man hitherto brought up to regard such revelations as a sealed book not to be opened by the person nurtured in moral and religious belief?

'Vice is a monster of such frightful mien,
As to be hated needs but to be seen,
Yet seen too oft, familiar with her face,
We first endure, then pity, then embrace.'

I can only sum up your contributor's article... as quite damnable, and I trust, sir, you will excuse the epithet as justified under gross provocation.[17]

Clearly, the repercussions of the Montagu trial were a mixed blessing for most homosexuals. Although it had instigated a national debate into the operation of the existing laws and thereby placed the possibility of reform firmly on the political agenda for the first time, by bringing the whole subject into the public arena it had inevitably sparked off deep fears held by the public who saw themselves about to be engulfed by a growing tide of vice, a view which was bolstered at every opportunity by Christian moralists. This situation naturally increased the everyday strains on individual homosexual men, as one of them later recalled:

The temperature of the time was quite unpleasant. We thought we were all going to be arrested and there was going to be a big swoop. The newspapers were full of it. I got so frightened I burnt all my love letters.[18]

Naturally self-preservation was at a premium and another man remembers using several ploys to protect himself from suspicion:

> I was fascinated that there were other people around doing the same thing I was doing. It was just a bit more serious because they'd been caught.... I just resolved to be inconspicuous and that would be why I even went out with women.... Nobody ever laughed at me or took the piss out of me like they did with people who were fairly obvious, and of course they got teased so much that I would avoid them like the plague. I probably took part in it, I've got to confess, because it would help to throw suspicion away from me. If I laughed at a queer, I could hardly be one: that's what I thought.[19]

Virtually the only area where positive images of homosexuality were appearing, almost unnoticed, was in a handful of novels which, for the first time, portrayed realistic homosexual characters as the heroes of stories set in the shadowy homosexual underworld of contemporary England. Mary Renault's novel, *The Charioteer*, was a powerful and moving story set in the Second World War about a soldier's struggle to accept his own sexuality and the choice he has to make between the pure, idealised love he feels for a young conscientious objector and his strong physical attraction towards a mature and confident naval officer.[20] *The Heart in Exile* by Rodney Garland used the device of an investigation by a homosexual psychiatrist into the mysterious suicide of his ex-lover to examine the prejudices against homosexuality which were prevelant in the early 1950s.[21] Today the book is perhaps more interesting as a social document than a literary classic, particularly in its apparently first-hand descriptions of the 'underground' of pubs and clubs which constituted the limited social environment available to homosexual men at this time in London.

Both these novels undoubtedly had a beneficial effect in countering the warped images of 'inverts' and 'perverts' so common in the popular mythology of the time, but the most significant contribution to presenting the human aspect of the problem was the appearance of Peter Wildeblood's autobiography, *Against the Law*, in November 1955.[22] The author's journalistic background enabled him to expose clearly the hypocrisy of the laws which had sent himself and his fellow defendants in the Montagu trial to prison for their unacceptable sexual behaviour. This account of his life, the horror of his arrest and subsequent imprisonment, and his emergence from the ordeal as a stronger and more honest person who was not ashamed to announce to the world 'I am a homosexual' was extraordinarily frank by the standards of its day. An attempt to prevent its publication failed – which doubtless gave a boost to its reputation and assured it a much wider audience.

According to Wildeblood the motivation behind the homosexual witch-hunt in the early 1950s was definitely political. This policy of repression originated in the United States where Senator McCarthy's hysterical anti-Communist campaign had been used as an excuse for a State Department purge of suspected homosexuals throughout the administration. There can be little doubt that the main reason for this move was the surprise defection in 1951 of the two British spies Guy Burgess and Donald Maclean, both of whom were known to be homosexual. Understandably the American security agencies put strong pressure on their British counterparts to weed out known or suspected homosexuals in sensitive government posts in order to prevent any further security lapses of this type.

After liaising with the FBI the new Commissioner of Police at Scotland Yard, Sir John Nott-Bower, initiated a full-scale policy of persecution. Of course, no mention of this appeared in the British press, but 12,000 miles away in Australia on 25 October 1953 readers of the *Sydney Sunday Telegraph* learned the full details of Sir John's crusade to 'smash homosexuality in London'.

> For many years past the police had turned a blind eye to male vice. They made arrests only when definite complaints were made from innocent people, or where homosexuality had encouraged other crimes.... Now, meeting Sir John's demands they are making it a priority job to increase the number of arrests.... Says Lieutenant Colonel Marcus Lipton, MP: 'The problem of homosexuality among Government officials... is of growing magnitude. These people, some of whom occupy important positions, are obviously a target for blackmailers.'

During his time in prison Wildeblood learned that the success of this campaign had been helped by the system of promotion in the

Police Force which depended very largely on the number of convictions secured by each officer.

> It is the number that counts, not the gravity of the offences concerned; and... it is very much easier to arrest a homosexual than a burglar. A policeman whose score is lagging behind that of his colleagues can always catch up by going to the nearest public lavatory, or merely by smiling at someone in the street.

The greatest impact of the book, now and at the time of its publication, lies in its honest and unsentimental examination of the emotional and practical difficulties facing an intelligent man whose sexual preferences made him a criminal. Wildeblood saw his abnormal sexuality as a disability:

> I am no more proud of my condition than I would be of having a glass eye or a hare lip. On the other hand, I am no more ashamed of it than I would be of being colour-blind or of writing with my left hand. It is essentially a personal problem, which only becomes a matter of public concern when the law makes it so.

This was certainly a more positive self-image than the notions of mental illness and deviancy offered by psychiatry at the time. Of course, the main reason why homosexual men were so often identified as psychiatric cases stemmed from the tremendous strains imposed upon them by the need to hide their true personality and feelings from a hostile world. For Wildeblood, his arrest was a welcome release from living a lie.

> I was forced to be deceitful, living one life during my working hours and another when I was free. I had two sets of friends; almost, one might say, two faces. At the back of my mind there was always a nagging fear that my two worlds might suddenly collide; that somebody who knew about me would meet somebody who did not know, and that disaster would ensue.... The strain of deceiving my family and friends often became intolerable.

Many men willingly accepted the advice of doctors and consultants who recommended them to develop their interest in women, marry and have children. In the long run this solution merely deepened their problem of leading a double life. Wildeblood rejected such a fraudulent and damaging charade.

I think it is more honest, and less harmful for a man with homosexual tendencies to recognise himself for what he is. He will always be lonely; he must accept that. He will never know the companionship that comes with marriage, or the joy of watching his children grow up, but he will at least have the austere consolations of self-knowledge and integrity. More than that he cannot have, because the law, in England, forbids it.

In the evidence he gave to the Wolfenden Committee it is likely that he made a considerable impact in arguing the case for reforming the law, although he had no way of knowing if his plea for justice would be heeded: 'The right which I claim for myself, and for all those like me, is the right to choose the person whom I love.'

2

TALKING
METAPHYSICS TO A
GOLDFISH: 1957-8

I believe that, ultimately, this reform will come. I am only
saddened by the fact that it should come only after a still
greater toll of human misery has been extracted by society.
Anthony Greenwood – House of Commons 26/11/58

IN PROPER PERSPECTIVE

On Wednesday 4 September 1957, after 62 meetings during which
it had gathered evidence from over 200 different organisations and
individuals, Sir John Wolfenden's Committee published its findings
in The Report of the Committee on Homosexual Offences and
Prostitution.[1] The Wolfenden Report, as it was more usually called,
made its final recommendations on both the topics it had been
asked to study on the basis of one simple fundamental principle.

We do not think that it is proper for the law to concern itself
with what a man does in private unless it can be shown to
be contrary to the public good that the law ought to inter-
vene in its function as guardian of that public good.

The section of the Report dealing with homosexuality started
with a comprehensive overview which examined and decisively
dismissed most of the common myths about the subject. It quoted
the relevant figures from Kinsey's American study and, although
accepting that most existing research on the subject in Britain had
been based on case histories of homosexual men in psychiatric or
penal institutions, stressed that the issue should not be seen predominantly in those terms since only a small proportion of these
cases had homosexuality as their root cause. The Committee concluded that:

homosexuality is practised by a small minority of the population, and should therefore be seen in proper perspective, neither ignored nor given a disproportionate amount of public attention.

There followed a review of the main arguments for retaining the existing laws against homosexual behaviour:

1 *Homosexual behaviour menaces the health of society and has led to the collapse of once-mighty empires.*
The Committee found no evidence to support this view.

> ... we cannot feel it right to frame the laws which govern this country in the present age by reference to hypothetical explanations of the history of other peoples in ages distant in time and different in circumstances to our own.

2 *Homosexuality has a damaging effect on family life.*
It was accepted that a husband with strong homosexual needs could certainly undermine his marriage and therefore his family, but that equally serious problems could arise if either partner in a marriage engaged in adulterous behaviour or if a wife had lesbian tendencies. There was no logical reason why homosexuality alone should be singled out for criminal punishment since in this respect it was no more damaging than these other practices.

3 *A homosexual man may corrupt young boys.*
The expert witnesses who advised the Committee distinguished between two separate categories of male homosexuals – the majority who sought other adult males as sexual partners, and the small minority who were attracted to pre-pubescent boys. These two types tended to be mutually exclusive; those who were attracted to one type of partner rarely showed interest in the other. It was pointed out that the legalisation of homosexual behaviour between consenting adults would actually reduce the risks of corruption by making boys less sought after:

> with the law as it is there may be some men who would prefer an adult partner but who at present turn their attention to boys because they consider this course is less likely to lay them open to prosecution or to blackmail than if they sought other adults as their partners.

The Committee admitted that any changes in the laws relating

29

to homosexuality could be misinterpreted by the general populace as condoning or approving such behaviour, and their Report contained repeated assurances that they did not intend to encourage or recommend homosexual activity in any way. However, it was recognised that the existing prohibitions did prevent some men from giving physical expression to their homosexual desires and that any reform of the law could lead to an increase in homosexual activity, but it shared the view that

> the law itself probably makes little difference to the amount of homosexual behaviour which actually occurs; whatever the law may be there will always be strong social forces opposed to homosexual behaviour.

In the light of these deliberations the Wolfenden Committee decided that there was no justification for retaining the existing laws forbidding homosexual activity. It therefore recommended that all forms of consensual homosexual behaviour between adults males in private should be decriminalised.

For the purposes of law the term 'in private' was considered to be defined under existing public order legislation as behaviour which took place anywhere where it was not likely to offend members of the general public. Similarly, 'consent' was defined in the same way as in corresponding heterosexual circumstances. If the Committee had had the courage to apply the same reasoning with regard to its definition of 'adult' and followed the example of the Church of England Moral Welfare Committee report which it had so often quoted, then the age of consent for homosexuals should have been fixed at 16, as for heterosexuals. But it was at this point that the fragile consensus that had united the members of the Committee broke down and personal prejudice was allowed to triumph over rational considerations – this crucial issue fell victim to the British vice of compromise. Having so firmly refuted the insidious 'corruption of youth' argument the Committee had to look for another justification to recommend a fundamental disparity between the heterosexual and homosexual ages of consent.

> While there are some grounds for fixing the age as low as 16, it is obvious that however 'mature' a boy of that age may be as regards physical development or psychosexual make-up, and whatever analogies may be drawn from the law relating to offences against young girls, a boy is incapable,

at the age of 16, of forming a mature judgement about actions of the kind which might have the effect of setting him apart from the rest of society.

After extensive discussions a decision, based on 'an element of arbitrariness', was reached on the age of 21 – for the simple reason that 'this is the age at which a man is deemed capable of entering into legal contracts, including... the contract of marriage, on his own responsibility'. Unwittingly the Wolfenden Committee had sanctioned the principle that homosexual acts should be treated by the law with greater severity than equivalent heterosexual behaviour – a principle which subsequently became enshrined in the law reform of 1967 and persists to the present day.

One of the members of the Committee, Mr James Adair, could not agree to the legalisation of homosexual activity at any age and produced a Minority Report to this effect arguing that his colleagues had paid too much attention to the opinions of 'expert' witnesses whose evidence had been flawed by 'a marked degree of sentimentalism'. According to this former Procurator Fiscal of Glasgow any liberalisation of this law would encourage further weakening in the moral force of the law generally, and would deter homosexuals from seeking treatment to cure them of their unfortunate urges. Despite all evidence to the contrary he warned of the danger of the corruption of youth:

> the presence of adult male lovers living openly and notoriously under the approval of the law is bound to have a regrettable and pernicious effect on the young people of the community.

VICE IN INCH-HIGH CAPITALS

Briefing the journalists of the nation's press about his Committee's recommendations prior to the publication of its Report, Sir John was pleasantly surprised by their sober and responsible attitude. He later recalled his astonishment at the outcome:

> It is difficult for me, and it must be nearly impossible for anyone else to realise the to-do that followed. It entirely filled the front pages of Wednesday's evening papers, with VICE in inch-high capitals as the main headline. And

Thursday's dailies, in their different styles, gave-it more column-inches than any of us had dreamt of.[2]

The 'conspiracy of silence' which the *Sunday Pictorial* had tried to puncture in 1952 was smashed forever when, on the morning of Thursday 5 September 1957, the topic of homosexuality was plastered over the front page of virtually every national and local newspaper in the United Kingdom. The headlines blazed out:

VICE OFFICIAL: NO WHITEWASH, NO PRUDERY AND NO HYPOCRISY – *Daily Mirror*

RELAX THIS SEX LAW – *Evening Standard*

VICE, THE STARK FACTS – *Scottish Daily Record*

Despite the sensationalism the majority of national dailies supported the Report's recommendations in their editorials on 5 September. *The Times* was unequivocal: 'Adult sexual behaviour not involving minors, force, fraud or public indecency belongs to the realm of private conduct and not of criminal law.' The *Daily Mirror* called it 'a sensible and responsible report', while the *Guardian* commented:

It is a fine piece of work, not merely or mainly in respect of its specific recommendations... but in its general outlook and temper, its interleaving of sympathy and stern-ness, its frankness of thought and word.

Even the *Daily Telegraph* called the findings 'clear, conscientious and courageous'. However, all these papers had reservations about the practicalities of implementing the proposals to decriminalise homosexuality. The *Daily Herald* was not alone in warning that 'Homosexual vice – or weakness – is so abhorrent to normal minds that public opinion will be slow to accept such a change'.

The few newspapers that disapproved of the findings were damning in their judgement. In the opinion of the *Daily Express* there was 'Nothing to Report'.

It is up to the Home Secretary to see that family life remains protected from these evils. If the law needs stiffening he should get on with stiffening it.... For all the help he will find in the Wolfenden Report he might as well tear it up.[3]

The *Evening Standard* was even more implacable: 'On no account must the Wolfenden recommendations on homosexuality ever be implemented. They are bad, retrograde and utterly to be condemned.'[4]

Most of the Scottish newspapers followed a similar line. The *Scotsman* gave Mr Adair's Minority Report considerable prominence and concluded that it was 'no solution to any public problem to legitimise a bestial offence'.[5] In the days and weeks that followed the debate raged on. Most provincial newspapers disapproved of the proposals and the *Sunday Express*'s self-appointed guardian of public prejudice, John Gordon, dubbed the Report 'The Pansies' Charter'.[6] The *News Chronicle* commissioned a Gallup poll on the issue which revealed that 38 per cent backed the proposal to decriminalise homosexuality, but 47 per cent disagreed.[7] North of the Border a readers' poll carried out by the *Scottish Daily Record* found that a massive 85 per cent were against changing the laws on homosexuality, with only 15 per cent supporting Wolfenden.[8]

It was no surprise, therefore, to find that the Church of Scotland staunchly opposed this reform; in the words one of its most senior Ministers, such an idea was

the last gasp so far as the moral life of the nation is concerned. We are down in the gutter, and the effect is going to be completely disastrous unless there is some resurgence of the spiritual and moral life of the nation which won't be from any committee appointed by any government.[9]

The Primate of the Church of Ireland agreed that existing laws should be retained: 'The existence of the penalty reflects the determined public judgement upon a certain line of unnatural conduct.'[10] The Archbishop of Canterbury, Dr Fisher, took the opposite view.

There is a sacred realm of privacy... into which the law, generally speaking, must not intrude. This is a principle of the utmost importance for the preservation of human freedom, self-respect and responsibility.[11]

The Bishop of Ripon and Dr Soper, former president of the Methodist Conference, agreed with his stand. The British Medical Association, the Howard League for Penal Reform and the National Association of Probation Officers also gave their backing to the Wolfenden recommendations.

A letter which appeared in the *News Chronicle* on 10 September summed up the whole business by homing in on the unpleasant aspects of the British national character which lay at the heart of the controversy.

> Within minutes of the publication of the Wolfenden Report down come the blinds of mock morality.... Thank you, Sir John Wolfenden, for trying. Alas! Not a dozen such sensible, powerful and honest reports will convince a people whose minds are choked with aspidistras. It is like talking metaphysics to a goldfish.

NO PROSPECT OF EARLY LEGISLATION

The political impact of the Wolfenden Report was more immediate, as the headline in the *Belfast Telegraph* on 5 September indicated: 'NO EARLY LEGISLATION ON VICE REPORT. TIME FOR PUBLIC OPINION TO FORM'. Although the paper accepted that the recommendation to decriminalise homosexuality would be widely criticised it went on to argue that the logic behind the proposal made it impossible for the Government to ignore: 'the Home Secretary will require almost as much courage to wholly reject it as to adopt it'. The new Home Secretary, Mr Butler, was too experienced a politician not to be aware of this danger and quickly made it clear that he would simply avoid considering the issue for the time being. According to the *Daily Mail*, this was because party loyalty would be strained 'beyond endurance' if the topic were debated in the Commons.[12] The *Daily Express*'s political correspondent offered a more convincing explanation:

> With a general election now less than two years away Ministers are reluctant to get the Government involved in a major moral controversy. This, I am authoritatively informed, means that the Government will not seek to alter the law to allow homosexual practices between consenting adults.[13]

Once again, the House of Lords proved unwilling to follow the Government line and on 4 December they held a full-scale debate on the Wolfenden Report and its findings.[14] Lord Pakenham, who wholeheartedly supported the Wolfenden reforms, called on his noble colleagues in his opening speech to show pity for the men who suffered from sinful homosexual impulses.

> when we reflect what torture is being suffered by many decent citizens... I hope we remember the injunction, 'Blessed are the merciful'. One day this change will be wrung from us without, if it were long delayed, much credit to anybody.

But, like the Committee, he felt the need to reassure people that by backing this reform he was not approving homosexual behaviour.

> Never let it be thought for a minute, even by the ignorant and ill-disposed, that if we bring our law into conformity with what is general practice in Europe, apart from Germany and Austria, we are condoning homosexuality. We are doing no such thing.

The Earl Winterton, whose reactionary opinions had dominated the debate he had initiated three years before, simply ignored the evidence presented in the Report and, elevating his prejudices above the weight of expert knowledge, proceeded to define homosexuality as a type of 'mania' (like kleptomania or nymphomania) which could only be effectively curbed by criminal sanctions. He dismissed the Report's conclusions for three reasons: firstly he felt that Sir John Wolfenden had been 'extraordinarily weak' in defending them during a radio interview; secondly he disapproved of one of the Committee's members whom he described as 'irresponsible'; and thirdly one or two of his 'aquaintances' disagreed with the findings! His final appeal was clear and simple:

> It is no doubt true that some homosexuals, but not all, are so constituted by nature that they cannot help being homosexual. But is that a reason for altering the law and making it easier for them?

From the ecclesiastical benches there emerged a considerable diversity of opinion. The Bishop of Rochester was well-informed about the seamier side of the subject.

> there are such things as sodomy clubs. There was one in Oxford between the wars, and I am informed there was another in Cambridge which even shamelessly sported a tie. And these clubs are plague spots wherever they exist.

He warned his audience not to be swayed by reasoned arguments on this issue.

> the emotion and moral indignation and horror which are aroused in the human heart by the thought and contemplation of unnatural vice, and which finds expression in the holy scriptures... are probably more right in teaching us our attitude to unnatural vice than academic discussion divorced from reality.

Although he admitted to being disturbed by these considerations the Archbishop of Canterbury repeated his commitment to the fundamental principle adopted by the Committee: 'The right to decide one's own moral code and obey it, even to man's own hurt, is a fundamental right of man.' Another Bishop, clearly not convinced by Lord Pakenham's assurances on the point, insisted that the general public would misconstrue the motives of the reformers: 'It would be assumed that abolishing the law means tolerating this – condoning it, not condemning it.' The Marquess of Lothian disagreed:

> if a change in the law is clearly and logically put before the British public they will see that as a just and not a weaker law and will not take it to mean a new attitude to the vice itself.

By courageously admitting that he was personally acquainted with homosexuals Lord Jessel for the first time introduced into the debate a human dimension which had been sadly lacking. He dared to suggest that their abhorrent physical activities might not deprive them of the ability to love:

> I myself have come across a case of a couple of men living together for years on terms of great affection and devotion, and I do not think any useful social purpose is served by prying into their exact physical relationship.

But Lord Brabazon of Tara, another firm advocate of reform, was the only speaker prepared to tackle this crucial but difficult area of human sexuality which lay at the heart of the issue. He dismissed the hysterical tirades which cast homosexuals as evil monsters and molesters, and considered them instead as the flesh and blood human beings they were:

when we speak of the repugnance and the disgust of the act, we have to face the fact that all sexual intercourse, be it heterosexual or homosexual, if it is looked at anatomically and physiologically, is not very attractive. But along comes the glamour of love; and that is a mystical, creative, Divine force which comes over two people and makes all things seem natural and normal. And what we have to get into our heads, although it is difficult, is that the glamour of love, odd as it may sound, is just as much present between two homosexuals as it is between a man and a woman.

The only coherent and rational opposition to the Wolfenden proposals came from the judge, Lord Denning, who dismissed the Committee's central premise that the sin of homosexuality should be exempt from criminal sanctions in the same way as other, equally culpable sins had always been: 'It is said that adultery and fornication are not criminal offences, so why should homosexuality be? The law answers that natural sin is different from unnatural vice.' In this respect homosexuality was in the same category as incest, abortion, bestiality and suicide – all of which were still crimes in 1957. He therefore concluded that homosexual behaviour should remain illegal because 'the law should condemn this evil for the evil it is, but the judges should be discreet in their punishment of it.' Speaking on behalf of the Government the Lord Chancellor acknowledged the fine work of the Committee but drew attention to the difficulties they had found in providing legal definitions of 'consent', 'in private' and 'the age of consent'. Although he did not dismiss the Report's recommendations he made it clear that the controversy they had aroused had been the major factor influencing the Government's response to the matter:

> Her Majesty's Government do not think that the general sense of the community is with the Committee in this recommendation, and therefore they think that the problem requires further study and consideration. There can be no prospect of early legislation.

Although there was no vote at the end of the debate those speakers supporting the Wolfenden recommendation slightly outnumbered those against it, which Lord Pakenham accepted as a fair representation of the deep divisions on the issue in the country at large. He acknowledged that those advocating reform now faced the daunting task of persuading the general public that their cause was a just one, but he felt certain that they would ultimately succeed.

GIVING A CONTROVERSIAL SUBJECT THE BENEFIT OF A CONTROVERSY

On 7 March 1958 a letter appeared in *The Times* calling on the Government to introduce early legislation to decriminalise homosexual behaviour between consenting adults.

> The present law is clearly no longer representative of either Christian or liberal opinion in this country, and now that there are widespread doubts about both its justice and its efficacy, we believe that its continued enforcement will do more harm than good to the health of the community as a whole.

Among the 33 distinguished figures who had put their name to this appeal were Isaiah Berlin, MP Robert Boothby, Julian Huxley, J.B. Priestley, Bertrand Russell and C.V. Wedgewood. A month later a similar letter signed by 15 'eminent' married women appeared.

The man responsible for organising these displays of concern was a university lecturer, A. E. Dyson, whose determination to pressurise Parliament into reforming the laws had been fired by a recurrence of the old-style 'chain' prosecutions against homosexuals. With the help of his friend the Rev. Andrew Hallidie Smith, Dyson persuaded a number of these highly respected signatories to become founder members of the Homosexual Law Reform Society (HLRS) which was pledged to campaign for the implementation of the Wolfenden proposals. Alongside this Honorary Committee of the 'great and the good' a smaller Executive Committee chaired by leading sexologist Kenneth Walker was set up to plan the details of a political campaign. A letter outlining the nature and aims of the Society was duly sent to the Home Secretary; Mr Butler's reply was suitably vague, but did suggest the strategy which he thought the organisation might be best advised to take if it wished to achieve success.

> The Government have not come to any final conclusion... we do however welcome the fullest discussion because it is essentially a matter on which public opinion should have the

opportunity of expressing itself before final decisions are taken.[15]

As with any pressure group the first priority for the HLRS was to raise funds. For this purpose the Albany Trust was set up as a registered charity with a young barrister, Antony Grey, as its Chief Executive. In order to ensure a regular annual income for the campaign he placed adverts in most of the national and provincial newspapers calling on those who supported homosexual law reform to pay an annual subscription to the Albany Trust. Of course, there was an inevitable delay before this money became available and during this period a homosexual couple, Len Smith and Reiss Howard, bravely offered the HLRS the use of their home as a temporary base. Reiss later recalled those early days:

> I was really in the background. I made the tea and coffee and addressed the envelopes. The neighbours didn't give us any trouble. We had a poster with 'Homosexual Law Reform Society' in black letters on a yellow background in the window, and one neighbour asked for one 'so that they'll think we're all queer'.[16]

By the autumn of 1958 the Society had sufficient funds to afford a permanent office at 32, Shaftesbury Avenue in London and to pay the Rev. Hallidie Smith to become its first full-time Secretary. Although the money from subscriptions kept the organisation funded for the first five years, regular appeals had to be launched from 1963 onwards to cover basic administration costs. In part this problem stemmed from the increasing resources which had to be channelled into supporting the homosexual men who came to the Society seeking emotional and practical help. This was inevitable since the HLRS was the first and only organisation publicly sympathetic to the problems of homosexuals, and as the years went by Antony Grey and his voluntary staff at the Albany Trust found their meagre resources stretched to the limit as the demand for counselling grew ever more rapidly.

The initial success of the HLRS proved that public consciousness had been irrevocably changed by the revelations of the Wolfenden Report (which had already sold over 15,000 copies in the nine months since its publication), and that the Government was not going to be able to go on ignoring the issue for much longer. In June 1958 the *Telegraph*, *Observer* and *Daily Mirror* all called for an end to the Home Secretary's 'shameful' prevarication. By the autumn even Sir John Wolfenden was publicly complaining about the Government's inaction which the *Observer* denounced on 7 September as a 'conspiracy of silence'. This barrage of criticism finally achieved its purpose and on 9 October Mr Butler announced that the House of Commons would be allowed to debate a motion to 'take note' of the Wolfenden Report (a formula designed to avoid the subject being put to a vote).

The *Spectator* was singularly unimpressed at the prospect of more talk and scathingly predicted:

> The Home Secretary will deliver himself of mellifluous ambiguities in the margin of this 'sad' and 'controversial' subject, and the challenge will then rest with the House. Will the other members be content to tread warily in his footsteps, or will they judge the occasion better served by giving a controversial subject the benefit of a controversy? This will be their chance to speak out. If they fail to do so they will fail not only themselves but... democracy itself.[17]

Writing in the *New Statesman*, the historian A.J.P. Taylor was equally pessimistic about the outcome of the debate: 'The homosexuals are likely to lose on a free vote. I am sorry about this... It is silly to have an elaborate enquiry by busy people and then do nothing.'[18] On the other hand, as a staunch opponent of Wolfenden the *Daily Mail* was relishing the prospect of inaction and reported gleefully that

> The leaders of both Parties have no wish to become embroiled in this issue. They say that arguments over homosexuality only 'confuse political issues' when a general election is so near.[19]

Undeterred by these negative predictions the HLRS launched its first attempt at parliamentary lobbying by sending copies of their pamphlet 'Homosexuals and the Law' to every MP along with a copy of Dr Eustace Chesser's book *Live and Let Live*, both of which argued the case for reforming the law. They also sent a deputation to put their case to the Home Secretary, who apparently promised that he would bear the Society's view in mind. But the issue must have already been very much on the Minister's mind since in the same week Ian Harvey, MP for Harrow East and Joint Parliamentary Under-Secretary at the Foreign Office, had been arrested in

St James's Park and charged with an act of gross indecency with a Coldstream Guardsman.

On Friday 21 November Mr Harvey tendered his resignation to the Prime Minister but Mr Macmillan, somewhat surprisingly, suggested that he might take a couple more days to consider the matter. On the following Monday Mr Harvey confirmed his decision and at Bow Street Magistrates Court on 10 December he pleaded guilty to the charges and was fined £5 for breaking park regulations. Although the press gave the story front page coverage, once the ex-Minister had resigned his parliamentary seat their interest soon faded. Only 'Brutus of the Recorder' gave consideration to Mr Macmillan's rather strange behaviour:

> The only interpretation that can be put on the Prime Minister's action... is that he was willing for a man who was going to be convicted of a disgraceful and degrading act to continue as a member of his Government.... It would be most reprehensible if it appeared that the Prime Minister of Great Britain, and presumably his chief colleagues, were ready to condone, or at least to overlook, the sort of behaviour with which Mr Harvey was charged.[20]

THERE, BUT FOR THE GRACE OF GOD...

Opening the debate on the Wolfenden Report in the House of Commons on 26 November[21] Mr Butler congratulated the Committee on its sterling work, praised its recommendations on prostitution which he intended to translate into law as soon as possible, and then proceeded to dismiss its proposal for homosexual law reform on the basis that

> there is at present a very large section of the population who strongly repudiate homosexual conduct and whose moral sense would be offended by an alteration of the law which would seem to imply approval or tolerance of what they regard as a great social evil.

Although he admitted that 'much human suffering derives from the operation of the existing law' he confirmed that the Government would not repeal it. In the meanwhile he suggested that further research into homosexuality was needed.

Labour's Front Bench spokesman, Anthony Greenwood, confirmed that his party agreed with the Government that the issue should not be treated as a party political matter since it involved 'so many considerations of public morality and private conscience'. But in a personal capacity he went on to give his unequivocal support to the Wolfenden recommendation, and pointed out the absurdities of the existing punishment meted out to homosexual offenders:

Life is harsh enough for these people without society adding to their burden. The fact that the law is largely unenforced, and, indeed, largely unenforceable, is certainly no reason for retaining it.... one is as likely to cure a homosexual of his perversion by sending him to an all-male prison as one is likely to cure a drunkard by incarcerating him in a brewery.

In a sincere speech advocating reform the Ulster Unionist MP, Montgomery Hyde, called on his audience to show sympathy and compassion for the problems faced by homosexuals. He read out a pathetic plea for understanding which had been sent to him by a homosexual.

I do so want to try and make you people look upon this coming debate with kindness and sympathetic consideration and think 'There but for the grace of God go I.' It is all right for people to condemn us so much, but they have no idea the life of fear and dread we live all the time, in case our friends find out or we are caught.... Just because I was cursed with the homosexual trait, I was no more able to get rid of it than a man could get rid of cancer. It's in you from birth – I feel sure of that. I have studied so many cases and men I have met. When you understand, you feel terribly sorry.

Sir Hugh Linstead (Con.) who had been a member of the Wolfenden Committee, also argued forcefully in support of its findings.

If we no longer impose on them a legal code of sexual behaviour which we do not expect from anybody else, we can surely expect homosexuals to accept the same responsibility as the rest of us accept for behaving themselves in public.

It was Douglas Jay (Lab.) who, for the first time, put the issue of homosexual law reform into the context of what would later become defined as 'human rights'. He insisted that the existing law infringed the basic principle of personal freedom and warned: 'Once we depart from that principle... it is a road that leads... eventually to concentration camps and to the persecution of heretics.'

But those favouring reform were in a minority; their opponents ignored the fruits of the Committee's research and clung tenaciously to the prejudices and fallacies which were still so popular in the tabloid press. For example, one Labour backbencher spoke for many when he described homosexuality as a disease which could be spread:

> Those who practise the cult are a malignant canker in the community, and if this were allowed to grow it would eventually kill off what is known as normal life.

A Conservative MP agreed with this theory and therefore saw the solution as a simple one: 'I do not believe it is beyond the power of medical science today to find some way whereby these people can be treated and cured.' One of Labour's few women MPs went into considerable detail about the dangers of the corruption of youth, and dismissed the findings of the Report because it had failed to discover the cause of homosexuality. Another of her colleagues agreed and, ignoring the fact that the proposed reform would only legalise homosexual behaviour in private, drew the following picture of its catastrophic results:

> I can envisage men walking down the street together arm in arm, possibly holding hands, and at dances perhaps wishing to dance together and even caressing in public places... it is a shocking example to young people.

It was left to Conservative Cyril Black to weigh in and finish off the litany with the final and familiar vision of apocalypse:

> These unnatural practices, if persisted in, spell death to the souls of those who indulge in them. Great nations have fallen and empires been destroyed because corruption became widespread and socially acceptable.

However, he and several other speakers gave a disturbing new twist to the debate by suggesting that a clandestine organisation of homosexuals had been formed to mount a high pressure campaign in support of the Wolfenden proposals. It was even suggested that this subversive group's influence had spread to the heart of West-minster:

> homosexuality sets up a society within a society, and this is indeed sinister.... It is perfectly true to say that in many spheres of activity today the ability and the willingness to enter into homosexual acts is a means of promotion. That is so in a great number of spheres, even in business and maybe in politics.

Although one Labour MP was prepared to support the Wolfenden recommendations, he was deeply disturbed by this idea of 'a *corps d'élite* of sexual perverts' and warned: 'I believe that the sort of propaganda which has been circulated round the House... has done much more harm than good to the cause it tries to serve.'

In addition to the deep psychological ignorance and fear running through these arguments against reform, there were more pragmatic political considerations, as one MP had the honesty to admit: 'I cannot believe that our constituents would thank us for what would be considered an act... of condonation if we altered the law.' With a general election expected soon some MPs were wary of supporting controversial legislation which might lose them votes and possibly their parliamentary seats.

NOT BUGGERY BUT HUMBUGGERY

The *Daily Express* was delighted at Mr Butler's stand which it dubbed 'A Victory for Public Opinion'.[22] The *Daily Sketch* agreed: 'the Government are wise to await the result of research into the problem of homosexuality before they take steps to alter the law.'[23] The *Sunday Times* was surprisingly neutral in its reaction:

> Parliament, always at its best in a non-party Council of State atmosphere, in its deliberative rather than in its legislative role, functioned with distinction and sincerity on the Wolfenden Report. Inevitably the subjects of prostitution and homosexuality brought forth on both sides overtones of special pleading and old-fashioned prejudice, but the over-all balance was enlightened.[24]

The paper went on to warn the HLRS of the clear dangers of over-zealous lobbying which might encourage those opposed to its aims to form themselves into an organised group.

This advice is slightly puzzling by contemporary standards, but the reasoning behind it is clear. However, the extraordinary spate of paranoid outpourings by MPs disturbed by visions of secret homosexual 'coteries' within the Establishment pressuring for reform seems very bizarre. One can only assume that these irrational fears hark back to the treachery and subsequent defection to Moscow of Burgess and Maclean who were both homosexual. Suspicions were clearly aroused that these same subversive cold war forces might again be at work, manipulating other highly placed and influential homosexual traitors to push for this reform which would ultimately, in some undefined way, undermine national security. Running alongside these fears was the idea that reformers were expecting Parliament to make such an enormous concession in excising such unnatural and sinful sexual deviations from the statute book that they should not be pressing the case too hard. Should the reform be granted it was to be seen as a great humanitarian gesture of the last resort exempting men who could not stop themselves from committing such disgusting acts from the justifiable wrath of the law. Homosexuals were expected to wait patiently for Parliament to grant them relief from their suffering in its own good time. The idea that homosexuals themselves could argue their own case was obviously totally unacceptable.

Perhaps it was simpler than that, as the *News Chronicle* commented at the time:

> too much emphasis was placed on appeasing popular prejudices and not enough on reform and justice.... It is regrettable that Mr Butler should pay so much deference to an unpleasant aspect of our national character – the valuing of respectability above reform.[25]

Or as the *Spectator* put it rather more pithily:

> 'The "*Vice Anglais*",' said Mr Leslie Hale, 'is not buggery but humbuggery.' It was the perfect epitaph for the House of Commons debate on the Report of the Wolfenden Committee.[26]

The *Observer* reported that Sir John Wolfenden had been disappointed by the Government's rejection of the recommendations on homosexuality but was confident that it would only be 'a matter of time' before public opinion swung round to support the Committee's view.[27] The scale of this exercise was revealed by the results of a Gallup poll in the *News Chronicle* on 17 December. People were asked if the Government's decision to reject the Wolfenden proposal on homosexuality was right or wrong: 48 per cent supported Mr Butler's policy, 25 per cent disagreed, but a substantial 27 per cent simply didn't know. This news could hardly have been welcomed by the HLRS, which was still shaken by the extent to which its well-intentioned parliamentary campaign had backfired. Future lobbying would clearly require a far greater degree of subtlety and sensitivity in order to reassure even the most sympathetic MPs. Furthermore, to disprove the repeated claims of the opposition that public opinion was against reform the Society had to change these uncompromising statistics in its favour. Kenneth Walker later recalled what a daunting prospect this seemed.

> It was clear... that a long and arduous fight lay ahead. To 'educate' the public upon such an emotional subject as homosexuality to the extent that the Wolfenden proposals might become palatable to politicians who feared, apparently, a massive constituency backlash from those who were totally ignorant of the subject was a formidable task for a small and slenderly financed organisation such as the HLRS.[28]

3

KEEPING WOLFENDEN FROM THE WESTMINSTER DOOR: 1959-63

I do not believe that a full case for a change has been made, nor am I convinced that we are yet in a position to make a final decision on the precise nature of the change which should be made. We need more information... and more time.

R. A. *Butler* – House of Commons 29/6/60

A RENEWED REFLECTION OF PUBLIC AWARENESS

1959 might well be considered one of the less memorable years in the history of the struggle for gay rights. On 18 March the distinguished Judge, Mr Justice Devlin, as the guest speaker for the second Maccabaean Lecture in Jurisprudence, took the opportunity to question further the fundamental principle behind the Wolfenden proposals. Developing the argument put foward by Lord Denning in the House of Lords a year earlier, Mr Devlin dismissed the premise that sin should be separated from crime. He contended that the very existence of criminal sanctions against homosexual activity, as opposed to other sins such as adultery and fornication, was a reflection of society's strong disapproval of this particular form of sexual behaviour. The logical conclusion to which he was led by this reasoning was reported in *The Times* the next day:

No society could do without intolerance, indignation and disgust; they were the forces behind the moral law, and if the genuine feeling of the society in which we lived was that homosexuality was a vice so abominable that its mere presence was an offence he did not see how society could be denied the right to eradicate it.

Given the paper's consistent backing for homosexual law reform its leader article might have been expected to question this dangerous assumption, but instead it actually applauded the Judge's sentiments.

There is a moving and welcome humility in the conceptions that society should not be asked to give its reasons for refusing to tolerate what, in its heart, it feels intolerable.

The following week the paper published a letter from a correspondent in Cambridge who pointed out the appalling consequences of such deeply flawed reasoning.

I am afraid we are less humble than we used to be. We once burnt old women because, without giving our reasons, we felt in our hearts that witchcraft was intolerable.[1]

A couple of months later, with the prospect of a general election not far from his thoughts, the Home Secretary gave the *News Chronicle* the benefit of his opinions on reform under the headline 'HOMOSEXUALS: WHY WE'RE NOT READY FOR A NEW LAW YET'. Although Mr Butler accepted the fact that the Wolfenden proposals would eventually be implemented, he revealed his determination to prevent this from happening until people were 'most accustomed to the subject'.

In this same month the *Scotsman* started a series of articles on 'Scotland and the Wolfenden Report' which showed the Home Secretary's views to be positively progressive in comparison with prevailing opinion north of the border. This wide-ranging investigation gave a clear account of the extent and nature of the homosexual subculture which existed in most of Scotland's major cities and claimed that it was spreading due to a lack of police action. The articles zealously trotted out the old chestnuts about the self-propagating nature of homosexual groups and the serious danger of the corruption of youth, before going on to label every homosexual a potential traitor:

homosexuals, by the nature of their disability, owe their primary allegiance to the homosexual group before any other authority or loyalty in their lives. Hence the connection between perversion and subversion, which is one of world Communism's greatest strengths in this country.[2]

It was therefore concluded that an immediate campaign of police repression was needed to control the problem, before greater attempts could be made to cure such men of their 'unnatural urges'.

To counter the emergence of this type of opposition the HLRS had already launched its own nationwide campaign of persuasion. This involved addressing meetings all over the country, keeping up regular correspondence in the letter columns of the national and provincial press, writing articles for magazines and newspapers, appealing for support and funding in publications that would accept its advertisements, and producing a newsletter and a journal to keep its growing membership informed about developments and progress. At the same time it was strengthening its parliamentary contacts and monitoring the continual changes in political circumstances. Although the Society was not aligned to any one political party, the return of the Conservative Government in the October general election with a substantial majority of 100 and Mr Butler still at the Home Office was not a cause for celebration.

On 12 May 1960 – the second anniversary of its foundation – the HLRS 'went public' by holding an open meeting at the Caxton Hall near Westminster with Kenneth Walker in the chair and the Bishop of Exeter; Kingsley Martin, editor of the *New Statesman*; Mrs Allen, a magistrate; and Dr Neustatter, an eminent psychiatrist, all speaking in favour of homosexual law reform. The organisers were overwhelmed when an audience of more than 1,000 people arrived on the night and an overflow meeting had to be hastily arranged in a nearby room. Bernard Dobson, a gay man who subsequently became actively involved in the HLRS, later recalled the impact of that exhilarating evening in terms which echoed the reactions of gay men attending GLF meetings more than a decade later:

I went with a friend of mine ... and we went early, feeling very self-conscious. It was packed out. By going to a place like that, you were proclaiming in a blaze of lights that you were one of these hundreds of homosexual men – they were mostly men – meeting, not in the usual situation, cruising the place, but going there to talk about law reform.... On the platform was a man called Antony Grey... I was very excited by the meeting, so I went up to him and told him that he had given a marvellous speech and that I was very interested. He gave me his address and I joined the society.[3]

At the end of the evening a resolution calling on the Government to implement the Wolfenden recommendations without delay was passed by a resounding majority. In a letter to the *Guardian* on 21 May Kenneth Walker claimed that the overwhelming success of the event was a strong indication that prevailing attitudes in the country were 'predominantly and increasingly in favour of reform'.

It was against this background of growing support that Labour MP Kenneth Robinson introduced a Private Member's motion into the House of Commons asking the Government to take 'early action' to implement the recommendations of the Wolfenden Committee. This type of motion allowed MPs to discuss and vote on a subject according to their private opinions, theoretically without pressure or interference from their party. An editorial in *The Times* on the morning of the debate reiterated the paper's unwavering support for reform and approved the fact that the issue was to be considered in this way: 'what is wanted is not hand to hand combat but a renewed reflection of public awareness and anxiety about this painful problem'.[4] This firm stand must have been much appreciated by the HLRS's parliamentary supporters especially since the *Guardian's* editorial on the previous morning, far from supporting their cause, was suddenly voicing strong reservations about the consequences of legalising homosexual behaviour.

> However the law may have come into being, what has to be considered is whether it can be in part abrogated without appearing to give a charter to conduct which is clearly immoral and anti-social. The conduct must be distinguished from the condition. While the latter is a grievous personal misfortune, the former cannot but involve others in moral detriment.[5]

LEADING THE COUNTRY FROM BEHIND

Opening his debate on 29 June Kenneth Robinson presented a strong case for reform based on the Wolfenden arguments.[6] He called on the Home Secretary to abandon his policy of prevarication on the grounds that in some matters it was 'the duty of Government to lead and not to follow public opinion and to do what they know to be right'. But Mr Butler was not to be persuaded; he continued to insist that no steps should be taken to introduce legislation until there was proof that it had the full backing of the country, and the extent of the damage to public interests which might result from such a change could be more accurately gauged. To this end his department was backing new research at Birkbeck College into the psychological and other characteristics of individual homosexuals. His refusal to act was unequivocal:

> In a period when religious and ethical restraints remain weak, as undoubtedly they are now, those of the criminal law acquire a special significance.... I would, therefore, not regard this and the state of progress we have made so far, with public opinion and with research, as being the time to let down our first line of defence.

The Minister's speech ensured that the battle was over before it had begun and he was followed by a string of speakers from his own party who prided themselves on their 'old fashioned' views and vied with each other to describe the most shocking repercussions of such a reform. As well as the usual familiar arguments, there was a new emphasis on the fear that an alteration in the law would bring about 'a substantial increase in homosexual activity'. Even worse was the prospect raised by one MP that the implementation of the Wolfenden Report would be followed by 'a campaign of self-justification... an effort to prove that homosexuality has its virtues'. Certainly the very idea that homosexuality could have any positive aspects was one that could never have been entertained in the worst nightmares of most MPs. Even some Labour MPs opposed reform because of the danger that it might bring about 'a development of a homosexual cult'.

But most speeches from the Labour benches were strongly in favour of the motion. Douglas Jay once again argued the case in terms of basic human rights.

> I do not believe, as a principle, that the State or the law has any right to interfere with the acts of private individuals, whatever they may be, however much you dislike them, which have no effect on other people. These are matters of conscience and not of law, and it is the mark of a truly free country to leave them to conscience and not to the Courts.

It was one of the few women MPs, Eirene White, who dared to offer an extraordinarily perceptive analysis of the irrational prejudice which was being so violently promulgated by those opposed to the reform: 'A number of men, consciously or subconsciously, are moved to vehement condemnation by some feeling that they have to assert their own virility in the process.' She went on to suggest that this reaction might be caused by unconscious or repressed homosexual inclinations within such men, a psychological condition which would only be recognised as a root cause of homophobia more than two decades later.

Despite the firm support of these and other influential front bench speakers including Roy Jenkins, Richard Crossman and Anthony Greenwood (who were all later to become Ministers in the Wilson Government), when the vote was finally called the motion was defeated by 213 votes to 99. Although the scale of the defeat was a serious blow to hopes of legislation for the remainder of that Parliament, the commitment shown by senior Labour politicians boded well for the future. Leo Abse, the exuberant Labour backbencher whose Private Member's Bill was eventually to allow the implementation of the Wolfenden proposals, voted in favour of the measure; and among the small minority of 22 Conservatives who backed the Bill was the name of Margaret Thatcher.

According to the *Sunday Times* the outcome of this debate was 'a pretty fair representation of the state of public opinion on the matter, perhaps a short way ahead of it in the direction of reform'.[7] The parliamentary correspondent of the *Guardian* agreed:

> It gave voice to extremes of enlightenment and compassion on the one hand and cruel stupidity on the other.... Mr Butler was still determined to lead the country from behind in this matter.[8]

But the *Glasgow Herald* approved of the Home Secretary's caution: 'medical and psychiatric research... should be intensively directed towards discovering a cure for, or a socially acceptable palliative of, homosexuality'.[9] 'Supporters of lax laws for homosexuals were routed in the Commons last night', reported the *Daily Express* with unrestrained delight;[10] while in the *Sunday Express* John Gordon applauded the high moral standards shown by the majority of MPs.

> The House of Commons with a splendid understanding of public opinion smacked the pansies down so hard that there hasn't been a cheep out of them since.... The Queers, as you might say, are in Queer Street.[11]

Around this time it was reported in the press that attempts had been made to suppress discussion of homosexual law reform at the Annual Conference of the Scottish Liberal Party on the grounds that mention of homosexuality in a Liberal publication had lost that party votes in Inverness at the general election. But according to Allan Horsfall, a local Labour councillor in Lancashire, similar attempts to hamper free discussion were also being pursued at a local level within his own party. In a letter to the *Guardian* he proceeded to list the ploys used to suppress pro-Wolfenden proposals and the arguments that could be marshalled to counter them:

> The most popular seems to be the contention that these sexual matters are not really political issues at all, but are questions for the individual conscience which are traditionally dealt with in the House, if at all, by a private member. In answer to this it is appropriate to draw attention to the method by which the Street Offences Bill [which in 1959 put into effect the Wolfenden Committee's proposals relating to prostitution] was enacted and then go on to ask how the dictates of individual conscience... are to be made effective, in a matter involving legislation, except through political action.
>
> The next move... is maintaining that this is a non-party matter which cuts clean across party lines. This is perfectly respectable when used by a party spokesman commenting upon a matter which his party has not considered, but when it is used to prevent discussion within a party it becomes a very shabby get-out indeed.
>
> Next comes the 'vote-loser' dodge from the expediency-before-principle-every-time boys and finally (Lord help us!) the claim that the matter is not one that can be discussed in mixed company.[12]

In parliamentary terms the matter rested in abeyance until March 1962 when Leo Abse introduced a Private Member's Bill which gave effect to some of the less contentious recommendations of the Wolfenden Committee without making homosexual behaviour between consenting adults legal. He wished to achieve three main objects:

> first, to ensure that all prosecutions between consenting adults in private were authorised by the Director of Public

Prosecutions; this was intended to act as some slight kerb on police enthusiasm and to impose some uniformity upon police practice. Secondly, to provide that prosecutions for offences of this kind must be commenced within twelve months of their commission; this was intended to minimise the likelihood of the prolonged blackmail of homosexual offenders. Thirdly, to make it obligatory for courts to obtain a psychiatrist's report before sentencing a man who had been convicted for the first time... of a homosexual offence: this very modest proposal was intended to let a little of the light of understanding into the darkness of the judicial mind.[13]

However, his approach to the Home Office for backing met with no success. Mr Abse later suggested that the Government's refusal to confront the issue owed a great deal to the attitudes of the Lord Chancellor, Lord Kilmuir, who had set up the Wolfenden Committee as Home Secretary Sir David Maxwell Fyfe, but was now so strongly opposed to any homosexual law reform that he refused to sit at the Cabinet table if the subject was to be discussed.

In the event official opposition to the Bill was never voiced – the debate in the Commons on 9 March lasted barely one hour and the time allocated having run out, the motion automatically lapsed without a vote.[14] Even in these restricted circumstances it was made clear that many Conservative MPs saw Mr Abse's move as a deliberately devious attempt to introduce 'some form of Wolfenden watered down'. The press largely ignored this brief skirmish, the *Guardian* being one of the few national dailies to consider it worth any mention: 'Members who oppose a more human law for homosexuals are at least as determined as ever they were to keep Wolfenden from the Westminster door'.[15]

Giving one talk in a series organised by the Albany Trust in the winter of that year Kenneth Robinson felt that these efforts had not been entirely in vain.

Perhaps the most encouraging aspect of these very disappointing debates was the widespread recognition that reform of some kind must come, and the absence of any serious attempt to justify the existing state of the law.... Parliamentary and outside pressure will continue until we have a Government and a Home Secretary willing to risk a brief storm – unlikely to be a violent one – which reform of this law may provoke.[16]

There is little doubt that these repeated airings of the subject in the House of Commons were ensuring that it remained firmly in the public domain despite the unwillingness of large sections of the media to give serious consideration to the issues.

A SORT OF COTERIE SOCIETY

There was evidence that the coverage of the purely legislative and moral aspects of law reform were beginning to be supplemented by articles dealing with the homosexual lifestyle and the difficulties associated with it. Initally these pieces tended to follow the sensationalist approach reminiscent of the Montagu witch-hunt period. For instance, in the *Daily Herald* on 26 November 1958 there was an investigation into the 'most delicate yet frightening problem' of 'MEN WITHOUT WOMEN'.

The paper's intrepid reporter had infiltrated the seedy back-streets of London's Soho with the aid of 'a drab little man well into his forties' who was nothing less than a 'self-confessed homosexual'. This man told of how he had been brought up in an Edinburgh orphanage where he had been tutored as a male prostitute.

> Soon I was upgraded and became a recognised, much flattered member of the club. To the ordinary men we were 'jessies'. I didn't mind hard names. From the start I had plenty of money, lovely clothes, a flat, and for 'friends' I'd rich men, professional men – University men, doctors, lawyers. And oh, such lovely parties when West End actors came to Edinburgh with the shows.

A police clamp-down had forced him to flee to London where he had quickly resumed his debauched lifestyle.

He was now a pathetic figure with frayed cuffs and traces of make-up on his face who haunted 'dark doorways in narrow streets'. From one such vantage point he and the reporter observed a 'wolf homosexual' attempt to engage the attentions of a respectable city gent in a bowler hat. An elaborate code of signals was employed which culminated in a newspaper being switched from one hand to another as a 'come-hither' sign and to the reporter's surprise the two men hurried off together.

'Is that the first time they've met?' I asked. 'Of course' said my guide. 'They'll spend the afternoon together. The wolf will have a nice present, and no regrets. But *he* might be sorry he ever walked down this street.' 'What do you mean?' I asked – and got this cryptic but significant answer: 'Well, the wolf doesn't mind who he knows. But *he* might. And the other one would blackmail his own father.'

On the evidence of this single sordid example of the homosexual underworld and the opinions of 'an experienced and well-educated policeman' readers were warned that any reform of the law would make it easier for homosexuals to convert others to their degenerate and unhappy way of life.

By the early 1960s a more constructive approach was becoming apparent with the appearance of informed articles which aimed to stimulate discussion rather than pass judgement. The description and analysis of the homosexual sub-culture which appeared on 21 June 1963 in the magazine *Peace News* was clearly provided by someone with an intimate, personal knowledge of it. Despite being hampered by the melodramatic title 'THE NIGHTMARE WORLD OF THE HOMOSEXUAL', the anonymous author of the article showed how the existing law often forced homosexuals into the type of promiscuous behaviour which heterosexual society so vehemently condemned.

One of its basic assumptions is that the homosexual must protect himself from the law, and this means primarily that as far as possible he must remain anonymous. You never know in what guise a policeman will appear or who will inform. There are cafés, clubs and pubs where the homosexual can go to make contact and he soon learns where they are, but even here the police will infiltrate. This sort of coterie society is not a glittering playground. It tends to frequent rather cheerless places and to develop hard, suspicious and selfish manners.... With anonymity at a premium, the homosexual finds his experiences in furtive situations which dehumanise the experience and degrade him.... He can risk meeting an *agent provocateur* by loitering in public lavatories, especially those at main line stations. There are turkish baths and open commons and parks which are the resorts of homosexuals.... Of course the criminal sanction is only one of the factors which induces this sort of behaviour, but the sanction does encourage it by militating against more desirable social behaviour.

In a hard-hitting criticism, entitled 'The Law and the Homosexual' in the *Daily Mail* a year later, journalist Monica Furlong also suggested that the more 'unacceptable' aspects of homosexual behaviour stemmed largely from society's oppression of that minority. She immediately homed in with deadly accuracy on the prevailing hypocrisy displayed by so many MPs when faced with the subject:

> There is the story of an MP who, having campaigned violently against the Wolfenden proposals in the House of Commons, asked someone, 'Tell me, is it true that these homosexuals actually find the idea of going to bed with a woman distasteful?'
>
> Nothing could better suggest the wilful blindness, the almost laughable ignorance with which the subject of homosexuality has become surrounded.

After discussing the nature and causes of homosexuality, the work of the HLRS and the slow progress of law reform in Britain, she went on to look at the homosexual community which had grown up in the Netherlands where homosexual behaviour between consenting adults had been legal since the end of the Second World War. Dutch homosexuals had set up their own organisation called COC in 1947; the group offered support and counselling for those having difficulty in accepting their sexuality as well as running a highly successful social club in Amsterdam.

> The kind of self-pity and exhibitionist behaviour which can be a distasteful feature of 'queer' gatherings in this country has disappeared; probably because the club enjoys complete social acceptance and no one has to live a life of pretence any longer. Respectable businessmen have no hesitation in taking a taxi from their office to the club; by contrast our own community appears pathetically riddled with hypocrisy and fear.

Miss Furlong then described how psychiatrists in Britain were using aversion therapy to 'cure' homosexual men of their sexual urges: a technique which involved giving them drugs to make them vomit while looking at pictures of naked men. In her conclusion she suggested that this approach to the problem was more sick and immoral than any form of homosexual activity.

> That brainwashing as a treatment can be seriously enter-tained suggests how unhealthy and unbalanced our thinking on the whole subject has become. It is clear that we need not only new laws but a whole new climate of thought and understanding.[17]

As early as October 1961 an article entitled 'CRIMINALS FROM BIRTH' in the *Socialist Leader* had offered a radical new persepec-tive on the problem of coping with homosexual maladjustment, based on the novel premise that homosexuals could lead happy and fulfilled lives. Its suggestions were humane and compassionate, but practical.

> so many young homosexuals grow up without any of the help which they need so badly.... Life is harder for the homosexual than for the rest of us. Our way of life is built round the family as a social unit... homosexuality precludes the joy and stability of married life, as well as the pleasure of children. Obviously, then, it is a disability.... We must concentrate on helping these people to live as happily as possible *as homosexuals*. We must make it possible for them, despite the disadvantages of their condition, to achieve worthwhile relationships with their own kind.... It is time we realised that legal persecution is no answer.[18]

THE LAW AS IT STANDS...

Although such articles were undoubtedly of value in countering public misconceptions their impact was limited by their rarity. Most people's awareness of the issue was kept alive by the unrelenting stream of reports of the prosecution of homosexual men in court-rooms all over the country. It was a recurrence of the old-style chain prosecutions by his local constabulary that prompted Labour coun-cillor Allan Horsfall to send a letter to the *Bolton Evening News* denouncing the existing law which allowed eight consenting adults to be arrested for behaviour which had taken place in private. Encouraged by the support his opinions drew he helped to found the North Western Homosexual Law Reform Society (NWHLRS) under the chairmanship of Colin Harvey, a senior social worker for the Church of England in Manchester, and requested affiliation to the national HLRS. As Mr Horsfall later recounted, his new provincial group attracted a far higher proportion of active homosexual members than its London counterpart, including the owner of a club for homosexuals in Manchester.

While the mailing list was predominantly non-gay, the active attendance at the policy-making meeting was the reverse. But these open meetings were soon proving too nebulous to form an effective controlling body and when the then Bishop of Middleton... urged that decisions should be made by an identifiable committee, we agreed. An immediate consequence was that half the people who used to come to meetings were never seen again! However odd it may now seem, in the very first years of the committee, an unwritten rule required that questions about individuals' sexual orientation were never asked. If this information was available it was because it had been volunteered.... Relations between the two organisations were equivocal from the beginning. London seemed to embrace us or reject us according to the mood of the moment.... They had taken the view that any new organisation was necessarily going to corner a proportion of finite financial support which had hitherto been at their exclusive disposal, and as a consequence weaken them. It never seemed to occur to them that there was a vast reservoir of people who remained unlocated and untapped either for their money or their energy. Long discussed proposals for a link-up between the two bodies came to nothing.[19]

Regardless of the growing pressure for reform the police were, of course, obliged to uphold the existing law but the degree of determination with which they tackled this task depended mainly on the extent of the crusading zeal of the local Chief Constable. In some areas ingenious new methods were employed by enterprising officers in their campaign to stamp out this type of crime. In Hertfordshire police lifted floorboards in Baldock Town Hall in order to spy through the ceiling of the public convenience below; and the technique employed by one West Country constabulary prompted the following letter to the *Spectator*:

If anybody really wants to know how childish we are, I will

take him to a public convenience in Bristol where a mirror
is fixed to the ceiling so that a police spy may stand outside
and see what is going on within.... Any passing woman or
child can take the place of the police.[20]

Concern about such methods was also being voiced in other quarters; at a conference on homosexuality an eminent QC told his
audience: 'I do not like these spies.... There is something about this
sneaking that is revolting to the English sense of fair play.'[21]

Although some judges clearly approved of repressive police
action and passed appropriately harsh sentences, there were others
whose opinions led them to show considerable leniency. The *West-
morland Gazette* on 16 January 1959 reported that one judge in a
multiple prosecution trial had refused to imprison any of the
convicted men

because it was obvious to him that the suffering had been
inflicted on the defendants and their relatives by the publicity and shame attendant upon such charges, and the
proceedings.

Another, at the Staffordshire Assizes in July of the following year,
commented: 'So long as they confine themselves to adults, while it
is illegal and repulsive, no great harm is done.'[22]

The clearest indication of changing judicial attitudes could be
seen in regard to blackmail cases where the homosexual victims
were usually allowed to remain anonymous during trials and were
not themselves prosecuted for the alleged sexual misconduct which
had given their blackmailer a hold over them. But public attention
was only really directed towards this particular aspect of the existing
law by a sensational trial at the Old Bailey in the autumn of 1962
when William Vassall, a homosexual Foreign Office clerk based in
Moscow, was charged with selling secrets to the Russians. In the
course of the proceedings it was revealed that, having discovered
Vassall's sexual inclinations, the KGB had lured him into a compromising situation and subsequently used photographic evidence
of the incident to blackmail him into providing them with confiden-
tial information. As a result of the uproar caused by Vassall's
successful prosecution and subsequent imprisonment, the Radcliffe
Tribunal was appointed by the Government to look into the security aspects of the affair.

Certain sections of the press were quick to use the case as an opportunity to stir up the old fears about all homosexuals being potential traitors. The most unpleasant example of this approach appeared in the *Sunday Mirror* on 28 April 1963 in an article entitled 'HOW TO SPOT A HOMO'. Astonished by the Radcliffe Tribunal's conclusion that Vassall's homosexuality could only have been discovered by 'active police detective work', the journalist asserted that the spy had been clearly indentifiable as a 'gilt-edged specimen of his type'. Obviously the Admiralty, the Foreign Office and MI5 needed his help in detecting homosexuals who apparently fell into two distinct categories: the 'obvious' effeminate homosexuals like Vassall, and the 'concealed' homosexuals whose normal appearance made them extremely difficult to detect. Almost every man was suspect:

> they wear silk shirts and sit up at Chi-Chi bars with full-bosomed ladies. Or they wear hairy sports jackets and give their wives a black eye when they get back from the working men's club. They wrestle, play golf, ski and work up knots of muscles lifting weights. They are married, have children. They are everywhere, they can be anybody.

The article then proceeded to list eight specific 'types' of men who would be on any 'suspect list'. This spiteful and paranoiac article concluded with the assertion:

> Anyone with a gram of sense can *smell* the homos amongst these men.... Most of us have an in-built instinct about possible, or probable, or latent homosexuals. The object of this lesson is to help sharpen that instinct.

However, elsewhere in the media the whole sorry business of treachery and blackmail was used as a further argument for reforming the laws against homosexuality. The *Daily Mail* argued that the present law forced homosexuals into pretence, concealment and a double life which made them easy targets for blackmailers and spies.

> If anyone wished to devise a school for secret agents the way Britain treats homosexuals could hardly be improved upon.... Although homosexuals are no more inclined to treachery than you are, the law as it stands gives the Communists a lever against them which they have over nobody else.[23]

The article went on to applaud the news that the incident had persuaded Lord Boothby to consider introducing a Private Member's Bill into the House of Lords to implement the Wolfenden recommendation to decriminalise homosexuality. The *Daily Herald* accused the British Establishment of being 'liars, hypocrites or fools' when it came to the problem of homosexuality and made a strong plea to the Government to 'SCRAP THIS LAW THAT BREEDS BLACKMAIL'.[24]

Antony Grey and his colleagues at the HLRS were quick to exploit this new public controversy over blackmail which the Vassall case had highlighted. Advertisements and articles in the national and provincial press drew attention to this aspect of the problem, and the Albany Trust's ever-growing file of cases of blackmail, extortion and assault against homosexual men was used to illustrate the personal tragedies involved. In July 1963 the magazine *Titbits* used some of these case histories in a piece about the growing blackmail racket run by petty criminals called 'rolling the queers' which involved the extortion of money by threat, physical intimidation and robbery.

> In South London two thugs lurked in the shadows waiting for their victim to come home. As he opened the door they pushed him inside and coolly and systematically rifled his home. They got away with £150 in cash and valuables.... Another case was that of a young university student who had his flat raided by a gang. They were not satisfied with taking his money and valuables. With a touch of sadism they ripped off his clothes and left him without a stitch to wear.

The criminals relied on their victim's fear of prosecution to prevent him approaching the police to report such incidents and more often than not this proved to be the case. This situation was not helped by the occasional reports of cases where police officers themselves were found guilty of blackmailing homosexual men who had approached them for protection.

Of course, for some homosexual men the fear of intimidation and violence added to the other pressures of hiding their sexuality became too much and suicide became the final desperate chance of escape. It was not uncommon for men awaiting trial for homosexual offences, as well as those who had been found guilty, to try to kill themselves rather than face the shame and humiliation of being dragged through the courts or spending years in prison. If they were unsuccessful in their efforts these unfortunates would find themselves facing futher criminal charges for their attempt to end their own lives.

WE WANT TO BE RECOGNISED AND TOLERATED

Since the topic of homosexuality was no longer taboo it was inevitable that playwrights and film-makers should want to explore the issue more openly. The lifting of the Lord Chamberlain's ban on plays with homosexual themes in November 1958 gave the green light to 'sincere and serious' portrayals of homosexuality in the theatre and, subsequently, the cinema. Oscar Wilde's life was the first to transfer from stage to the screen in two films both released in 1960. Shelagh Delaney's play *A Taste of Honey* was released as a film in 1961 with Rita Tushingham in the main role and Murray Melvin as her homosexual friend. The same year saw the release of *Victim* which starred Dirk Bogarde, Sylvia Sims and a host of well-known British character actors in a contemporary drama which, for the first time in the history of British cinema, had homosexuality as its central issue.

Bogarde played an affluent barrister with homosexual inclinations whose marriage and professional reputation are put at risk by a blackmail threat following the suicide in police custody of a young man he has been seeing. Although in tone the film is sombre and unremittingly serious, its uncompromising case for law reform and the quality of the performances still make it compulsive viewing. At the time of its release its role in changing popular attitudes cannot be underestimated; even the *News of the World* was impressed by its treatment of its chosen subject:

> Soberly, intelligently and unobtrusively the film presents and argues the problems of these men and illustrates the agonies of mind some must suffer. It pulls no punches, yet it is not sensational. Nor is it offensive.[25]

Televison, too, began to be influenced by this new openness; in 1960 Granada Television put Oscar Wilde *On Trial*, and three years later their Play of the Week entitled *Dangerous Corner* had a homosexual character. In June 1963 some BBC viewers were shocked by an episode of the popular police drama series *Z Cars* which featured a homosexual couple who were being blackmailed. The topic was periodically aired on discussion programmes such as *Gallery* in 1962 and *Table Talk* in 1963; *This Week* created a sensation by showing the first full-blown documentary in 1964 which compared the situation of British homosexuals with that of their counterparts in the Netherlands. Viewers saw scenes of homosexual men dancing together and kissing in a Dutch club, and heard a number of anonymous British homosexuals talking about their lives and the difficulties caused by the law.

Throughout this period fiction and non-fiction books dealing with homosexual characters and themes were becoming increasingly common. Novels included Elliot George's *The Leather Boys* (which was released as a film in 1963) and a book of *Victim* ; while for those who preferred autobiographies there was Lionel Fielden's *The Natural Bent* and John Morris's *Hired to Kill*. More facts and figures based on research were provided in 1960 in Gordon Westwood's book *A Minority* and in Richard Hauser's Home Office sponsored survey of *The Homosexual Society* in 1962.[26] The moral and religious arguments in favour of law reform received a significant boost with the publication of *Towards a Quaker View of Sex* which firmly rejected the notion that the Christian Church should automatically condemn all homosexual behaviour. It also put forward the very progressive notion that homosexual relationships were not necessarily any less valid than heterosexual ones.

> we see no reason why the physical nature of a sexual act should be the criterion by which the question of whether or not it is moral should be decided. An act which... expresses true affection between two individuals and gives pleasure to them both, does not seem to us to be sinful by reason *alone* of the fact that it is homosexual.[27]

One book which seemed to sum up all these various aspects of the problem was *Queer People* published by W. H. Allen in 1963. In this frank and interesting 'personal survey' of the world of one well-balanced professional homosexual man, the author (writing under the psuedonym Douglas Plummer) was uncompromising about his sexuality.

> I am a homosexual, a so-called 'queer' or 'pansy'. I admit it without shame... I am a respectable citizen with a good job and decent record. I volunteered for the army directly war was declared in 1939 and I was an infantry officer for six

years, fighting in three major tank battles, in the last of
which I was wounded. If you met me you would not know
I was a homosexual.

Several national newspapers had rejected the work in the form of
a series of articles on the grounds that 'public opinion was not ready
for them'. Mr Plummer's call for an end to persecution was certainly
bold and unequivocal, demanding that homosexuals were no different to heterosexuals and deserved to be treated equally:

> We want to be recognised and tolerated, not abused and
> thrown into jail for being something we cannot help and
> time cannot cure. We wish to be integrated into society, and
> to be allowed those measures of freedom which should not
> be denied civilized people.

However, these arguments and his attempt to rally his fellow
homosexuals to fight for their own freedom were nearly a decade
ahead of their time.

> I sometimes think we homosexuals are absurdly tolerant.
> The way some newspapers attack us would not be accepted
> by any other group of a million people.... We are completely
> disorganised and rather pathetically fail to speak with one
> voice being absurdly afraid of public censure. Yet a million
> or more voices should not be negligible, if raised in defence
> of a way of life which the world is powerless to alter.

Despite this explosion of media coverage opinion polls seemed
to indicate that the deeply rooted prejudice against homosexuality
amongst large sections of the British public was not going to be
swept away easily. In fact, there were signs that this new openness
might be alienating those who had initially supported the Wolfenden recommendations. An in-depth study carried out for the
Albany Trust by the British Market Research Bureau (BMRB) in
1963 revealed that 67 per cent of the 2,500 people questioned
opposed the decriminalisation of homosexual behaviour between
consenting adults in private, with only 16 per cent supporting the
proposal. A survey in *New Society* in the same year found that 59 per
cent of respondants believed that some legal restriction of homosexuality was unavoidable, although there was a substantial
minority of 39 per cent who disagreed.

One had only to look in the correspondence columns of local

and national newspapers to find the concrete proof of this deeply rooted opposition to homosexuality. Whereas in the political arena the debate had become focused more on the social and psychological aspects of the issue, those who still rested their faith firmly in biblical condemnation were being given every encouragement to express their passionately held views in print. This example from the *Gloucester Echo* was typical of its type:

> God doesn't call homosexuality a sin. He calls it an abomination. He is very definite what should be done with these perverts – death.... I have heard of other suggestions, including slinging the whole lot on some far-away distant island.[28]

Christian concern was frequently combined with patriotic fervour to bolster the argument, as in this letter to the *Birmingham Post*.

> those of us who love our nation are not going to allow homosexuality to be advocated as a way of life. First comes the decline, then the Fall. Homosexuality means the death of family life and the end of our Christian heritage.[29]

A significant section of the Great British public felt that the existing prohibition against homosexuality permitted them to ignore its very existence: what the eye cannot see, the heart cannot grieve over. Or as Lady Lloyd put it in a letter to the *Daily Telegraph* on 5 July 1960:

> All decent people long to see a cessation of the discussion. Behind a drawn blind a corpse may be rotting; the blind will not stop the smell, but at least it will hide from the passer-by the horrors of putrefaction.

Faced with such extreme views some brave homosexuals were prepared to risk their livelihood and reputation in order to speak out and defend themselves; and in doing so took the first small but significant step towards gay liberation. Very few had the courage to follow the example of the three men whose letter appeared in the *New Statesman* on 4 June 1960 who deliberately chose to sign their real names in order to make what was possibly one of the earliest public gestures of 'coming out' in the British press.

> We are homosexuals and we are writing because we feel strongly that insufficient is being done to enlighten public

opinion on a topic which has for too long been shunned....
Over the past few years an enormous amount has been
spoken and written about the homosexual situation. Most
of it has been realistic and sensible, some has been vicious
and ill-informed. But whatever its form we welcome it
because we must welcome anything which brings this topic,
for so long taboo, into open discussion. Only in this way can
prejudice, which is born of fear and ignorance be overcome.

It is a problem only because of the prevailing attitude
towards it, and because the law encourages such an attitude
and hinders every attempt to overcome it. Even so, law
reform, although essential, is only a first step; there will
remain the much larger and longer task of dissolving centuries of accumulated and deeply ingrained misconception.

Roger Butler, Raymond Gregson,
Robert G. Moorcroft.

4

BURBLING ON ABOUT BUGGERY: 1964–67

> I say unequivocally that it was a bad Bill to begin with, that
> it is a bad Bill now, and that it will be a bad Bill till the end
> of time.
>
> *Mr Peter Mahon* – House of Commons 19/12/66

PARLIAMENT'S RIGHT TO DECIDE

By the spring of 1964 it was becoming increasingly clear that a
general election was imminent. In the midst of the end-of-term
atmosphere at Westminster it was therefore something of a surprise
to find a distinguished right-wing Tory MP, Sir Thomas Moore,
tabling a motion on 16 April calling on the Government to implement the Wolfenden recommendations on homosexuality. Leaving
aside the inappropriate timing, this was hardly the type of initiative
which Sir Thomas's colleagues would have expected someone of
his deeply conservative opinions to be promoting. The explanation
was, apparently, that he had been very disturbed by the confidences
of a close friend who was homosexual and had been forced to
conclude that the existing laws were vindictive and unjust. His
motion did not attract enough support to force a debate, partly
because MPs knew that the impending dissolution of Parliament
would prevent it making any real progress, but also because most
Labour politicians did not want to be seen co-operating with such
an eminent figure in the Conservative Party. In June the Prime
Minister let it be known that an autumn election was certain and
the political parties immediately began to prepare their respective
manifestos – none of which mentioned homosexual law reform.

On 7 July a front page exclusive in the *Sunday Mirror* revealed 'a
top level investigation into the alleged homosexual relationship

between a prominent peer and a leading thug in the London underworld'. Although he was not mentioned by name, the peer in question was the ardent supporter of homosexual law reform, Lord Boothby; the thug was one of the notorious Kray brothers. Scotland Yard denied that any such inquiry was in progress. Lord Boothby, who was holidaying abroad, returned home to refute the allegations, and a few weeks later the publishers of the *Sunday Mirror* issued a statement apologising to Lord Boothby for the articles and paying him £40,000 compensation.

This somewhat bizarre business was followed on 16 July by an unexpected announcement that

> the Director of Public Prosecutions, in exercising his responsibilities for prosecutions policy... has advised Chief Constables informally that in order to achieve greater uniformity of enforcement of the law regarding homosexuality in private they should seek his advice before bringing proceedings.[1]

There was intense press speculation as to whether this move was in any way connected with the *Sunday Mirror*'s story; but with hindsight it seems more likely to have been a Government ploy to placate the growing concern of senior backbenchers like Sir Thomas Moore, while at the same time removing one of the reformers' principal objections to the existing law. Furthermore, the new Attorney General was Sir Peter Rawlinson, who had defended Peter Wildeblood at his trial in 1954, and was one of the parliamentary sponsors of Leo Abse's Private Member's Bill in 1962.

Although a number of newspapers supported the principle behind the request most disapproved of this underhand method of achieving it; as the *Daily Herald* put it: 'the way to change the law is not by administrative action. The issue must be decided in the open, and it is Parliament's right to decide.'[2] The *Evening Standard* used the announcement as an excuse to run a series of articles exposing 'LONDON'S HIDDEN PROBLEM'. These contained the now familiar, sympathetic accounts of the difficulties facing homosexual men and described the existing underworld of clubs and pubs in the capital where they could meet. But the most interesting fact they revealed was that London's homosexual community had begun to use a new word to define themselves:

> The old opprobrious names, 'queer', 'pansy', 'nancy boy', 'pouf' were given them. 'Gay' is what they prefer to call

themselves. A light, unwounding, inconspicuous word that has a useful double meaning... the present use is largely American, but has caught on here.[3]

In October 1964 the Labour Party won the election on a manifesto promising an extensive programme of reforms – but found themsleves with only a tiny majority of four in the House of Commons to achieve it. MPs on the Executive Committee of the HLRS advised against any immediate parliamentary initiative since the new Prime Minister, Harold Wilson, was expected to call another election in the near future to secure a larger working majority. However, the Liberal peer and newspaper journalist, Lord Arran, had different ideas, and approached the Society to inform them that he intended to raise the issue of the Wolfenden recommendations in the House of Lords. In preparation for the debate he duly wrote to more than 200 peers across the entire political spectrum asking for their assistance. On the day before his motion was scheduled for consideration a letter appeared in *The Times* backing reform and carrying the signatures of five bishops and three peers including, most significantly, Lord Devlin, who had argued such a strong case against the Wolfenden Report in his 1959 Maccabaean lecture.[4]

Lord Arran's eloquent and impassioned plea to the Lords on 12 May 1965 for an end to the legal persecution of homosexual men was supported by 17 of the 22 speakers who contributed to the debate – including the Archbishops of Canterbury and York.[5] The Home Office spokesman, Lord Stonham, indicated that the Government would retain the traditional neutrality with regard to this type of issue, but it was clear that this neutrality would be more sympathetic to reform than that of its Conservative predecessor. Although the procedure adopted by Arran did not permit a vote on the matter, the clear majority in favour of the motion encouraged him to bring forward the following simple one clause Sexual Offences Bill less than a fortnight later: 'A homosexual act in private shall not be an offence provided that the parties consent thereto and have attained the age of 21 years.'[6] At the Second Reading debate on 24 May it was the opponents of reform who dominated the proceedings; two former Lord Chancellors, Lord Dilhorne and Lord Kilmuir, led a succession of speakers issuing dire warnings of the disastrous repercussions of passing this Bill. Although he was convinced that he had lost the argument, Lord Arran was still determined to press for a vote; he later recalled his surprise at the outcome.

> as I stood in the lobby holding my wand – I was a Teller – I saw coming towards me a sweet and seemingly endless stream of 'contents'. Lord Stonham... my strong though officially neutral supporter, gave me the thumbs-up sign, and I knew we had won. The *Guardian* called the majority of 94 to 49 'a splendid palindrome'. It was I think the only great moment of my small life.[7]

Although this was certainly the first step along the legislative path to reform there was still a considerable distance yet to be covered, with many pitfalls along the way, before the Wolfenden proposals would find their way on to the statute book. Having passed the formal First Reading in the Lords, and its general principle having been approved by this Second Reading, the specific details of the Arran Bill would now have to be thrashed out in Committee session before it could receive its Third Reading and be sent on to the House of Commons.

Assuming that the Government was not prepared to sponsor the Bill (which was usually the case on issues of 'individual conscience') it would have to be introduced into the Commons by an MP as a Private Member's Bill. This could be done in three ways: by winning a place in the yearly ballot for Private Member's Bills which enabled a small proportion of such bills to pass into law; by introducing the bill under the Ten Minute Rule which allowed its sponsor a ten minute speech to argue his or her case and one ten minute speech in opposition, followed by a vote; or by bringing it forward as an 'unballoted' bill at the end of the main debate on a Friday when it had to receive an unopposed Second Reading – an attempt which could be thwarted by any MP shouting the word 'Object'. Those bills sponsored by MPs who had won high places in the ballot stood the strongest chance of becoming law; bills introduced by the other two methods were rarely successful.

Once a Private Member's Bill had been introduced into the Commons it had to pass its Second Reading before being sent to a Standing Committee consisting of MPs interested in the measure and reflecting the balance of opinion shown during the debate. When its details had been discussed and all amendments considered then the bill would return to the floor of the House for its Report Stage. If a majority was achieved in that debate a Third

Reading would automatically be assured. However, all these stages were hampered by the very limited amount of time available for Private Members' legislation and the need for at least 100 MPs to vote in favour of the bill at every division. The bill would now return to the House of Lords where it might once again be required to win a vote before being passed into law.

THE OUTCOME IN THE COMMONS

Although most of the national newspapers were impressed by such a progressive decision by the traditionally conservative Upper House none of them underestimated the obstacles which still lay ahead. In the *Daily Mail* on 26 May Bernard Levin commented: 'Their Lordships... have shown more wisdom, courage and humanity on this question than the Lower House, and also than any Government in recent years.' The accuracy of this observation was demonstrated on that same day when the House of Commons considered a very similar bill to Lord Arran's, which Labour MP Leo Abse had introduced under the Ten Minute Rule procedure.[8] The puritanical right-wing Conservative backbencher Sir Cyril Osborne put himself forward as spokesman for the opposition and made an impassioned plea to the House to defend the Victorian values of the nation against declining morality and the rising tide of permissiveness. The main thrust of his argument was not particularly sophisticated:

> do we wish to encourage sodomy? It is as simple as that. This
> is an age of lawlessness, violence and crime. What we need
> is sterner discipline and not more licence.

In the vote that followed the motion was defeated by 178 votes to 159. Senior Conservatives voting against the motion included Edward Heath, Peter Walker, Francis Pym and George Younger. They had been joined by a significant number of old-style trade union MPs led by the Chairman of the Labour Party, Manny Shinwell, whose radical political beliefs and non-conformist religious views would not countenance approval of this decadent vice. One consolation for Mr Abse was that the majority against reform had fallen from 114 in the 1960 debate to a mere 19. And further encouragement could be drawn from the list of Cabinet Ministers who had voted in favour, including Home Secretary, Roy Jenkins,

Housing Minister, Richard Crossman and John Silkin, the Government Chief Whip.

The Times had mixed feelings about the result, but seemed to consider it inevitable.

> the outcome in the Commons was probably a wise one. While public sympathy has increased for those afflicted as homosexual, it is not yet ready to countenance the state on a broader scale. Or so Parliament believes.[9]

The *Guardian* was unimpressed: its report on 27 May suggested that the Commons had 'struck a brave blow for reaction', but its editorial noted that the outcome of both votes indicated that 'an appreciable shift' in public opinion was beginning to take place. In the *Daily Mail* Monica Furlong was concerned that nearly half the MPs had not even bothered to vote on the matter and suspected that this was partly because they were afraid of upsetting or offending their constituents.

> It is when one considers this sort of possibility that one begins to feel that a moral rot may well have set into our national life, though not the kind envisaged so dramatically by Sir Cyril Osborne.[10]

In the meanwhile Lord Arran's Bill continued its passage through the Upper House. Shortly before it was due for its Third Reading its sponsor persuaded the Editor of the *Daily Mail* to commission a National Opinion Poll to find out the extent of public support for his reform. In a remarkable shift from the findings of the BMRB poll in 1963 there emerged for the first time a clear majority of 63 per cent in favour of decriminalising homosexual behaviour between consenting adults in private. However, some MPs must have been disturbed to learn that 21 per cent of respondents felt they would be less likely to vote for their MP at the next election if he or she supported such a measure.[11] The result of this poll undoubtedly helped the Bill pass its Third Reading on 28 October by a decisive 116 votes to 46 after 27 hours of debate.[12] It was not taken up by any backbench MP in the Lower House and automatically lapsed at the end of that parliamentary session.

In the first session of the 1966 Parliament Conservative backbencher Humphrey Berkeley decided to use his high placing in the Private Member's ballot to introduce Lord Arran's Sexual Offences Bill. Although this news was a cause for cautious optimism, the

Observer warned on 6 February that the success of the initiative would depend to a large extent on the personal attitude of Harold Wilson.

> The Prime Minister is expected once more to stay away – a strategem attributed by some of his colleagues to excessive caution. It is said by those who know him better to represent the typical North-country nonconformist approach.

At the Second Reading of the Bill on 11 February, after five hours of debate and in the absence of the Prime Minister, the House of Commons recorded its first ever vote in favour of homosexual law reform by 166 votes to 109.[13]

The next morning the Fleet Street dailies were virtually unanimous in approving this decision: the *Daily Mail* called it 'one of the outstanding free vote debates in recent years', while the *Telegraph* recorded its firm approval thus –

> It will end a law that is equally disreputable for being largely unenforceable and often cruel where enforced; it will shift a great fear from many people, no more sinful than most of their neighbours; it will cut the blackmailer's income; not least it will end a controversy that has become unseemly and disproportionate, and rob homosexuality of the false glamour which always attaches to persecuted minorities.

The *Daily Express* stood alone in its condemnation: 'it does not represent the views of the great majority of people in Great Britain. They would reject it given the opportunity.' As might have been expected this situation was completely reversed north of the border where the *Scotsman* was virtually the only newspaper to support the Commons' decision. The *Scottish Daily Herald* berated MPs who had stayed away from the debate and consequently allowed such a 'misguided' measure to pass; the *Sunday Post* rallied its readership to 'stop the rot and kill this Bill by sheer weight of public opinion'.[14] The irony was that Scotland, along with Northern Ireland, was not affected by the Bill which applied only to England and Wales!

AN AWAKENED CONSCIENCE

By now the debate over the issue had spread well beyond the parliamentary arena, but since the national dailies largely supported the reform, those opposed to any relaxation of the existing law often found their case received more sympathy in the correspondence pages of the local press. In Scotland the debate, almost inevitably, had a distinctly spiritual edge. The *Dunfermline Press* printed a very balanced consideration of the issues in its editorial on 12 February which left its readers to ponder for themselves on the fundamental question at stake: 'Homosexuality, *if it is to be condemned*, must be condemned as a sin. *But can or should one legislate against sin?*' One of its most regular and most religious correspondents was a certain Mr Sinclair of Kelty, who had written several times to condemn the Arran Bill as it passed through its various parliamentary stages and rally his fellow countrymen to 'raise their united voice over the harm which the passing of this Bill will do to the cause of Jesus Christ in this Scotland of ours'.[15] He was appalled by the even-handed editorial, which he dismissed as 'a piece of sophistry', and continued in characteristic style to lambast anyone who refused to condemn the proposed reform.

> The fact is that sodomy is a sin against God and a crime against society and as such ought to receive due punishment. There is no cult about it, but an acquired vice, and a disgusting one at that.... You say, if I understand you aright, that we should stifle our conscience and accept this Bill as necessary.... But 'conscience doth make cowards of us all' and an awakened conscience is a hundred hells. *I know*.[16]

But some people were heartily sick of this sort of blind religious bigotry, and on 26 February the paper gave another writer space to launch a swingeing attack on Mr Sinclair's 'smug, self-rightous, holier-than-thou diatribes'.

> There is no logical reason why the current Bill should not be passed. No one is going to be endangered by the ending of the illegality of homosexual practices between consenting adults. Outraged morality and righteous indignation aside, there is, I repeat, no *logical* reason. I am painfully aware, of course, that expecting a bible-walloper to see logic is like expecting snow in the Sahara.

Having noted the prevailing tendency for Bible quotations to be bandied about he offered the Kelty correspondent a selection of half a dozen which included 'Thou shalt love thy neighbour as thyself' and 'Judge not, that ye be not judged'. He went on:

Mr Sinclair is a typical religionist, all righteous talk, Sunday Kirk, and all the rest of it, but singularly lacking in any charity or understanding to those most in need. If Mr Sinclair is not prepared to act upon the words of his own Bible, then may I offer him a final quotation from the same source: 'And weigh thy words in a balance and make a door and bar for thy mouth'.

South of the Border there was no shortage of professionals who felt it appropriate to offer calmer and more superficially reasoned objections to liberalising the law, but almost always they eventually fell back on the 'moral' argument. An anonymous 'Northern Barrister' warned of 'The Dangers behind the Wolfenden Bill' in the *Yorkshire Post* on 10 June 1965:

There is a danger that good-hearted people will support abolition because, without knowledge, they are persuaded that all homosexuals are creatures to be pitied however abominable their actions.... I have both prosecuted and defended men charged with homosexuality. This experience convinces me that the majority are completely sane, fully aware of the evil of their lives, but glorying in it. Such men cannot be tolerated in decent society. Is it irrelevant to remember the fate of the Cities of the Plain?

In the *Birmingham Post*, an eminent QC opposed the reform on the grounds that: 'if the law was relaxed... unnatural practices would increase and multiply'.[17] But when, in a spate of correspondence in the *Manchester Evening News* in June 1965, a supporter of the Arran Bill had argued that those who had voted for it were 'intelligent, well-educated, Christian men who understand the problem',[18] he was immediately taken to task by another writer who demanded to know:

Who do they speak for? Not the majority of people who try to live by good moral codes. Poor 'illiterate' people like myself, who on behalf of their children resist these progressives – how can we bring up our children to live decently and be clean-minded when moral standards are flouted by people like [this]?[19]

Another local 'expert' blamed all the ills of contemporary society on homosexuals.

The present upsurge in crime, immorality, vandalism, delinquency, and drug-taking must be checked. To condone homosexuality would only aggravate the position and lead to more thuggery and blackmail.... Respectable millions must not be contaminated by a few minions.[20]

The advocates of reform fought back stroke for stroke, often displaying considerable humour in the face of such grim and uncompromising hostility. After an editorial in the *East Anglian Daily Times* propounded the view that homosexuals were responsible for all present day problems – including the decline of contemporary art and sculpture – a certain Mr Cranbrook attempted to put the matter back into perspective.

I cannot think... that you really believe that these ordinary people... with homosexual tendencies 'could do irreparable damage to public morality and to the decent and honest conduct of public life' if the Bill now before Parliament becomes law.... Like you I find homosexuality and some forms of modern art repugnant, but I am also repelled by many other things: by left-wing politics, by young, but obviously heterosexual men with hair like girls, by robbery with violence, and, if you don't mind my saying so, by your rather turgid prose. Of these the only one which could reasonably be thought to be affected by the others is the last, which doesn't really help us when we are dealing with a difficult social problem which... demands balanced thinking, sympathy and understanding – not woolly phrases.[21]

WILDE WINS AS LAST

Back on the parliamentary front line Mr Berkeley's success was very short-lived; less than a month after his Bill had been passed Parliament was dissolved to allow a general election to take place on 31 March 1966. Not only was the Bill automatically void, but the MP himself was not re-elected and promptly blamed his defeat on his support for such a politically sensitive subject. Of course, in an election which had given the Labour Party a majority of nearly 100 in the Commons many other Conservative MPs also lost their seats, including 21 who had voted against the Berkeley Bill. The new session of Parliament seemed to offer little immediate prospect for homosexual law reform since the Private Member's ballot was not supposed to take place until the autumn. Lord Arran therefore decided to re-introduce his bill in the Lords where it received a Second Reading by a majority of 70 votes to 29 on 10 May.[22] Its successful Third Reading on 16 June was accompanied by a number of appeals to the Government for time to be found so that it could be considered by the House of Commons.[23]

In the meantime an early Private Member's ballot had been permitted by the Government, but despite behind-the-scenes encouragement from the Home Secretary Roy Jenkins none of the MPs who had won a high place in it could be persuaded to take on the Arran Bill. When Jenkins learned that Leo Abse had already decided to propose the Bill for a second time under the Ten Minute Rule procedure he informed the MP that if a decisive vote could be gained in its favour he would insist on the Cabinet finding time for it to be debated fully. As soon as the Upper House had passed the Sexual Offences Bill Mr Abse introduced it into the Commons and on 5 July 1966 was rewarded by a handsome majority of 264 votes to 102.[24]

According to Richard Crossman's diaries Roy Jenkins used this result early in the new session of Parliament to put a persuasive case to the Cabinet for the Government to abandon its traditional neutrality on this issue. But at the Cabinet Meeting on 27 October there were objections from a number of Ministers including the Prime Minister and the Chancellor of the Exchequer James Callaghan; and the argument might well have been lost without the intervention of Crossman himself who, as Leader of the House of Commons, was responsible for arranging the legislative timetable. He later recorded the clever reasoning he had employed to overcome this opposition.

> I was able to point out that we couldn't really be neutral in this case because both Houses had already expressed a clear will for legislation. In that case it was clearly better to let the Commons debate the matter freely now and to provide time for this rather than let the subject drag on until nearer the election. With this highly tactical argument we persuaded the P. M. to drag the rest of his colleagues with him.[25]

A special evening sitting of the Commons on 19 December was arranged for the Bill's Second Reading with the co-operation of the Chief Whip, John Silkin. During the debate the opponents of the Bill rallied and concentrated their efforts on the issue which had been raised by the National Maritime Board as to whether Merchant Seamen should be exempted from the provisions of the Bill as members of the armed forces already were. Mr Abse used this controversy to his advantage: he initially resisted the calls for homosexuality to remain a criminal offence in the Merchant Navy, but once the House had voted to continue its debate after 10pm he grudgingly agreed to consider amendments to that effect during the Committee Stage of the Bill. Due to a technicality of parliamentary procedure this meant that no further vote need be taken and the Sexual Offences Bill was automatically through to its next stage![26] The majority of the press approved of the outcome: 'GO AHEAD FOR VICE BILL' was the triumphant headline in the *Daily Mirror* on the following morning; the *Liverpool Post* considered it 'a debate of high quality' while the *Aberdeen Evening Express* applauded Mr Abse's clever tactics under the heading 'COMMONS MIX-UP FOOLS OPPOSITION'.

In order that the Bill was not delayed in the queue of other legislation waiting for Committee scrutiny a special Standing Committee was set up to consider it separately. At its first meeting Mr Abse performed an immediate volte-face and agreed to the demands over the Merchant Navy. The opponents of the reform who had been appointed to the Committee (three of whom did not even attend its first meeting) had expected a prolonged dispute over this point and had therefore not put forward other amendments for discussion; but since the matter had been resolved the Committee stage was duly completed within an hour and the Bill was ready to return to the floor of the House for its Report and Third Reading. Extra time was allocated for this stage on the morning of Friday 23 June.[27] Infuriated by Leo Abse's brilliant tactics the opposition embarked on a determined effort to talk the Bill out by tabling a long list of new amendments and indulging in protracted and rambling speeches. In this way they ensured that all the new clauses had not been discussed by the end of the sitting and therefore the final vote could not be taken.

At this point the measure would probably have failed if Roy Jenkins had not been fully committed to it – once again Crossman and Silkin arranged further time for debate by allowing the House to continue in session after 10p.m. on Monday 3 July.[28] But the adversaries of law reform, although clearly in a minority, continued their filibuster tactics and as the debate droned on into the small hours of the morning tempers frayed and angry insults were flung across the Chamber. A weary Richard Crossman recorded in his diary:

> at two in the morning it looked as if it was going to last 30 hours. But the opposition conked out. Neither Cyril Osborne or Cyril Black, the leaders, could get there.[29]

Leo Abse later explained how close he came to defeat.

> To close the debate on each amendment I had to obtain leave of the Speaker to move a closure, and then to have a minimum of a hundred MPs to join me in the Lobby to enforce the leave granted. Nine times during the long night I went through the Lobbies, and on each occasion I had but a handful over the hundred required with me.[30]

When the final vote was taken after dawn on the morning of 4 July 1967 the Sexual Offences Bill was passed by 101 votes to 16. One homosexual man who had been part of the HLRS contingent which sat patiently in the public gallery through to the small hours of that morning later recalled his reaction to this final victory.

> I came out of the House of Commons with Antony Grey and all the crowd and we all said goodnight to one another. I walked down to the Embankment and I stood and lit a cigarette and was looking down into the water and I was very aware that I'd been part of making history. Part of something people will be very glad about.[31]

Although some newspapers played up the drama of the long debate, most of the press coverage was limited to short but approving pieces which expressed a general sense of relief that the issue of homosexual law reform had finally been dealt with. There were still a few papers which continued to echo the prejudices of the previous decade; the *Daily Express* stood almost alone in continuing to dispute the outcome of the debate.

> What benefit can this proposed legislation bring to anyone – least of all to the unfortunate men most directly affected? Unnatural practices will become more easily indulged. A social stigma will be weakened... Parliament only brings discredit on itself when it separates itself so decisively from the moral sense of the people.[32]

The *News of the World*'s leader column agreed that the decision was 'a blot on the country' and its main article highlighted opinions of the MPs who had opposed the Bill which it dubbed 'THE CHARTER FOR CORRUPTION'.[33]

For the third time the Bill now passed back to the House of Lords where it received final approval on 21 July.[34] In his victory speech Lord Arran quoted from one of Oscar Wilde's letters written just after the unfortunate dramatist had been released from Reading gaol:

> 'Yes, we shall win in the end; but the road will be long and red with monstrous martyrdoms.'
> My Lords, Mr Wilde was right: the road has been long and the martyrdoms many, monstrous and bloody. Today, please God! sees the end of that road.

Six days later the Bill was given Royal Assent and passed on to the Statute Book as the Sexual Offences Act. By this time press interest had dwindled away and most newspapers carried a few column inches under such headings as 'Wilde Wins at Last' or 'Arran says Mr Wilde was Right'.[35]

CHRISTIAN COMPASSION, NOT CHRISTIAN CONTROVERSY

Without any doubt Lord Arran and Mr Abse had scored a significant victory in enacting the main recommendations of the Wolfenden Report, namely that homosexual activity in private between consenting males over the age of 21 should be decriminalised. However, Wolfenden had argued that homosexual activity was no more or less culpable than many other heterosexual sins, and therefore should be subject to the same legal constraints as the equivalent heterosexual activity, with the one major exception of the age of consent. But the Sexual Offences Act not only endorsed the Committee's acknowledged inconsistency in setting the homosexual age of consent at 21 years, it actually imposed a number of further significant restrictions on the freedom of homosexual men. The need for these constraints was implicit in the arguments which the reformers had put forward to win their case.

In every debate even the most fervent of the Bill's supporters had repeatedly asserted that they did not wish to suggest that Parliament was encouraging or approving of homosexual activity

81

by removing criminal sanctions against it. As Lord Arran himself proudly asserted in a speech on 16 June 1966:

> No single noble Lord or noble Lady has ever said homosexuality is a right or good thing. It has been universally condemned from start to finish by every single member of this House.

Consequently, although this sinful and distasteful behaviour was to be permitted in the sphere of private relations, it was essential to ensure that it was entirely banished from the public arena once and for all. During the debate on 19 December 1966, Conservative MP Norman St John Stevas explained this concept bluntly.

> If this Bill were passed, homosexuality would remain unlawful, although not criminal. The Bill would create no recognised status of homosexuality. It would remain contrary to public policy.

In order to achieve this end, and also to stifle the oft-repeated argument regarding the corruption of youth, young men had not only to be protected by a higher age of consent, but needed to be shielded from any public manifestation of homosexuality which might encourage them to adopt such a disastrous lifestyle. To cover the first case, the sentence for consensual buggery with a young man between the ages of 16 and 21 was fixed at a maximum of five years, while the prison sentence for anyone found guilty of commiting or attempting to commit gross indecency with a youth over 16 but under 21 years old was actually increased from two to five years. Furthermore, a dangerously imprecise clause imposed a maximum prison sentence of two years for 'any man who procures another man to commit with a third man an act of buggery', which pandered to the prevailing notion that homosexuality could be spread by deliberate recruitment. But for a number of Peers this was still not sufficent to protect society from the undoubted dangers of an explosion in 'sodomitic societies and buggery clubs', and so to prevent the horrific possibility of homosexual orgies they forced through an amendment stating that a homosexual act would not be considered private:

(a) when more than two persons take part or are present; or
(b) in a lavatory to which the public have or are permitted to have access, whether on payment or otherwise.

Due to the insistence of the Service Ministries, homosexual acts by members of the armed forces continued to remain illegal on the grounds that discipline would be irrevocably undermined if senior officers were known by lower ranks to be homosexual or could use their authority to corrupt subordinates into such activities. Sex between merchant seamen on board their ships was still forbidden (although this did not apply if their partner was a passenger), thanks to the insistence of the National Union of Seaman and the National Maritime Board. Finally, the new Act applied only to England and Wales – in Scotland and Northern Ireland all homosexual acts continued to be illegal.

It is tempting simply to cite the atmosphere of ill-informed prejudice and irrational fear which had surrounded the whole subject of homosexuality since it had surfaced in the early 1950s to explain away these illogical but important restraints. In spite of the detailed findings of the Wolfenden inquiry and the sterling efforts of the HLRS the myths and misconceptions which defined homosexuality as some sort of insidious sickness which could be spread by infecting others remained firmly rooted in the national consciousness. This view was not only nurtured and perpetuated by a moralistic, sensation-seeking press and a deeply conservative broadcasting system, but was rarely, if ever, challenged during the parliamentary debates. Antony Grey later observed:

> As a consequence of this continuing unwillingness of politicians to face up to the needs, in the first instance for any action at all, and subsequently for a really frank and searching debate, the discussions which did take place in Parliament between 1965 and 1967 contained elements of unreality and to that extent were in fact irrational.[36]

In his book *Parliament and Conscience*, Professor Peter Richards noted that by adopting this over-cautious approach the Bill's proposers had ensured that

> the fundamental moral issue was consistently avoided.... Clearly, it was not in the interests of the reformers to raise contentious issues.... Their task was to arouse Christian compassion, not Christian controversy. Their tactic was to keep parliamentary debate as rational and moderate as possible because of the danger that an upsurge of emotion and prejudice would ruin their chances of success.[37]

But the motives and methods of the men who steered the

legislation through the complex and treacherous channels of the parliamentary process also exerted a considerable influence on its final form. Essentially the Bill was shaped by a relatively small group of elderly peers – protected from considerations of electoral gain by their privileged status – in the strange hot-house atmosphere of the Upper Chamber in the spring and summer of 1965; the alterations made in the House of Commons were merely cosmetic by comparison. Its chief architect, Lord Arran, was a married man suffering from poor health, who had no history of reforming zeal on contentious sexual issues. In a magazine article in 1972 he admitted that his motives for getting involved in the matter were far from clear.

> Exhibitionism? Because I went to Eton and I knew what it was all about? A hatred of injustice...? I do not know my own motives any more. Most probably my – or Parliament's – liberation of the male homosexual here and elsewhere derives from my unhappiness at that time over a purely domestic matter (nothing to do with homosexuality). I have known more than one man in his distress turn to matters which will give him a new anxiety.[38]

Leo Abse, who had also pondered this question at the time, subsequently met a man who claimed to have been the homosexual lover of Arran's older brother.

> This older brother, who over many years had received psychiatric aid, died tragically only a matter of days after becoming the Earl. Arran succeeded to the title: it must have brought him much guilt. But it brought him, too, the opportunity to make a massive and brave act of reparation.[39]

Whatever the reasons, Lord Arran was undoubtedly committed to his chosen cause, but he had no experience of piloting such a controversial piece of legislation through Parliament. As his campaign progressed he found himself living in 'a little private hell': he began receiving a barrage of obscene and anonymous letters; he became so afraid of blackmail that his female secretary was present whenever he saw young men at his office; and in November 1965 the walls of his office, his Club, and virtually every railway and underground station in London were daubed with graffiti which read 'ARRAN HOMO'. He later confessed: 'It was at this time that I began to drink, not heavily or, I like to think, noticeably. But for over a year I was permanently, if slightly pickled.'[40] This was certainly not the ideal state of mind for anyone who required mental agility and swift manoeuvering to ward off the vitriolic and irrational opposition that the subject of homosexuality aroused.

Given these circumstances the Government's offer to lend the expertise of the parliamentary draftsmen to assist Lord Arran in drawing up the details of the Bill must have come as a welcome relief. However, in this way the Government was able to exercise considerable power in dictating the final form. When supporters of the HLRS later proposed amendments to reduce the age of consent and to offer a more precise definition of 'procuring' – which were clearly disapproved of by the Government – their motions were rejected on the grounds that they were badly drafted and would be unworkable in practice. Antony Grey, who was the key figure in the HLRS's lobbying campaign, tried to make Arran aware of these subtle influences but found him unwilling to risk losing this invaluable support, arguing that it was better to make compromises of detail to achieve final success since in his opinion politics was 'the art of the possible'. He never accepted Antony Grey's argument that greater firmness on his part might have persuaded the Whitehall Establishment that it was possible to dispense with some of the 'safeguards' which they had incorporated into the Bill.

Lord Arran's policy of political pragmatism was shared by his 'unexpected and indefatigable ally' in the Commons: Leo Abse. But in virtually every other respect the two men were very different. Mr Abse was already well known for his advocacy of social reforms in areas connected with morality and family life. Perhaps his late marriage contributed to his obsession with the nuclear family as the ideal form of social organisation which, combined with an adherence to Freudian psychology, produced his rather eccentric view of the world. His main argument for homosexual law reform was clearly outlined in his opening speech of the Second Reading debate on 19 December 1966.

The paramount reason for the introduction of this Bill is that it may at last move our community away from being riveted to the question of punishment of homosexuals which has hitherto prompted us to avoid the real challenge of preventing little boys from growing up to be adult homosexuals. Surely, what we should be pre-occupied with is the question of how we can, if it is possible, reduce the number of faulty males in the community. How can we diminish the number of those who grow up to have men's bodies but feminine souls?

Antony Grey later confirmed that the MP had genuine compassion for the problems of homosexual men.

He had this idea about the sanctity of the family – those that don't procreate are deprived or stunted. And he was able, perfectly sincerely, to put across this viewpoint in the Commons. But however much one disagrees with Leo Abse's philosophical attitude towards homosexuality, he was a master tactician and probably the only person in the House who could have got the Bill through in the way he did.[41]

According to Mr Abse himself, the most important of these tactics was to present the case for reform in such a way that the personal sexual insecurities of the male-dominated House of Commons were not threatened by it.

it was only by insisting that compassion was needed by a totally separate group, quite unlike the absolutely normal male males [sic] of the Commons, could I allay the anxiety and resistances that otherwise would have been provoked. Homosexuals had to be placed at a distance, suffering a fate so different from that enjoyed by Honourable Members blessed with normality, children and the joys of a secure family life. Because of their wealthy endowment, they could surely afford charity.... I was, however, not to eschew all psychological arguments in presenting my case, but the arguments were, perforce, highly selective and to that extent my case was fraudulent.[42]

WHERE DISTASTE SO QUICKLY TURNS TO MORAL INDIGNATION

When the angry tirades and extravagant accusations of the opponents of reform are taken into account it is easy to appreciate the wisdom of this policy. The elderly Peers in the Lords were particularly unpleasant in this respect. War hero, Lord Montgomery of Alamein made no attempt to tone down his vituperation:

I regard the act of homosexuality in any form as the most

abominable bestiality that any human being can take part in and which reduces him to the status of an animal.

Another peer was in full agreement: 'I cannot stand homosexuals. They are the most disgusting people in the world.' Antony Grey who attended almost every debate on the issue finally decided to miss one in the House of Lords on the grounds that he could not bear to hear them 'burbling on about buggery any more'.[43]

But similar opinions were by no means absent from the debates in the Commons, and although usually delivered in calmer tones, the views expressed were no less vehement. Backbench Conservative MPs repeatedly condemned homosexuality as 'a filthy business', 'an abomination', or simply 'this odious topic'. Some were a little more humane; one suggested that the existing law should be retained since it offered some, albeit inadequate, protection for society, but that it should be allowed to fall into disuse as time passed: 'I would rather leave the scab on the wound to wither and fall off than wrench it off prematurely and cause a hæmorrhage at this stage.' It was ironically a Labour MP who most honestly summed up the general attitude of those who were resisting reform: 'I am against the Bill lock stock and barrel, root and branch, hook line and sinker, warts and all.' It is tempting to argue with hindsight that given the irrational nature of this opposition those proposing reform could have pushed the Wolfenden proposals through without so many compromises. But a contemporary advocate of such a policy would probably have been considered incredibly politically naive.

Of course, repeated attempts to amend certain clauses in the Bill were made by a number of Peers on behalf of the HLRS. Despite the essential role played by Antony Grey and his voluntary team in supporting the campaign by raising money and sending out whipping letters, neither Abse nor Arran consulted the Society over the details and drafting of the Bill and resisted its suggestions for altering the proposals. Consequently the Society was forced to seek the assistance of other politicians. For instance, the Earl of Huntingdon repeatedly argued that the proposed age of consent was too high:

It seems to me very illogical that women do not have to be protected after 16, and that, suddenly, we say that men are so incapable of looking after themselves that they have to be protected up to 21.

He suggested that a compromise age of 18 was more acceptable, but this move was decisively defeated. Lord Arran felt unable to offer his support because he was 'afraid lest we go too far', although he admitted that the case was a strong one. Leo Abse's personal conviction that young men passing through a homosexual 'phase' might be prematurely fixated at that stage if they were subjected to the sexual attentions of older men confirmed his belief that 21 was the most appropriate age.

There were also a number of other individual speakers, mainly in the Lords, who made effective challenges to the prevailing view of homosexuals as a wicked and depraved sub-species. The Marquess of Queensbury, whose ancestor had hounded Oscar Wilde to prison, offered appropriate atonement for the deed by making his maiden speech in favour of Lord Arran's Bill. He suggested that some of his colleagues might gain a better insight into the human aspect of the problem if they actually talked to real flesh and blood homosexuals.

> I have certain friends with whom I have done this, and I do not think they are in any way more depraved or immoral than either myself, or any other normal man of my acquaintance.... I believe these laws will be changed and that when my children grow up they will be amazed that laws of this sort could have existed in the middle of the twentieth century.

The most consistent good sense, once again, came from the lady Peeresses. The reasons why women politicians generally seemed to feel less threatened by the issue was hinted at by Lady Wootton when she questioned the motives of her male colleagues who so vehemently opposed the reform.

> They cannot be afraid that these disgusting practices will be thrown upon their attention, because these acts are legalised only if they are performed in private. They cannot be afraid that there will be a corruption of youth, because these acts will be legalised only if they are performed between consenting adults.... I can only suppose that the opponents of this Bill will be afraid that their imagination will be tormented by visions of what will be going on elsewhere. Surely, if that is so, that is their own private misfortune, and no reason for imposing their personal standards of taste and morality on

the minority of their fellow citizens who can find sexual satisfaction only in relations with their own sex.

Lady Gaitskell, whose comments were like a welcome breath of fresh air in the stuffy atmosphere of the Upper House, made it clear that she was also determined to keep the debate grounded firmly on common sense.

I do not believe that homosexual conduct in private between two consenting adult males injures the public, nor does its influence or its example have a harmful effect on the young. Young people should not be kept in ignorance about the complexities of human behaviour. I do not believe that the present laws keep homosexuality in check, and I do not believe that homosexuality would be increased if the laws were liberalised.... What kind of loyalty can we expect from these people towards a society which hounds them, often in such a humiliating way. What could be more squalid than the police spy in the public lavatory?

Ultimately, however, it was not rational, cool arguments like these that had won the day. The tone of exaggerated moral rectitude continued to characterise the discussions in the House of Lords through to the Third and final Reading of the Bill on 21 July 1967. In a highly emotional speech Lord Arran thanked his allies in both Houses of Parliament and paid tribute to Sir John Wolfenden and to Antony Grey of the HLRS. But the chief architect of the reform could not resist using the opportunity to preach an austere message to the men who had been liberated by this change in the law.

Homosexuals must continue to remember that while there may be nothing bad in being a homosexual, there is certainly nothing good. Lest the opponents of the Bill think that a new freedom, a new privileged class, has been created, let me remind them that no amount of legislation will prevent homosexuals from being the subject of dislike and derision or at best of pity. We shall always, I fear, resent the odd man out. That is their burden for all time, and they must shoulder it like men – for men they are.

5

GETTING RADICAL ABOUT THE WHOLE THING: 1967–73

> Any form of ostentatious behaviour, now or in the future,
> any form of public flaunting, would be utterly distasteful
> and would, I believe, make the sponsors of this Bill regret
> that they have done what they have done.
>
> *Lord Arran* – House of Lords 21/7/67

THE NEXT AGENDA

When Sir John Wolfenden had presented his Committee's recommendations at the Home Office in 1957 he had been warned by the Permanent Secretary there that he should not expect them to be implemented in the near future; according to this senior civil servant: 'In a thing like this, where deep emotions are likely to be aroused, I would guess fourteen years as the average time-lag between recommendations and legislation.'[1] Although the subsequent ten year campaign must have seemed a remarkably long haul to the reformers and the homosexual men on whose behalf they fought, to bring about such a fundamental change in the law relating to a complex moral and social issue like homosexuality within a decade was a remarkable achievement. The British parliamentary system has always been notoriously slow to accept social reform in general, mainly because the major political parties have fought shy of controversial 'issues of conscience' and left them to the uncertainties and difficulties of Private Member's legislation. In the mid 1960s increasingly permissive attitudes towards sex and religion had undermined this consensus and led to a spate of Private Member's reforms on issues like divorce, abortion and censorship which had succeeded thanks mainly to the active co-operation of the Labour Government. In his diary on 3 July 1967

Richard Crossman was clearly concerned about the political reper-cussions of the Government's support for this particular measure.

Frankly it's an extremely unpleasant Bill and I myself don't like it. It may well be twenty years ahead of public opinion; certainly working class people in the north jeer at their Members at the weekend and ask them why they're looking after the buggers at Westminster instead of looking after the unemployed at home. It has gone down very badly that the Labour Party should be associated with such a Bill.

Writing in the *New Statesman* on 28 July 1967, C. H. Rolph agreed that the Sexual Offences Act was certainly ahead of its time.

Ten years would not be long for a campaign to modify the criminal law in any respect whatever, but to have done it in respect of a sexual offence is as the speed of light. The Western world has always felt unchallengeably righteous when punishing its sexual minorities.

But he went on to dispute the opinion of Conservative MP, Quentin Hogg (now Lord Hailsham), that the Act was 'a small measure which will have very little effect on our social life'. Although con-cerned over the anomalies in the new legislation, Rolph was confident that these could be removed in the review of the law relating to all sexual offences which Roy Jenkins had promised would be undertaken by the Criminal Law Revision Committee. In conclusion he predicted that the majority of homosexual men simply wanted to be left in peace, although there would remain the problem of helping a significant minority who needed care and counselling to adapt to their sexuality in a hostile world.

An editorial in the *Sheffield Morning Telegraph* warned that the passing of the new law was not an end of the problem, but the beginning of a more complex and daunting challenge.

The Bill's passage is a victory for reason and compassion. Parliament cannot legislate these into existence: it can only liberate. Nor can it make people tolerant, sympathetic and understanding towards sexual deviation. This is the next task for the reformers, and an even more difficult one.[2]

In the *Sunday Telegraph* on 9 July an article entitled 'ABSE, AND AFTER: THE NEXT AGENDA' revealed that this view was ac-cepted by Leo Abse who predicted that it would take 'almost as long to dismantle the social prejudices against homosexuals as it did the legal ones'. It seemed likely that this task would naturally devolve on to the already hard-pressed Albany Trust, which was also facing the daunting prospect of a further increase in the growing number of homosexuals seeking support from it. In the previous two years the Trust had advised 300 cases, while more than 100 men had already approached it in the first six months of 1967. The main problem facing Antony Grey and his small staff was funding; the possibility of Government assistance had been withdrawn and negotiations with large private foundations were under way to raise money. The article concluded by looking at the future of the HLRS, which seemed to have campaigned itself out of a job:

> One possibility now being canvassed is that it will go into a state of 'animated suspension'... with a watching brief on the way the law is administered. Or it may remain alive to offer the fruits of its nine years experience to Mr Roy Jenkins in his promised review of all sexual offences. But its Commit-tee... reflects such conflicting attitudes to everything except the law reform itself that its unity may not long survive its success.

Meanwhile, the initial reaction of many homosexuals to their new legal status was simply one of relief, as journalist Roger Baker later recalled:

> far from imparting a new sense of liberation and identity to homosexuals, the passage of the Sexual Offences Act through Parliament actually contrived the opposite effect.... Queer spotting became a great game, as it had been ten years earlier at the time of the Wolfenden Report. This sudden focus of attention, naturally enough, scared most homosexuals to death. This climate created a threat far greater than any relief promised by reform. We kept a low profile.[3]

Historian Jeffrey Weeks remembered that while he simply didn't feel the reform was very relevant to his own life, some homosexuals actually resented the freedom thrust upon them:

> there were others I met in the pubs and the cottages of London and South Wales who were actually hostile, nervous

that the new legality would ruin their cosily secret double lives.[4]

At the time the *Guardian* was one of the few papers which thought it appropriate to seek out the views of men directly affected by the Act:

> Neville, who is a homosexual and living alone, feels that some small sense of shame has been lifted. John and Eric, who have been together for the past 20 years, reckon it hasn't made a ha'p'orth of difference to them... [they] don't need to worry about being blackmailed any more or about visitations from the police. Not that this seems to have troubled them overmuch in the past few years, with cops among their heterosexual friends attending poker parties in their council flat.... They are men without problems, unlike Neville, who still has to find the partner he badly wants. The Act hasn't made it easier, he thinks, to do that. Basically he still finds it difficult to declare himself for what he is.[5]

The article suggested that for the majority of homosexuals the main problem was one of loneliness and social isolation which could only be solved if they had 'respectable' places to meet others.

Some reformers seemed to believe that new legislation would be necessary to achieve this modest demand – particularly in the light of the antagonism shown in the parliamentary debates towards the idea of 'buggers clubs'. There was a distinct feeling that with the passing of the new law the whole unsavoury matter had been satisfactorily resolved and should now be removed from the political agenda. The very idea of its practitioners attempting to move out of the shadowy world to which they had been safely assigned to indulge their unacceptable sexual habits in the strictest privacy was inevitably at odds with the views of many of their staunchest parliamentary supporters. In terms of public morality all manifestations of homosexuality were still deemed inadmissible. However, in September 1967 this issue did not seem a matter for concern – more attention was being paid to the Latey Committee's recommendation that the age of majority should be lowered to 18, putting an end to Wolfenden's principal justification for fixing the homosexual age of consent at 21.

Freed from the fear of imprisonment more homosexuals may

have found the courage to seek out their fellows for social and sexual intercourse, but there was no evidence of a significant increase in the numbers attending the network of bars and clubs which already catered for a homosexual clientele. The floodgates did not seem to have opened in the way which so many opponents of reform had predicted. This was somewhat surpising given the general atmosphere of sexual freedom which young heterosexuals had been enjoying since the mid 1960s. There is little doubt that antagonism against homosexuality was still deeply rooted in all areas of society, and to expect the younger generation to conceive of it as an integral part of their sexual revolution was clearly premature. It was therefore only to be expected that many people strongly disapproved of the idea that homosexuals should be allowed the basic freedom of association in order to achieve emotional and physical relationships which were no longer criminal.

The *Sunday People* newsaper reflected this view when it revealed 'shocking practices' in a Midlands pub; its censorious reporter posed the question: 'Even in these permissive times do we want pubs like this?' The answer was definitely in the negative:

> The new law makes it quite clear that acts offending public decency will not be tolerated. It allows stiff prison sentences for people who do not comply with it. But last week I witnessed conduct which I consider way beyond the bounds of decency.... I saw men – dancing cheek to cheek to the music of the juke box. Kissing passionately on the dance floor and in secluded corners. Holding hands, petting and embracing unashamedly in the packed room.... It's about time the authorities took some notice of the Crown & Anchor. It's about time, in fact, that the police put a stop to the odd goings-on there.[6]

It might have been surmised from this report that an increasing number of pub landlords were going to be at risk of a homosexual invasion, but a statement on the matter from the Licensed Victuallers Association revealed a quite different picture:

> We were very worried when the Sexual Offences Act was passed because it looked as though some pubs, particularly in the West End of London, would become meeting places for more and more homosexuals. It did not happen as much as was feared. But then many of the queers are difficult to

detect. It is even more difficult to bar them when they cause no trouble.[7]

OPEN FLAUNTING OF A NEW AND LEGAL FREEDOM

In Manchester the North Western Homosexual Law Reform Committee (NWHLRC) headed by Allan Horsfall was not content to sit back now that the law had been reformed. As early as June 1967 they suggested that the Albany Trust should set up a network of social clubs along the lines of the Dutch COC organisation, but their proposal was rejected on the grounds that public opinion would need greater reassurance before such a move could be considered. Undeterred, the NWHLRC advertised a telephone advice service for homosexuals operating from a private house. As Allan Horsfall later admitted:

> we were really testing the amount of unhappiness and frustration that there was. It was an information and recruiting service done quite cheaply. And it did prove how tremendous was the unhappiness, frustration and fear.[8]

Writing in *New Society* on 29 August 1968, Ray Gosling, one of NWHLRC's members, revealed that of those who phoned 25 per cent wanted to know where they could get treatment for venereal disease and another 25 per cent specifically wanted a place to meet. The committee of NWHLRC decided to form Esquire Clubs Ltd in order to provide social facilities for homosexuals.

> Go to the club with your friends. Take your sister, to meet your friends and their friends. A humbler Playboy. Viable, and the profits from the bar go two ways: to help members who want to run activities – magazine, trips to the theatre, holiday tours – and to operate a counselling service for members in distress. The one sure place where homosexuals need not be afraid.

It was, of course, too good to be true. Lord Arran was quick to condemn the project as 'an open flaunting of the new and legal freedom of outlet'. He reminded the club organisers of the Act's provisions regarding privacy, and continued: 'I imagine that they obtained permission of the police and of the Home Office. If not, they would be wise to do so.'[9] Leo Abse agreed; he told the Albany

Trust's committee that he did not want to see 'the creation of homosexual ghetto communities'. In a letter to *New Society*, Antony Grey suggested that such premature demands for clubs might unnecessarily arouse public alarm without actually solving their members' real problems.

> 'Integration' for the homosexual means being brought to a full personal understanding of him or herself as a homosexual person. 'Clubs' can undoubtedly help in this respect, but only if the provision of a physical meeting place is not regarded as the be-all and end-all. Much more immediately important is the need to build up new personal and community attitudes, which will replace the too common cynicism and loneliness of the sexually different with a new sincerity of comradeship and concern for one another.[10]

An anonymous correspondent heartily agreed, calling the idea (of 'properly run social clubs') 'the most nauseating and degrading I, as a homosexual, have yet come across. If there is one thing the homosexual does not want, it is organised tolerance.'[11]

Local reaction seemed muted: the *Burnley Evening Star* ran a short matter-of-fact piece about the proposal, while the *Sheffield Morning Telegraph*'s report that Esquire was considering their city as a possible venue was dealt with in three column inches. But in the same week readers of the *Manchester Evening News* were told of a police raid on the Baton Rouge Club. Plain clothes officers had visited the premises and seen men dancing together; one policeman had even been forced to join in this 'indecent and improper' behaviour to avoid having his cover blown. The manager suggested in his defence that 'it was better to have these types concentrated in one club rather than spread them all over the city'.[12] The magistrates obviously did not agree – he was convicted, fined £50 and dismissed from the management of the club, which had its licence revoked.

Despite the determination of the members of Esquire they met resistance at every turn and by the end of 1969 had not succeeded in setting up a single club. Other attempts to establish social facilities for homosexuals had also failed. In the *Daily Mirror* on 12 January 1968 it was revealed that the Canon of Coventry Cathedral wanted to set up a centre where homosexuals could meet but the Provost had immediately stepped in to squash the idea. That same month the *News of the World* exposed a plan to set up a social group in

Wolverhampton called The Male and Female Homosexual Association of Great Britain (MANDFHAB).[13] Its founder, 19 year old John Holland, was very frank about their plans.

> There is hardly a paper or magazine in the country that will accept our advertisements. Society will not allow us to communicate. We need to improve our public relations, make sure our talents are not wasted and establish a better image. The best way is through organised groups. Some of us are prepared to parade with banners proclaiming our homosexuality if it will help. We are in the position of the old suffragettes, struggling for our democratic rights.[14]

He also claimed that Wolverhampton had the best social club for homosexuals in Europe. Two months later the police raided the club and brought charges in respect of 'obscene and indecent acts committed on the premises' – this meant that men were dancing together. The police also visited some club members in their homes in connection with enquiries into alleged teenage homosexual relationships. MANDFHAB was never heard of again.

But as the 1960s drew to a close there were signs that some progress was being made towards establishing a specifically homosexual sub-culture. A few magazines had sprung up which contained contact adverts for homosexual men; these were soon supplanted by more professional publications like *Timm*, *Jeremy* and *Spartacus*. Peter Marriott revealed the editorial policy for his magazine to the *Daily Mirror* on 5 August 1969:

> *Jeremy* will be designed to appeal to gay people and bisexuals. It will not be at all crude, but very sophisticated and camp, and its motto will be: 'Who cares about sex?'.

John Stamford's *Spartacus* was the first publicly available magazine which catered openly for homosexual men: featuring full-frontal male nudes and making explicit references to gay sex. It also contained news, articles and short stories; and published a Gay Guide which by 1970 covered 60 gay venues in London and over 200 in the United Kingdom.

As an alternative to the 'commercial' establishments listed in *Spartacus* the NWHLRC had decided to form a number of local social groups as the beginning of a grass-roots homosexual community. In order to emphasise its dissatisfaction with the restrictions of the new law, it also changed its name to the Committee for Homosexual Equality (CHE). By November 1970 it boasted 500 members in 15 local groups and had renamed itself the Campaign for Homosexual Equality. This change undoubtedly reflected a need for assertion in the face of continuing police harrassment of the emerging gay community: Home Office figures showed that prosecutions for homosexual importuning were continuing at the same rate as they had before the passing of the Sexual Offences Act and it was clear that some police forces still used *agent provocateur* tactics.

Meanwhile, others also acknowledged the need to press for tangible improvements in gay rights and in *New Society* on 27 March 1969 Antony Grey and sexologist D. J. West argued that there was a 'NEW LAW BUT NO NEW DEAL' and called for further reforms. The Albany Trust was certainly not in a position to take any initiatives of this type – a report in *The Times* on 9 April 1969 revealed that its case-load had doubled in two years and that it was facing a deficit of £5,500. In a *Spartacus* editorial of May 1970 John Stamford expressed his view that law reform was a matter of 'extreme urgency'; and suggested a radical new strategy:

> I feel the time has come for the homophile movement in this country to be more militant in the protection of our rights as citizens and in the struggle for freedom from persecution... Let us unite in raising our voices against oppression and persecution and fight tooth and nail in any effort to rob us of the rights and privileges to which we are all entitled.

HONOUR, IDENTITY AND LIBERATION!

While in Britain the call for a mass movement of homosexuals must have seemed a wasted effort, in the USA this very ideal was already being realised. In the United States homosexual men and lesbians had begun to organise themselves into self-help groups as early as 1948 and by the late 1960s there were nearly 150 such societies active in the country. Although the radical and revolutionary youth movement which had its climax in the international student unrest of 1968 had given them a new impetus and increased support, they remained essentially liberal in outlook, advocating persuasion instead of confrontation. However, in June 1969 when the New York Police carried out one of their periodic raids on a gay bar in the city's artisan quarter, Greenwich Village, the homosexuals there started to fight back and a riot began which spread throughout the neighbourhood and lasted for three days and nights. The newspaper, *Village Voice*, chronicled the birth of what was to become an international gay liberation movement.

> The forces of faggotry, spurred by a Friday night raid on one of the city's largest, most popular, and longest lived gay bars, the Stonewall Inn, rallied Saturday night in an unprecedented protest against the raid and continued Sunday night to assert presence, possibility, and pride until the early hours of Monday morning. 'I'm a faggot, and I'm proud of it!' 'Gay Power!' 'I like boys!' – these and many other slogans were heard all three nights as the show of force by the city's finery met the force of the city's finest. The result was a kind of liberation, as the gay brigade emerged from the bars, back rooms, and bedrooms of the Village and became street people.[15]

From this euphoria the Gay Liberation Movement was born and it spread rapidly across America as homosexual men and lesbians began to throw off the negative attitudes imposed on them by heterosexual society and instead assert that 'Gay is Good'.

The Gay Liberation Movement in Britain had a less dramatic start: its first meeting took place on 13 November 1970 in a basement classroom at the London School of Economics and was attended by 18 men and one woman. Bob Mellors and Aubrey Walter who had spent their summer vacation in America shared their experience of the new 'gay consciousness' which was transforming the lives of thousands of homosexuals and lesbians on the other side of the Atlantic. Their message fired their audience and within a month meetings were attracting nearly 200 people and a larger venue had to be found. Those who attended were largely young homosexual men under 30, but women and older men were always in evidence. On 27 November the new Gay Liberation Front (GLF) went public by holding a torch-light parade on Highbury Fields to protest against the arrest of a prominent young Liberal activist accused of committing indecent acts there. The event attracted little media attention, although there was a short mention of the demonstration in *The Times* on the following day. The GLF drew up its demands and printed them in its magazine *Come Together* which was also used to publicise forthcoming events such as the first GLF disco at the London School of Economics on 4 December.

By the spring of 1971 the GLF had established an office at Caledonian Road, had moved to larger premises for meetings which now attracted up to 400 people, had produced three more issues of *Come Together*, and was running a highly successful programme of social events and discos. At the meetings there was little structure or formality – the emphasis was on participation and exploration as a former GLF regular remembers:

> People stood up and had their say and had arguments across the room or whatever. So it was a great mish-mash and, at that point there was a common bond – the important thing was being out of the closet. The important thing was being political. The important thing was no longer hiding. The important thing was to be honest and say that you were gay.[16]

New sub-groups were constantly being set up to consider exciting and novel ways of raising each individual's gay consciousness through 'think-ins', 'awareness groups' and communes. Out in the streets they distributed leaflets, performed street theatre, 'zapped' established gay pubs and clubs. A large contingent joined in a Trades Union Congress march against the Industrial Relations Bill which had just been introduced by Edward Heath's Conservative Government. However, this gesture of solidarity with their trade union brothers was far from welcome; the anti-gay working class prejudice which had motivated many union-backed MPs to oppose the Sexual Offences Act in Parliament was clearly evident on this occasion.

For gay men and lesbians who belong to the post-GLF generation it is impossible to imagine the revolution of attitudes that the movement brought about. With hindsight its aims and methods seem rather naive and Utopian, but these were its greatest strengths at a time when the simple act of being openly gay was in itself a revolutionary gesture for most of the gay community. The power of its message is most clearly felt in this early handout which was distributed on the streets in the winter of 1970–1.

WE BELIEVE that apathy and fear are the barriers that imprison people from an incalculable landscape of self-awareness. That they are the elements of prejudice and the enemies of truth.

That every person has the right to develop and extend their character and explore their sexuality through relationships with any other human being, without moral, social or political pressure.

That no relationships formed by such pressure, or not freely entered into, can be valid, creative or rewarding.

To you, the others, we say:

We are not against you, but the prejudice that warps your life, and ours.

It is not love that distorts, but hate.

On your behalf, and ours, we demand:

The same right to public expressions of love and affection as society grants to expressions of hate and scorn.

The right to behave, without harm to others, in public and private, in any way we choose, in any manner or style, with any words or gestures, to wear whatever clothes we like or to go naked, to draw or write or read or publish any material or information we wish, at any time and in any place.

An end to the sexual propaganda which distorts the innocence of children, conditions their image of human relationships, and implants guilt and nurtures shame for any sexual feelings outside an artificial polarity.

An end to the centuries of oppression and prejudice that have driven homosexuals from their homes, families and employment, have forced them to cynicism, subterfuge and self-hatred and have led them, so often, to imprisonment or to death.

In the name of the tens of thousands who wore the badge of homosexuality in the gas chambers and concentration camps, who have no children to remember, and whom your histories forget,

WE DEMAND honour, identity and liberation.

Although these aims were awe-inspiring in their scope, their achievement rested squarely in the hands of each individual. At the heart of the GLF's philosophy was the process of 'coming out' which required every gay man and lesbian to root out from their own minds the idea that their sexuality was bad, sick or immoral and develop in its place 'gay pride'. This in turn would generate gay

anger against the existing social and political system which oppressed all gay people and lead to individuals 'coming together' to
create a mass movement to challenge the status quo. A former GLF
member later recounted his personal memories of that extraordinary process:

> It did all sorts of things to me which are very difficult to
> explain. I think it was being able to be open, and also the
> support – not just from one or two people, but from lots of
> people. I felt a kind of strength that I'd never experienced
> before. Using the word 'gay' was symbolic – I was casting off
> the word 'homo' and using a word which was a good word...
> I was casting off a tag that society had put on me. It was some
> sort of liberation of the spirit and the mind.... I thought that
> everybody was going to change; everything was going to get
> better; everybody was liberated, and all these young people
> were growing up and they were going to lead quite different
> lives – they were going to conquer everything. Everybody
> was going to be accepted and there wasn't going to be a
> stigma about being gay.[17]

According to GLF, at the heart of society's oppression was the
concept of sexism whereby men and women were defined by their
gender which gave them certain rights and obligations, and led to
a culture dominated by heterosexual men who maintained their
power by means of the family unit. The GLF manifesto published
in October 1971 explained these complex inter-relationships in
simple, clear language. There was no pretence that the fundamental changes required to bring about this revolution would happen
overnight.

> The long-term goal... is to rid society of the gender role
> system which is at the root of our oppression. This can only
> be achieved by the abolition of the family unit in which
> children are brought up.... To achieve our long-term goal
> will take many years, perhaps decades. But if at the moment
> the replacement of the family by a system of communes may
> seem a very long way ahead, we believe that, in the ever
> sharpening crisis of western society, the time may come
> quite suddenly when old institutions start to crack, and
> when people will have to seek new models. We intend to
> start working out our contribution to these new models now,

by creating an alternative gay culture free from sexism, and by setting up gay communes.

As the message spread across the country GLF groups sprang up in other cities including Manchester, Brighton and Sheffield.

CHALLENGING THE STATUS QUO

In the early months of 1971 press coverage of the new movement was sporadic: in January the *Spectator* carried an article describing the beginnings of the London GLF,[18] while the *Observer* reported on its mixed success within London's gay community.

the homosexual population in general remained aloof – 'I enjoy my double life', said a delicate youth wearing a gold chain belt in a Chelsea pub, 'I don't want to come out.'[19]

In the *Watford Evening Echo* some radical and outspoken members of the new organisation were interviewed under the headline 'THE GAY REVOLUTION – or how politics got mixed up with the campaign to allow men who like it to hold hands in public'.

'We don't care a f--- what straights think about us. We've been beaten up and murdered for centuries. We're going to force the rest of you to accept us.'[20]

Despite this rather sensational opening what followed was a fair and accurate summary of the aims and activities of the GLF. On 12 April in the *Guardian*, Jill Tweedie confirmed that 'Gay's the Word' in a comprehensive and sympathetic article.

these young homosexuals, by their very acceptance of the normality of homosexuality, challenge the status quo.... And they are beautiful to see. It is lovely to be with men and women who are not ashamed to express their affections openly, in the normal heterosexual ways, the hand in hand, the arm in arm, the occasional cuddle, the quick kiss. Suddenly, watching them, the whole evil, squalid image of homosexuality crumbles – are these bright young faces corrupters of children, lavatory solicitors, the something nasty in all our woodsheds?

By August Vera Brittain writing in *The Times* was calling the GLF 'an alternative to sexual shame'. Almost without exception press coverage at both national and local levels seemed to be generally favourable and understanding in its treatment of the GLF. One notable, if unsurprising, exception to this was the magazine *Penthouse*, better known for its naked women than for its social conscience, which took a rather jaundiced view of the new sexual phenomenon.

Whereas the old homosexual was more often than not a parody of the heterosexual's marriage or even heterosexual promiscuity, the new is spontaneous, freewheeling, orgiastic and frequently bisexual – in a group grope, if one sees an open orifice, any open orifice, one fills it.... The trouble with Gay Lib as it stands is that they are not attacking the fundamental problem. Despite the changes in the law, the gay life remains as unacceptable to straight people as ever. Their difference from us cuts deeper than other differences like religion, race or class. Cursed without a cause, afflicted without a cure, they are an affront to our rationality and a threat to our stability.[21]

More surprising was the lack of coherent opposition GLF's somewhat outrageous public behaviour seemed to provoke from a bemused heterosexual population; this letter is a rare example of its type:

There's no need to be gay: such sick-minded people have existed in many civilisations; now we are informed they are essentially a political organisation. What utter rot! It amazes me that under the guise of liberal thinking free publicity should be given to yet another group of 'drop outs' whose only aim is to overthrow any form of self-disciplined society. Is it not time this unwholesome minority were swept under the mat and not lauded as intellectuals?[22]

It was a sad irony that many of those who publicly disapproved of the movement were homosexuals who felt threatened by its open and provocative tactics. In the *Leyton and Leytonstone Guardian* on 9 April 1971 an 'outspoken' homosexual launched a bitter attack on the membership and methods of the GLF:

The Gay Liberation Front is for left-wingers and people who want to jump on bandwagons.... It's when you start shoving the idea up people's noses that oppression and discrimination really become apparent.... Getting radical about the whole thing can only serve to alienate.

The leaders of CHE were also worried by activities of its radical rival. On the one hand they seemed to fear that the public militancy of GLF was alienating liberal heterosexual backing for further law reform, but on the other they resented the amount of support that this policy seemed to be attracting among gay men. CHE's Secretary, Paul Temperton, assured readers of the *Guardian* that there was 'Nothing queer about the CHE' in a letter which appeared on 17 April.

GLF is as unrepresentative of the mainstream of the homophile movement in this country as the weird-looking people in your photograph of so-called 'homosexual street theatre' are unrepresentative of 98 per cent of homosexuals. Publicity of this kind does a great deal of harm to the cause by helping to perpetuate the popular myth that homosexuals are a bunch of freaks.

In the *New Statesman* ex-Conservative Minister Ian Harvey, who was now a prominent member of CHE, suggested that the GLF would create a backlash against further freedoms for homosexuals.

Its members, who include both sexes, incline to display a neurotic state of emotionalism which is out of date in the light of recent reforms and creates hostility rather than sympathy even amongst the most liberal minded. The organisation has associated itself with Marxism, although Marx had no homosexual tendencies, and has demanded 'all power to oppressed people'. A great deal of this oppression is now more imaginary than real.[23]

Perhaps this was the case, but police harassment of the emerging gay community still continued in a series of sporadic, but significant incidents. The first GLF disco in December 1970 was raided by police ostensibly searching for drugs; in the spring of 1971 the magazine *Spartacus* was forced to close down after its editor John Stamford had been charged with sending indecent material through the post; during the summer the police tried to pressurise publicans in London's Notting Hill Gate to ban GLF supporters from their pubs; and in Burnley CHE's second attempt to establish a gay social club was defeated by a storm of local controversy.

THE ADVANCE FROM THE GAY GHETTO

Throughout 1972 GLF maintained a wide range of events and activities, but its rejection of a formal structure led to increased fragmentation and encouraged extremist elements to press for greater militancy. In February the lesbian 'sisters' split away from the movement to campaign on their own and left behind them a growing conflict between the remaining factions over tactics and targets for furthering the cause. Although 2,000 gay men and lesbians took part in the first ever 'Gay Pride' march on 1 July walking through the centre of London with banners and balloons, this show of strength was largely illusory. One year later divisions and disagreements hampered the organisation of a second march and only a few hundred people attended. By the end of 1973 the Caledonian Road office had closed and GLF had ceased to function as an identifiable national movement.

In his book *Coming Out* Jeffrey Weeks examined the meteoric rise and equally dramatic collapse of the GLF.[24] He concluded that sexual orientation alone was not a sufficiently strong platform on which to build a large-scale movement, since individual gay people are divided by a wide range of social, political and cultural influences which are as much a basis for conflict as co-operation. In the early 1970s, too, the general British political climate was already moving away from consensus as Edward Heath's Conservative Government came into repeated confrontation with the trade union movement over wages and industrial relations which resulted in the miners' strike of 1973 and the subsequent defeat of the Heath Government in the April 1974 general election. Exposed to the harsh light of these political realities the GLF's idealised 'promised land' of equality and harmony must have looked increasingly quixotic and unreal. By the time the first meeting of the London GLF took place the radical 'alternative' youth culture of the late 1960s had already given way to disillusionment and dissension. Weeks argues that the very success of the movement's liberation of its individual members undermined its strength to survive.

> The essence of GLF was to change consciousness. But once it had begun to change it – and without a revolution! – it seemed less necessary to build the sort of radical movement that GLF claimed as essential to carry it through.

I would suggest that another cause of the GLF's swift demise was its lack of secure roots within the gay population. Unlike its American counterpart the British movement had not stemmed from a spontaneous rebellion against oppression – it had no such reservoir of anger, energy and excitement to draw upon, and no cry of 'Stonewall!' to rally flagging supporters. Reactionary repression by the British Establishment might have nurtured it, but instead the tacit acceptance of its cause by the media and the apathy of the general public further undermined its case for revolutionary change.

Brief though its existence had been, the GLF left behind a considerable legacy for the emerging gay community it had dragged, somewhat unwillingly, out of the closet. One of its founders, Aubrey Walter, later described this rich inheritance in his book *Come Together*.[25]

> The immediate achievement of the GLF was to have led the advance from the gay ghetto, very confined and repressed, to a somewhat less inhibited gay community. After GLF had blazed this trail, the gay community ramified in many different directions. A great deal of the new infrastructure involved the encroachment of commercial interests: new clubs, the big discos, as well as dating services, hotels, travel agencies, etc. What is more important, though, is the great expansion of the community services run by gay people for gay people on a non-profit basis.... Many institutions of the gay community today had their roots directly in the London GLF. The Icebreakers counselling service grew out of the GLF counter-Psychiatry Group, Gay Switchboard out of the office collective, 'Gay News' from people involved in the GLF Action Group and so on.

With the appearance of the new fortnightly newspaper *Gay News* in June 1972 the gay population had found its own distinctive voice. According to the collective who produced the first edition the paper was aimed at a broad spectrum of gay readers.

> It should never get across just one point of view, it should get as much in as possible. The feature ideas reflect this: there will be articles on such differing aspects of our society as Marlene Dietrich and queer bashing. The paper also intends to campaign for the reduction in the homosexual age of consent and changes in Scotland and Northern Ireland that were unaffected by the 1967 reforms.

For revenue *Gay News* ran contact adverts for homosexual men, flying in the face of a recent controversial House of Lords judgement which upheld a ruling that the underground magazine *International Times* (*IT*) was guilty of a 'conspiracy to corrupt public morals' by allowing homosexual men to advertise in this way. *IT*'s publishers, through their 'progressive' young barrister (and future Home Secretary) Mr Leon Brittan, had argued that since the Sexual Offences Act had decriminalised homosexual behaviour it could not be illegal to allow two men to contact each other for such purposes. But according to Lord Reid, one of the five Law Lords giving judgement, 'there was a difference between exempting certain conduct from criminal penalties and giving licence to others to encourage that conduct'.[26] *Gay News* retorted by heading its personal advertisement column with the quotation 'Love Knoweth no Laws' and claiming that the adverts' intentions were not sexual. An article in the paper a few months later by Dr George Weinburg identified the root cause of these continuing attempts to oppress the gay community as an illness called 'homophobia'.[27] This was described as 'a form of acute conventionality' which manifested itself in 'a morbid and irrational fear of homosexuals and the hatred of them'. Somewhat surprisingly, the acutely conventional police force did not pounce on the fledgling publication and by May 1973 its sales had reached 7,500 and were only being restricted by continuing reluctance on the part of newsagents to stock the paper.

The basic freedoms demanded by the GLF were patently still to be fought for, despite the small but significant progress which had been made. However, the success of the GLF went far beyond its tangible achievements. Jeffrey Weeks sums up:

> For the gay community it had an immensely stimulating effect in ways that are still being realised. GLF did not cause the changes that have taken place, but it suggested that they might be possible. That was its historical function.... GLF helped make homosexuality a political issue in the broadest sense. In terms of legislative change, the effect so far has been nugatory; but in terms of homosexuals' ability to conceptualise their social position, the change has been immense – and it is this which portends most for the future. The historic wave that GLF seemed to promise has not surged forward; but the undercurrents have had a deep effect on many gay people's lives.[28]

6

STANDS ENGLAND WHERE IT DID?: 1973–7

I do not know anything about the law on the subject, but I would leave it as it is; we are too fond of poking our noses into the law. Let us leave it to the people and not go messing about with it.

Lord Strathclyde – House of Lords 10/5/77

DON'T ASK – DEMAND!

A group of us might go into a shopping centre and hold hands. But I think that if people are intelligent they will see the point and think a little.... If I hold hands with my lover in the street we are doing the normal thing. It's your problem not ours. I would encourage my friends to do this when they can but they are very frightened of being beaten up and spat at.

This interview with a spokesman for the local branch of the Campaign for Homosexual Equality (CHE) which appeared in the *Romford Recorder* on 7 September 1973 reveals clearly the extent to which the philosophy and methods of GLF had already spread throughout the emerging gay community. Although CHE had initially made a concerted effort to dissociate itself from the overt and uncompromising tactics of its more radical rival, as GLF declined it was CHE who benefited directly from the increased awareness and expectations it had awakened.

From early in 1972 CHE's national network of social groups began to experience considerable growth in membership. By October 1972 there were over 20 local CHE groups in London with a total membership of more than 700, and by the time the Campaign held its first National Conference in Morecambe in April 1973 its overall membership exceeded 2,700. A reporter in the *Luton Evening Post* of 25 May commented:

> I was delighted to read that the first homosexual conference – held for some reason in a building at the end of a pier in a northern seaside resort – was such a success. The place was not struck by lightning, there was no tidal wave, and neither dogs nor children came to harm. In fact the proceedings were entirely normal – naturally.

Some newspapers still adopted the Sixties approach of pitying homosexuals for their sad disability: a report in the *Northampton Chronicle and Echo* about local CHE members attending the conference was headlined 'THERE'S NOTHING "GAY" ABOUT THEIR WORLD'[1] and concentrated on the problems and disadvantages faced by homosexuals; while the *Lincoln Chronicle* on 17 May 1974 still felt the need to apologise to its readers for mentioning the subject at all!

However, in many areas local newspapers were writing about the emerging gay world in informed, accurate and positive terms. These pieces were very often written by women journalists and concentrated on individuals coming to terms with their sexuality through their membership of local CHE groups. A typical example appeared in the 'Mainly for Women' section of the *Oldham Weekly Chronicle* on 16 November 1974. Owen, the Convenor of the three week old Oldham CHE group, discussed his sexuality and his three-year relationship with his partner Simon under the heading 'FIGHTING FOR THE RIGHT TO BE THEMSELVES...'.

> Owen defines homosexuality as meaning a feeling that you want to love someone of your own sex. He doesn't want to corrupt little boys, wear make-up, go out in drag, take part in orgies, have sex in public, destroy marriage. 'We are both men', he said. 'It isn't true that one of us plays the dominant male and the other the passive woman. The pressures we felt when we were younger taught us the senselessness of role-playing. All we want is to be treated as equals with heterosexual people.'

This new-found tone of unapologetic self-confidence had been bolstered and boosted at CHE's second National Conference held at the 'straight-laced, no nonsense, Victorian aunt'[2] resort of Malvern in April 1974. Out of a membership of over 3,000 more than 800 delegates converged on the town 'to congratulate themselves, pass motions by the score, listen to and rapturously applaud overseas gay activists and assume all would be well'.[3] In this atmosphere of heady optimism a proposal to lobby for the age of consent to be reduced to 12 was defeated and instead the Executive Committee was instructed to prepare more realistic draft legislation to give homosexuals equal rights in law with heterosexuals. The delegates overwhelmingly endorsed the findings of CHE's Law Reform Commission which had concluded: 'the continuing legal imposition of second-class citizenship upon homosexuals is a scandal requiring urgent action'.[4] In the *Guardian* on 28 May Nicholas de Jongh reported that the homosexual lobby had found 'a new vocal confidence': 'This, the homosexual year books of the future may well tell us, will come to be counted the period of the "gay breakthrough".' *Gay News* summed up the theme of the conference as 'DON'T ASK – DEMAND!'[5]

This affirmation of law reform as the main plank of CHE's campaigning strategy must have seemed timely since a general election had just returned the Labour Party to power with Roy Jenkins once more at the Home Office. CHE's survey of the views of prospective parliamentary candidates had revealed that a majority supported the need for the age of consent for gays to be lowered and for penalties against homosexuality in the armed forces to be removed.[6] Two members of the CHE Executive Committee had been accepted as official Liberal Party candidates although the party leader, Jeremy Thorpe, had been at pains to point out that homosexuality was not a subject for official party policy. A pre-election survey carried out by *Gay News* revealed that this line was also being taken by the leaders of the other two main political parties, and the paper observed that: 'Of all three leaders, Wilson's attitude seemed to be the least sympathetic.'[7]

CHE had very little practical experience of parliamentary lobbying upon which to base its new campaign. Apart from established contacts with supportive MPs the organisation's only formal meeting at parliamentary level had been back in 1972 when Labour MP, Will Hamling, had invited a number of gay groups to the Commons to discuss the implications of the *International Times* judgement banning gay contact advertisements.[8] However, the Scottish Minorities Group (SMG), although a far smaller organisation than CHE, had made some significant advances in finding politicians who were prepared actively to promote the cause of homosexual law reform in Scotland. It was now suggested that the two organisations should pool their resources to further the aim of legal equality for gays throughout the United Kingdom and join forces with the fledgling Northern Ireland gay rights group, the Union for Sexual Freedom in Ireland (USFI), to produce a draft Bill to put before Parliament. In order to launch this new campaign the three organisations held a rally in Trafalgar Square on 2 November which attracted the support of more than 2,500 men and women. *Gay News* described the event as 'the largest public gathering of homosexuals of all time in this country'. After speeches from representatives of the national gay rights organisations the crowd marched to 10 Downing Street where a letter was delivered to the Prime Minister calling on the Government to implement the Bill.

It read: 'Our demands are: Age of consent at 16 for everybody; law reform in Scotland and Northern Ireland; equal freedom with heterosexuals to express affection in public; removal from civilian law of sanctions against the armed forces and merchant navy. We hope that you will implement this legislation at the earliest possible moment...'[9]

On 9 January 1975 an article in the *Guardian* revealed that Home Office attitudes seemed to be hardening against any further reform of the age of consent for homosexuals. In the Commons on 6 February Labour MP Dr Colin Phipps asked the Under-Secretary of State for the Home Office if his department had any plans to lower the homosexual age of consent, since 21 was generally considered too high. In his reply the Minister indicated that the Government was satisfied that the decision to fix the age at 21 made in 1967 was the correct one and he therefore saw no reason to make any changes.[10] In the wake of this disappointing answer Dr Phipps told *Gay News* he would be launching a campaign to persuade MPs to put pressure on the Government to change its view.[11]

On 3 July 1975 a draft Homosexual Law Reform Bill was launched by CHE, SMG and USFI. Media interest was considerable: there were items on BBC radio, some local independent radio stations and both national television channels. The *Morning Star*'s article gave prominence to the challenge issued to politicians of all parties by CHE's General Secretary, Alan Clarke:

'We want the Parliament of this country to give one tenth of the population exactly the same rights as the other nine tenths. We ask for nothing more, and we will be satisfied with nothing less.'[12]

Less than a fortnight later the Home Secretary, Roy Jenkins, announced that he would be asking the Criminal Law Revision Committee (CLRC) to undertake a review of all laws relating to sexual offences, starting with the age of consent. On 15 July the *Guardian* revealed that some lawyers were concerned that these sensitive issues were to be considered by the cautious and conservative Criminal Law Revision Committee rather than the more liberal Law Commission. Although Mr Jenkins would be appointing a policy advisory committee to advise the CLRC this would be chaired by Lord Edmund Davies, who was well known for his traditional views on moral issues. *Gay News* admitted that the review would probably prove a mixed blessing for the new parliamentary campaign.

> Opponents of homosexual law reform will certainly use the CLRC as an excuse to defer any consideration of CHE's proposals.... On the plus side, the Committee's review means that reform is at least on the Government's agenda, whether they eventually decide to take action or not. If, however, the Committee issues a reasoned report against gay law reform, this would certainly set the CHE Bill back – almost certainly by years rather than months.[13]

It was expected that the CLRC would not issue its report for at least two years.

Despite this development the gay rights organisations continued to receive messages of support for their Bill from a number of backbench MPs, including the Scottish Labour MP Dr Dickson Mabon, who offered to act as its parliamentary sponsor if he won a place in the Private Members' Ballot. Along with a copy of the Bill all MPs were sent a booklet entitled 'No Offence' which set out the case for homosexual equality at law, arguing cogently and forcefully that the existing state of the law could not be defended credibly 'on medical, political, social, ethical, legal or psychological grounds'.[14] In *The Times* on 17 October columnist Bernard Levin reviewed this 'excellent pamphlet' and the CHE Bill itself, which he described as 'a most sensible and judicious document':

> It seeks to place the position under the law of heterosexuals

and homosexuals on the same footing, and it is interesting, and indeed admirable, that in many respects the Bill's provisions against the abuse of women by men are more rigorous than those of the present law; the Bill's sponsors have not simply aimed to ease life for homosexuals, but to bring decency as well as justice into the whole range of sexual activity as the law impinges on it.

WHEN CIVIL LIBERTY MEANS SEXUAL LICENCE?

To coincide with the new session of Parliament a rally to launch the CHE Bill was organised in Trafalgar Square on 23 November. After the rally, which attracted an estimated 3,000 gays and lesbians, the officers of the campaign met interested politicians from all parties who had been invited to the Commons by Dr Mabon and the Liberal Peer Lord Beaumont to discuss the prospects for the proposed legislation. The 14 MPs and Peers who attended this gathering felt that there was no chance of gay law reform being considered by Parliament until the CLRC had reported back, but in the mean time Lord Beaumont offered to put a motion before the House of Lords setting out the main principles enshrined in the CHE Bill. If this were passed it would be a clear statement to put before the CLRC. In addition Liberal MP Clement Freud agreed to set up a group to liaise with the gay organisations to take advantage of parliamentary opportunities which might arise in the future.[15]

In the mean while CHE set to work on the submission it, and other interested groups, had been invited to make to the CLRC by the Home Office. On 20 November 1975 *Gay News* published the results of a National Opinion Poll it had commissioned on the subject of homosexuality, expressing the hope that the findings would benefit gay rights campaigners. This in-depth study of nearly 2,000 people revealed that attitudes were somewhat inconsistent and confused: the existing state of the law was approved by the majority of respondents who did not want to see homosexual acts re-criminalised, but some felt that greater measures should be taken to prevent the public display of homosexual behaviour. While 40 per cent felt that homosexuals should be allowed to live openly together (against 31 per cent who disagreed) 53 per cent did not believe that they should be able to get married (only 16 per cent supported this idea). Finally 48 per cent felt that homosexuals should not be allowed to be Doctors or Teachers – 30 per cent disagreed. The main findings indicated a fair degree of tolerance, but the Report warned that this might easily change:

> Currently homosexuals seemed to be regarded as a minority group on the very edge of society. Their presence was more rumoured than witnessed. They were not therefore perceived as a threat to the mainstream of contemporary society.... It seems likely that this overall tolerance will last for as long as homosexuals are not perceived as a positively disruptive force in society. If their presence is ever perceived as extensive enough or blatant enough to undermine 'normal' society, it seems likely that this tolerance would become modified into a harder attitude.[16]

On 12 December in the *Police Review* the Police Superintendents' Association became one of the first public bodies to offer its views to the CLRC:

> We must register our strong opposition to any relaxation of the law on sexual offences of a non-heterosexual nature, particularly in regard to buggery with another human being or animal. The very nature of this type of offence is so abhorrent to all police officers that we cannot conceive any right-minded, caring body recommending any alteration to the existing law.

During the spring of 1976 it became clear that the Association was not alone in its stance. In an article in *The Times* on 22 January journalist Ronald Butt posed the question 'WHO REALLY WANTS A CHANGE IN THE AGE OF CONSENT?'. His arguments centred round the familiar and time-honoured myth of the corruption of youth, but with a sinister new twist. There was much emphasis on 'the lobby of child molesters who are now euphemistically called paedophiles', who he claimed had recently formed themselves into a group called the Paedophile Information Exchange (PIE) to pressurise the Home Secretary into liberalising the laws against sex with children – against the wishes of the general public.

> It is important for the politicians who represent the people to be vigilant in the face of the subtlety with which the law

115

can be changed, and the standards of a growing generation manipulated, by the activities of self-styled experts.

The storm broke on 10 March when the National Council for Civil Liberties (NCCL) suggested in its submission to the CLRC that the age of consent for both homosexuals and heterosexuals should be reduced to 14. *The Times* led the majority of the national dailies in rejecting the NCCL's recommendation; according to its Leader column the reasoning behind the proposal was 'a bit too simple' and the current age of consent should be retained 'for the protection of adolescents' until an overwhelming case for changing it had been made.[17] An editorial in the *Daily Telegraph* used some remarkably twisted logic to suggest that lowering the age of consent was somehow connected with the old fears about homosexual spies, and under the heading 'SEXUAL SUBVERSION' it warned of a possible threat to national security:

> If some members of society publicly pursue, with the sanction of the law, lifestyles which to a large number of their fellow citizens seem poisonous and degrading, is that society likely to be able to withstand the assaults of enemies who in their own affairs sacrifice everything to social cohesion?

On the following morning the *Daily Express* described the NCCL submission as a case of 'WHEN CIVIL LIBERTY MEANS SEXUAL LICENCE'. In the *Methodist Recorder* on 18 March, under the heading 'PERMISSIVE SOCIETY NONSENSE', Mr Johnston of the fundamentalist Christian organisation, The Festival of Light, commented: 'Such proposals are a gift to the commercial manipulators of sex who were never stronger in our society, and those whose aim is to break down family life.' Letters in the columns of many newspapers not only applauded this line, but took the opportunity to call for the laws on homosexuality to be made more restrictive. According to one 'horrified' mother of three teenagers: 'Leave the laws as they are. Or, better still, make them stricter. It is a better country we want, not a more depraved one.'[18] Questions were raised in the Commons on 11 March and the Government was urged to condemn the NCCL's proposal. The Home Office Minister gave suitably evasive answers and suggested that it was best to await the outcome of the CLRC's deliberations.[19]

On the day before these exchanges had taken place the Ulster Secretary, Merlyn Rees, had revealed in a parliamentary answer that although his Department had no existing plans to extend the 1967 Act to Northern Ireland he would be reconsidering the matter in the light of continuing direct rule.[20] Any optimism generated within the gay groups by this unexpected statement was quickly dampened by news from the Parliamentary Liaison Group that Lord Beaumont had been forced to drop his plans to table a motion in the Lords for fear of a massive defeat – presumably because of the backlash of opinion caused by the NCCL recommendations. The group advised that nothing more than 'piecemeal reform' should be attempted in the immediate future; any wholesale changes would have to wait until the CLRC had reported back.[21]

On 10 May the political Establishment was shaken by the resignation of Jeremy Thorpe as leader of the Liberal Party. Mr Thorpe's career had been hanging in the balance since 30 January when a former male model, Norman Scott, claimed to have had a homosexual relationship with the politician. Naturally the press had seized on the story with glee; the *London Evening News* front page headline 'MAN'S SEX AFFAIR WITH JEREMY – COURT STORY'[22] was representative of the general standard of the coverage by the national tabloids. Allegations and counter allegations about love letters, blackmail and death threats were splashed across every newspaper and as the story grew increasingly convoluted it was even suggested that the whole thing had been a plot by the South African Secret Service. The *Daily Telegraph* on 3 February urged the Liberal Party not to ditch its leader, the *Lancashire Evening Post* on 5 February was appalled that Mr Thorpe's future could be jeopardised by this 'uncorroborated attack': 'It does not seem right, and yet somehow it seems inevitable. To quote two proverbs: mud sticks, and Caesar's wife must be above suspicion.' The *Sun*, in its usual forthright manner, told the politician that he should stand down.

In the wake of the resignation the *Sunday Times* was not convinced that the public did believe any longer that 'good personal morals' were incompatible with sexual relationships between men.[23] The *Observer* disagreed, suggesting that continuing public prejudice against homosexuals had been the major factor in making Mr Thorpe a victim of 'British sexual hypocrisy and moral confusion':

> Talking to experienced political agents on this theme is a depressing experience... they say, unanimously, that the effect on a candidate of an admission of homosexuality

would be 'a disaster' – a word that recurred. In London, a Labour agent... said that the more working class the party, the more votes would be lost by any known homosexual candidate.[24]

The *Daily Telegraph* was sorry that the politician had become 'a sacrifice to the well-established convention in British politics that a public man must be free from all publicly sustainable suspicion about his personal morals'.[25] It was these unexplained suspicions which were to bring far greater misfortune for Mr Thorpe less than a year later.

ALICE IN WONDERLAND STUFF

At the beginning of June CHE published its submission to the CLRC; this argued that homosexuals should have complete legal equality with heterosexuals and included the draft Law Reform Bill enshrining that principle in law. However, when a delegation delivered the document to the Home Secretary on 15 June, Roy Jenkins could offer no hope of early legislation and advised the campaigners not to promote their Bill during the present Parliament.[26] An article in the *Justice of the Peace* on 26 June strongly supported the submission but once again highlighted the gay lobbyists 'Catch 22' position by expressing concern that the growing visibility and 'exhibitionism' on the part of homosexuals might be damaging to their cause: 'Homosexuals... are virtually alone in parading their sexual inclinations, and while they continue on this course prejudice is more likely to grow than diminish.' Prospects for legislative improvements in the new parliamentary session starting in the autumn were clearly very poor, but gay rights campaigners were certainly not expecting to find their energies directed into fighting a rearguard action.

In October 1976 the Government introduced a Bill to consolidate most of the existing sexual offences laws in Scotland, including those which continued to make homosexuality illegal. Ronald King Murray, the Lord Advocate of Scotland (with powers similar to the English Director of Public Prosecutions) insisted that this type of consolidation measure simply brought together a group of existing laws and tidied them up by creating one new law. He tried to reassure those who felt that the move might prejudice reform:

some will say that the enactment of the present Bill might

be taken as an illiberal act, as a hardening of the law against homosexual behaviour. I can give a categorical assurance that there is no legal basis for that view.[27]

Alerted by the Scottish Minorities Group, Conservative MP Malcolm Rifkind and Labour's Robin Cook led a number of Scottish MPs to oppose the measure. In a reply to a parliamentary question from Mr Rifkind the Lord Advocate had confirmed that he was continuing the policy adopted by his predecessors of not prosecuting private homosexual activities between consenting adults over 21.[28] In the Commons debate on the Bill on 25 October Leo Abse made a swingeing attack on the contradictions of this situation.[29]

What is the utter hypocrisy and humbug that could bring the House of Commons to consolidate Acts and then give the firm assurance that they will not be implemented? What will the general public think about that?

During the Report Stage on 3 November a concerted effort was made to remove the clause from the Bill.[30] Malcolm Rifkind argued forcefully that the decision to consolidate the existing law would be 'totally wrong as a matter of basic constitutional principle.... Parliament should not be asked to make a fool of itself or to stand on its head.' In the face of Scottish Office intransigence his fellow MPs were not convinced and the motion was defeated by 37 votes to 27; what the Scottish National Party MP, George Reid, dubbed 'Alice in Wonderland stuff' went on to become law.

The gay rights lobby was kept on the defensive by the Government's new Criminal Law Bill which proposed to remove the right of trial by jury for men accused of public importuning; such cases would be considered instead by a Magistrates Court. CHE succeeded in mobilising considerable opposition to the proposal; their main cause for concern was explained in the *Sunday Times* on 19 December:

MPs and lawyers with experience in these cases say the innocent man would stand a statistically smaller chance of acquittal before magistrates courts where most JPs are socially opposed to homosexuality.

Although CHE's protests were received with 'reasonable sympathy' by the Home Office, the department claimed that it had been 'inundated with letters' from people who felt that the existing law dealt with homosexuals too lightly.[31]

Clear evidence that similar views were held at the highest level of the judicial Establishment was provided in an article in *New Society* on 23 December which quoted recent remarks made by Lord Justice Wilberforce:

> Whatever new attitudes Parliament, or public tolerance, might have chosen to take with regard to the behaviour of consenting adults over 21... those should not entitle the courts to relax... the vigilance and severity with which they should regard the risk to children at critical ages being exposed or introduced to ways of life which might lead to severence from normal society, to psychological stresses and unhappiness and, possibly, even to physical experiences which might scar them for life.

In the face of this determination to ignore the rights of homosexual men it was inevitable that they would sooner or later attempt to get direct representation for themselves in Parliament. CHE member Peter Mitchell became Britain's first gay civil rights candidate by contesting the Westminster and City of London by-election in February 1977. Although he only polled 499 votes the exercise was significant in that ten years earlier the very idea of an openly homosexual candidate would have been inconceivable.

At the beginning of the following month those doughty veterans of the first reform campaign of the 1960s, Lord Arran and Lord Boothby, both introduced Bills into the House of Lords – the former to lower the age of consent for homosexuals to 18, and the latter to make homosexual behaviour in Scotland legal between consenting adults in private. Meanwhile, the Northern Ireland Human Rights Commission, which had been set up by the Government to consider whether recent social reforms which only applied in England and Wales should be extended in the Province, had recommended that the Sexual Offences Act should be implemented there. It was expected that the Northern Ireland Secretary, Roy Mason, would fulfil his earlier promise to act on the Commission's findings. 'THE HEAT'S ON!' was the exultant headline in *Gay News* on 24 March.

CHE and SMG hoped that the Bills would generate valuable discussion in Parliament and the media, but the campaigners admitted that it was highly unlikely that the House of Commons would find time for them even if they passed all their stages in the Lords. In the June issue of its magazine *Out*, CHE admitted that it was anxious

> that legislators and journalists should not be led to believe that a male gay age of consent at 18 would be any more acceptable to the gay movement than the present age of 21. Legal equality with heterosexuals remains the sole aim.

The debate on the Second Reading of Lord Boothby's Sexual Offences (Scotland) Bill took place in the Upper House on 10 May.[52] In the light of the statement made the previous year that the Lord Advocate had no intention of prosecuting homosexual activity in Scotland which would be legal under the 1967 Act, the opponents of this reform had no logical grounds on which to base their objections. While stressing the Government's traditional neutrality in these matters, its spokesman, Lord Kirkhill, had to admit that even he could see no reason why the reform should not be enacted since it was merely recognising existing practice. Lord Boothby assured his fellow peers that he simply wished to bring the law of Scotland into line with England but had proposed 18 as the age of consent in anticipation of Lord Arran's Bill being successful. Since consideration of that Bill had been delayed by its sponsor's ill health he undertook to increase the age to 21 before the Third Reading of his Bill if Arran's proposal was subsequently defeated.

Lord Monson once again put the issue of gay rights in the broader context of international human rights by drawing an uncomfortable parallel between the existing law in Scotland and the notorious South African Immorality Act which forbade sexual intercourse between white and non-white individuals:

> so long as in any part of the United Kingdom there exists a state of affairs in which our policemen rummage around bedrooms to discover what individuals of the same sex are doing together we cannot in all honesty, in all conscience, condemn what happens in other countries.

Lord Ferrier led the opposition by tabling an amendment seeking to defer consideration of the measure because Parliament was debating the need to devolve legislative power on Scottish issues to a new Scottish Assembly. He later admitted that this was merely a diversionary tactic and that his prime concern was to save his beloved country from this attack on its moral standards. Attempts to deny the Bill a Second Reading were defeated by a resounding 125 votes to 27. All remaining resistance crumbled during the Committee stage and on 7 July the Bill passed its Third Reading and was sent to the Commons.

REACTIONARY TWADDLE

In the euphoria generated by what *Gay News* pointed out was 'the first Parliamentary victory in ten years'[33] the overwhelming defeat of Lord Arran's Bill on 14 June came as a considerable shock.[34] In his *London Evening News* column on 9 March its sponsor had voiced doubts about his chances of success:

> I am by no means certain that our House will give me a majority. There are many peers who have a dislike of the whole thing and others will take the view that enough is enough and that there must be an end to permissiveness.

However, the extent to which he had underestimated the strength of such opinions became clear very early in the debate.

The Earl of Halsbury, as opening speaker for the opposition, triumphantly laid before the House the fruits of his 'thorough researches' which 'proved' that by ceaselessly demanding recognition of 'the false doctrine that homosexuality is a valid alternative to heterosexuality', social groups such as CHE along with *Gay News* and similar publications were responsible for the 'alarming increase in homosexual activity' which had taken place since 1967. Furthermore, according to the noble Earl,

> when it comes to procuring, pimping, soliciting and prostitution, *Gay News* is in it up to the neck through its advertisement revenues, thereby involving the social group [CHE] willy-nilly in its own degradation.

Finally, he regaled his listeners with lurid stories of the promiscuous behaviour of homosexuals which was responsible for a massive increase in venereal disease. In language reminiscent of pre-reform days he described such men as 'sick indeed' and he therefore called upon the House to throw out this 'sick Bill' 'in view of the growth in activities of groups and individuals exploiting male prostitution and its attendant corruption of youth, debasement of morals and spread of venereal disease'.

Old favourites of yesteryear about 'attempts to unseat the moral law' and causes of the decline of the Roman Empire were still very much in evidence, but new, modern objections were also exploited to the full. Bacteriologist Lord Stamp confirmed that 80 per cent of new cases of syphilis reported in one teaching hospital were apparently in young male homosexuals. He also felt obliged to draw the attention of his colleagues to the subject of paedophiles 'who indulge in sexual practices with children and whose increasing proselytising activities are closely related to the gay liberation movement'. Without producing a shred of evidence for this highly dubious assertion he went on to claim that his principal concern was to prevent young men being lured or seduced into a way of life which would cut them off from a happy heterosexual family existence. He quoted from a letter he had received from a senior probation officer who blamed the 'evil' and 'cruel' campaign which tried to persuade society that homosexuality was 'as natural as being red-haired or left-handed' for pushing many young men into a 'hell of alienation'.

A fellow peer had received a letter from a teacher who took a similar view, as well as a note from a hospital-worker which described in graphic detail the horrible anal injuries which could apparently be caused by sodomy. Yet another noble Lord read a letter from Lord Baden-Powell which argued that the present legislation was woefully inadequate to protect young Boy Scouts from the traumatic experience of being approached by older homosexuals, and that any further relaxation of the law could be disastrous.

The Countess of Loudoun clearly felt no need to quote the opinions of others to support her view that her male colleagues were failing to address the real issue at stake:

> Are we to encourage the infectious growth of this filthy disease by giving the authority of Parliament to the spreading of corruption and perversion among a new generation of young men and the younger boys in contact with them?

Whereas the tiny minority of lady Peeresses who had spoken in the debates of the mid 1960s had been unanimously in support of reform, this was clearly no longer to be the case in 1977 and was to become even less so over the next decade.

While the residents of the ecclesiastical benches could still be relied upon for their Christian charity, they were certainly not in favour of translating that into practical support for change. While denying that he was adopting a 'holier than thou attitude' the Lord Bishop of Birmingham's opinion was quite clear:

> I believe that the community has a real obligation to meet the needs of homosexual men and women and to do so with sympathy and understanding... but without giving their sexual activities, if and when they occur, the cloak of normality and respectability at any age, whether below or above the age of 21.

Lord Beaumont tried to present a few pertinent facts to stem this tide of hostility; he drew attention to the Dutch Government's Speyer Report which had concluded in 1969 that boys between the ages of 16 and 21 did not need greater protection from the sexual advances of adults than girls of the same age. He went on decisively to reject the 'corruption of youth' theory which he described rather aptly as 'a fairy tale'. Even Lady Gaitskell, that indefatigable defender of common sense, found herself on the defensive for asserting that homosexuality was 'a perfectly natural thing'. Dismissing the fearful apparitions of a tide of permissiveness engulfing the younger generation as nonsense, Lord Monson warned that the real dangers lay in blocking the reform, which would cause widespread resentment within both the gay and heterosexual community.

> What could engender more cynicism, more resentment, and more contempt among young people for the values, the teachings and the traditions of their elders than the prospect of the older generation conferring the privileges of adulthood upon the 18 to 21 year olds with one hand in order to get their vote; while seeking to remove an important aspect of those privileges with the other hand, at least so far as the private lives of young males are concerned.

But the supporters of reform were in a clear minority; their attempts at rational discussion stifled by a coherent, well prepared and highly articulate opposition appealing to popular fears and prejudices.

Those who advocated what Lord Chorley termed 'reactionary twaddle' were in the ascendant, and it was only the size of their majority that was a surprise – Lord Arran's Bill was decisively defeated by 146 votes to 25. This result undoubtedly owed something to the attempt by the Government to persuade Lord Arran to withdraw his proposal on the grounds that it was pre-empting the recommendations of the Criminal Law Revision Committee. The message was clear: the Home Office was sticking to the line that there would be no extension of the rights of gay men without the CLRC's approval. The emergence of Lord Halsbury as a highly articulate and skilful standard-bearer for the anti-gay lobby was of considerable significance, and his efforts to roll back the tide of homosexual liberation were to have an even more devastating effect on gay rights some ten years later.

In its front page story on 30 June *Gay News* revealed that there had been 'a most careful, most secret – and most successful – piece of organised lobbying by a motley collection of evangelical and anti-gay groups'. Apparently some of the letters from 'professionals' which had been read out by peers had, in fact, been sent by members of the Festival of Light. The newspaper savagely dismissed Lord Halsbury's attack on itself and other gay organisations as 'at best slovenly, at worst, scurrilous and defamatory'; its conclusion was bitter: 'If there is one lesson that gay lobbyists have learned from the debate it is that the road to Parliamentary success is apparently through deception and defamation.'[35]

Lord Arran was devastated by the defeat and told *Gay News* that his reaction was one of 'utter despair'. The tabloids ignored the whole business, while *The Times* and the *Telegraph* confined themselves to brief summaries in their parliamentary reports. In the political comment section of the periodical *World Medicine* on 29 June it was suggested that the House of Lords had simply proved, once again, that it was 'a collection of silly old buffers, reactionary over-privileged aristos, and pensioned-off political hacks'. And according to its final analysis: 'Stands England where it did? Yes.'

In the summer of 1977 many gays found their attention being diverted from events at Westminster by a bizarre case at the Old Bailey. On 11 July Denis Lemon, editor of *Gay News*, was found guilty of 'wickedly publishing a blasphemous libel villifying Christ'; namely a poem by James Kirkup entitled 'The love that dares to speak its name' in which Jesus was depicted as a homosexual. The last successful prosecution under this ancient law had taken place in 1921. Mr Lemon was fined £500 and given a nine month prison sentence suspended for 18 months, while *Gay News* itself was fined £1,000. Mary Whitehouse had initiated the prosecution, which had subsequently been taken over by the Director of Public Prosecutions. There had been considerable disquiet in the gay community over the case and the newspaper's readers had donated £21,000 to its fighting fund.

In the aftermath of these discouraging events it was inevitable that the tenth anniversary of the passing of the Sexual Offences Act in July was hardly a cause for celebration. A gay couple interviewed by the *Sunday Times* on 17 July believed that the 1967 Act had actually made homosexual equality harder to achieve because it had removed 'the extreme and ugly injustices that were obvious'. Tory MP Teddy Taylor was also of the opinion that the decriminalisation of homosexuality was a mistake. He felt 'that people were more understanding before the Act. Now they're fed up with all the noise and shouting.' In the *Spectator* on 9 July Leo Abse blamed the backlash on the 'the shrill and near-paranoiac extreme gay libera-tion lobbies' who had rejected heterosexual society and created their own alternative, thereby undermining the fundamental aims of the reformers.

> The goal was integration; but the ghetto walls we believed we had knocked down for ever have been rebuilt and, although the hostile heterosexual has sometimes lent a hand, the real construction workers have been the homo-sexuals themselves.... For many homosexuals our more civilised law has freed them to gain fresh insights, to come to terms more readily with themselves, to gain a personal integration and both they and the community have gained. For others the new freedom to come out has meant only that they have freaked out: their exhibitionism arouses resent-ment and indeed, in those lacking certainty in their own heterosexuality, it arouses fears which can only be warded off by repressive legislation.

He further suggested that complaints about discrimination under the 1967 Act were simply a cover, and that the massive increase in convictions for indecency between males in public showed that what most gay activists were actually seeking was 'the freedom to act out their sexual lives in public places'.

A letter which appeared in the magazine's next edition accused Mr Abse of displaying 'an alarming degree of prejudice':

> There is still oppression against homosexuals everywhere as there is no equivalent of the Race Relations Act to protect us. We can be harassed by police, thrown out of our homes,

or, as happened to me recently, lose our jobs simply for being gay.... I'm afraid the fact that Mr Abse's Act was ever needed in the first place is an insult to all gay people. We will not be fobbed off with patronising little bits of legislation like the 1967 Act which merely gives us what should be our right. Until we get equality, Mr Abse and his colleagues can count on being lobbied by angry gays.[36]

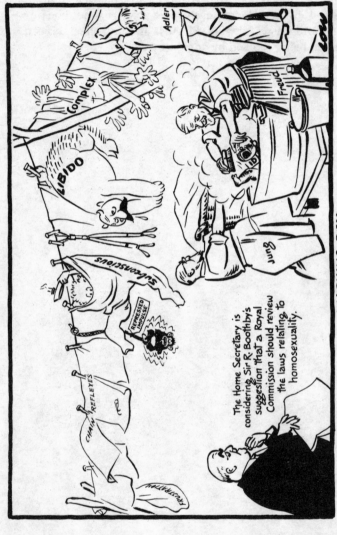

WASHING DAY

'Washing Day' by David Low. © Solo Syndication. First appeared in the *Manchester Guardian*, 23 February 1954.

'Wolfenden Report' by Vicky. © Solo Syndication. First appeared in the *Daily Mirror*, 6 December 1958.

'Free Vote on Wolfenden', © Bill Papas 1965. First appeared in the *Guardian*, 13 May 1965.

As a great reforming Government, Abse, we'd like to sponsor it but we feel that acts committed in private should be dealt with by a Private Member's Bill.

Trog, at the *Observer*, 16 May 1965

'Make It Legal', © text – Colin MacInnes Estate 1975 and Tony Reeves at *Gay Times*. First appeared in *Gay News*, 17 July 1975.

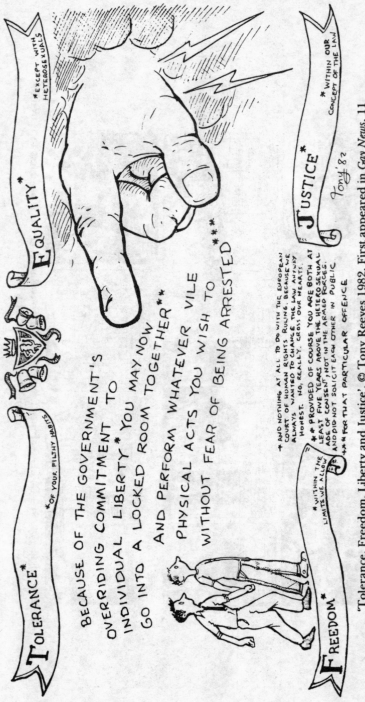

'Tolerance, Freedom, Liberty and Justice', © Tony Reeves 1982. First appeared in *Gay News*, 11 November 1982.

'Captain Condom', © Steve Bell 1986. First appeared in the *Guardian*, 21 November 1986.

'Controlled hysteria…', © David Shenton 1988. First appeared in *Capital Gay*, 1 March 1988.

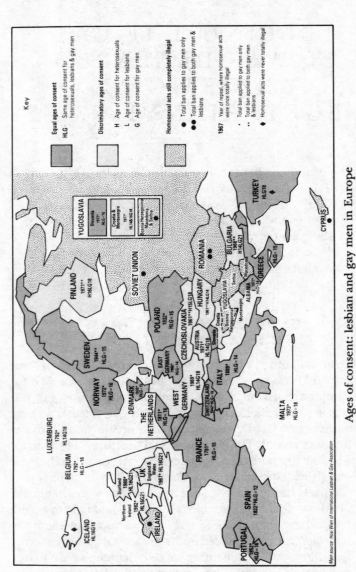

Ages of consent: lesbian and gay men in Europe

Source: Tatchell, P. (1990) *Out in Europe: A Guide to Lesbian and Gay Rights in 30 European Countries,*
London: Channel Four.

7

TELLING THE CAT IT WAS DECLARED AN OFFICIAL VEGETARIAN: 1977–82

> those of us who believe in individual freedom, especially
> where strictly private activity is concerned, and who want,
> therefore, to bring the laws throughout the United King-
> dom into line with the laws that prevail on this matter in
> virtually every other civilised country, do not have to justify
> ourselves. It is for those who wish to retain archaic and
> draconian laws... to make a convincing case for doing so.
>
> *Lord Monson* – House of Lords 21/10/80

UNPLEASANT NATIONAL CHARACTERISTICS

In the Autumn of 1977 the sensational news broke that there was a lesbian in Parliament. Maureen Colquhoun, Labour MP for Northampton North since 1974, revealed that she was 'gay and proud of it' after her local constituency party had voted to deselect her as their candidate for the next election on the grounds of her unsatisfactory record. The MP was certain that they, in fact, disapproved of the rumours relating to her sexuality which had become increasingly widespread. After confirming that many members of her local party had approached her subsequently with promises of support Mrs Colquhoun announced that she would fight to get the vote overturned. She expressed her bitter disappointment at the lack of support she had received from the national party hierarchy. The *Daily Mirror* on 28 September backed Maureen's right to stay on regardless of her sexual preferences and claimed that it was hypocrisy to dismiss her on her performance as an MP. The battling politician told the press:

I am not 'Britain's Lesbian MP'. I am the working Member of Parliament for Northampton North and I am carrying on with my job. My sexuality is of no more relevance to that work than is the sexuality of heterosexual MPs – something people do not continually question.[1]

Maureen Colquhoun went on to reverse the decision of her local branch and stood as the official Labour candidate at the next election. Unfortunately she lost her seat, along with many other Labour MPs, in the Conservative landslide victory of 1979.

Given the Labour Government's record on issues of gay law reform it was not surprising that the party at Westminster were unwillinging to rush to the aid of their first lesbian MP. Although plans to remove the right to trial by jury for homosexual men on soliciting charges had been dropped during the committee stage of the Criminal Law Bill the Government blocked Leo Abse's attempt on 13 July to reduce the penalties for this offence from two years to three months. The Home Office Minister rejected the amendment on the grounds that it was a matter under consideration by the CLRC; while one Conservative MP used the occasion to assert that importuning had attracted severe punishment as it was behaviour aimed at the corruption of youth: 'there are obnoxious and vicious adult men who will consistently importune teenage boys. As a last resort prison may be necessary to deal with such cases.'[2] It was this sort of prejudice which undoubtedly motivated the backbench MPs who repeatedly frustrated attempts by MP Robin Cook (Lab.) to introduce Lord Boothby's Scottish Reform Bill into the Commons in the Spring of the following year and ensured that it automatically lapsed at the end of the Session.[3]

On 4 August 1978 the Jeremy Thorpe saga entered a sensational new phase when the former leader of the Liberals was charged together with three other men with conspiracy to murder former male model Norman Scott. Committal proceedings began in November and further shocking allegations about the politician's past homosexual relationship with Scott once again filled the front pages of the popular press. Although Mr Thorpe was finally acquitted in June 1979 he had lost his parliamentary seat and his political career was clearly over. An article in the *Observer* on 24 June commented:

In an ideal world, Jeremy Thorpe's sexual preferences should have been of not the slightest interest to any but his sexual partners. But we do not live in an ideal world. Even

today, 12 years after the passing of the Sexual Offences Act...
for anyone in public life, let alone a politician, to admit
openly that he is a homosexual is to court disaster.

It was to be five more years before an MP challenged that assessment and proved it false.

Meanwhile, back in the late summer of 1978 Mr Thorpe's
successor as Liberal leader, David Steel, was preparing to withdraw
his party from the Lib–Lab pact which had kept James Callaghan's
minority Labour Government in power for nearly a year. All the
parties were expecting a general election before the year was out
and their campaigns were well prepared. On 1 September the *New
Statesman* revealed that the gay pressure groups within each of the
parties – the Labour Campaign for Gay Rights, the Conservative
Group for Homosexual Equality and the Liberal Gay Action Group
– were planning a joint initiative to draw attention to the issue of
homosexual law reform. The Liberals were still the only party firmly
committed to gay rights. Many backbench Labour MPs clearly
supported the cause but there was no sign that their Government
had any intention of abandoning its recent policy of obstruction.
The Conservative leader Margaret Thatcher was known to oppose
further homosexual law reform, and a recent poll of Tory MPs
carried out by the Gay Conservative Group had shown that nearly
half the 180 respondents agreed with her.[4]

On 15 February 1979, with the recent Thorpe committal proceedings very much in mind, author Michael Schofield pondered
the question 'Why is homosexuality still something to hide?' in the
magazine *New Society*. He noted that the 12 years since the passing
of the Sexual Offences Act seemed to have had little effect in
diminishing the predominantly hostile reaction of the Establishment towards homosexuality.

Yet all the evidence from polls and surveys shows that
ordinary men and women have become much more tolerant
about homosexuality over the last few years. The change in
the law seems to have brought about a welcome reduction
in prejudice.

In subsequent correspondence about the article Robert Palmer,
Chairman of CHE, backed up Schofield's observations by drawing
attention to the findings of a Gallup Poll in August 1977 which
showed that 58 per cent of the public were in favour of homosexual

relations between consenting adults being legal, against only 22 per cent who disapproved. A year later in an NOP survey young people aged between 15 and 21 agreed that homosexuals should be treated the same as everyone else by a majority of 61 per cent to 22 per cent.[5] Another correspondent suggested that the explanation for this striking difference in public and private attitudes was to be found by examining certain aspects of the British national character.

Amongst our unpleasant national characteristics are censorious-ness, hypocrisy, and intolerance, for all three of which homosexuals provide ideal raw material. You don't help a mouse much by telling the cat that it was declared an official vegetarian in 1967.[6]

When the long-awaited general election was called for 3 May the Liberal Party was the first and only one of the three major parties to announce a formal policy on gay rights. A 'Special Manifesto' backed CHE's Sexual Offences Bill and confirmed that discrimination against gay men and women would be made illegal as part of a proposed Bill of Rights modelled on the European Convention of Human Rights.

Mrs Thatcher's election victory in May 1979 was considered a bitter blow by many gay rights campaigners as the Conservatives had made it clear that their party would not find time for 'this type of reform'.[7] But *Gay News* suggested that this particular cloud might have a silver lining.

Whatever next...? A new Prime Minister, a new Parliament. Fears that the going will get tough for minorities like us, hopes that human rights will be treated with more respect than they were under Labour.... William Whitelaw [the new Home Secretary] has, in the past, indicated to his constituents that he believes that there is a case for lowering the age of homosexual consent.[8]

The first indication of the Thatcher Government's attitude to homosexual issues came on 6 March 1980 when a Labour amendment to the Housing Bill was defeated.[9] The suggestion, originally proposed by CHE, which would give gay couples security of tenure in council accommodation was firmly rejected by the new Environment Secretary as 'quite unacceptable,... it is not part of the philosophy of this Bill to take the lead on an issue of social policy'.

In June there came the mixed news that the advisory body set up to make recommendations to the Criminal Law Revision Committee had proposed that the homosexual age of consent should be lowered – but only from 21 to 18. Although public attitudes to homosexuality were recognised to have become more liberal it was argued that there was still too much unease and uncertainty over the whole subject to suggest lowering the age to 16 on a par with heterosexuals. Having accepted that sexual orientation was fixed by the age of 16, the group used the British Medical Association's rather dubious assertion that young men mature more slowly than their female counterparts to assert that they therefore need greater protection because 'the homosexual way of life is likely to be less satisfactory'. Once again it was left to the women members of the group to reject these feeble attempts to justify continuing the legal discrimination against gays and five of them produced a minority report firmly in favour of reducing the age of consent to 16.

The *Guardian* shrugged off the recommendation as inevitable since 'only the naive can expect the law to be in the vanguard of our moral code',[10] but on 2 July it published a spate of angry responses to the report from members of the gay community in its correspondence columns. Martin Johnson attacked the hypocrisy of the committee's justifications:

> What the committee should have realised is that the unsatisfactory aspects of the gay lifestyle are all imposed on us from outside the gay community.... The mixture of half-truths and evasions that usually passes for sex education teaches the kids, both straight and gay alike, to despise homosexual people. The law reinforces that attitude; the police and courts enforce the law. Although we cannot change people's attitudes overnight, we can and must change the law. Indeed... the law should protect all homosexuals from discrimination, whether they are at work, or in bed together, or any place in between.

Ian Harvey of CHE agreed:

> Young men of 16 are no more vulnerable than young women, and the danger to which they are exposed is much less serious: they cannot produce illegitimate children. Furthermore there is a law against sexual discrimination which admittedly was basically designed to enhance the position of

women. But this is tantamount to sexual discrimination against men.

The attitudes of a wider cross-section of gay men towards political issues were revealed for the very first time in a survey carried out by the gay pin-up magazine *Him* in April 1980. Of the 200 respondents 93 per cent agreed that legislation to protect the rights of gay people was needed along the lines proposed by the Liberal Party. Rather disconcertingly, it found that gay men were themselves split over the age of consent issue – although a majority of 66 per cent backed a reduction to 16, a substantial 30 per cent preferred 18. A startling 83 per cent of the readers felt that the police could not be trusted to deal fairly with gay people. Only one third of those who replied were openly gay at work.

This latter statistic was highly significant in the light of the disturbing case of John Saunders, who had been dismissed from his job as a handyman at a residential camp for schoolchildren in Scotland simply because his employers had discovered he was homosexual. Both his employers and the Employment Appeal Tribunal he approached agreed that his work was satisfactory, that he had no criminal record, and that he had never made sexual advances to children at the camp. However, the Tribunal rejected his appeal against unfair dismissal on the grounds that

> there are people who believe that homosexuals are a greater risk to the sexual integrity of children than heterosexuals, and that in deference to that prejudice they would refuse Mr Saunders a declaration that his dismissal was unfair.[11]

In an impassioned article in *The Times* on 24 April, columnist Bernard Levin called the decision 'deplorable and dangerous' and warned of the consequences if Mr Saunders intended appeal to the Scottish Courts failed:

> if he does not get legal redress it will have been judicially established that a citizen who is wholly blameless may be punished because some people believe that *other* people, not including the citizen in question, might, in certain circumstances behave wrongly.

Mr Levin was not confident that the Courts would reverse the ruling, a prediction which sadly proved to be completely accurate. The gay campaigning organisations quickly took up the case; the

Scottish Minorities Group (SMG) produced draft proposals to amend the Employment Protection Act, and jointly with the National Council for Civil Liberties (NCCL) agreed to address a meeting of MPs on 18 June at the Commons which would also be attended by representatives of CHE and the Northern Ireland Gay Rights Association (NIGRA). The organisations launched a petition which condemned the Tribunal's findings in the Saunders case and called on the Government 'to take immediate action' to abolish all discriminatory laws affecting lesbians and gay men in the United Kingdom'. Trade union leaders, show business personalities and politicians all signed the petition which was handed in at Downing Street at the end of the Gay Pride March on 28 June. Liberal leader David Steel described the situation as 'scandalous': 'This issue deserves the fullest possible support from all those who value civil liberties and human rights.'[12]

THAT LUDICROUS LEGAL LIMBO

One of the biggest stumbling blocks facing the campaigners, and a point which doubtless influenced the Tribunal's decision, was the fact that homosexuality was still illegal in Scotland. Back in 1957 Scotsman James Adair had been the only member of the Wolfenden Committee to oppose the recommendation that homosexual behaviour should be decriminalised and his view had been consistently promoted by the majority of the Scottish press throughout the reform campaign of the 1960s. In spite of this sustained antagonism and the lack of any organisation like the HLRS to counter it, a gay self-help group called the Scottish Minorities Group (SMG) was formed in May 1969. Although the continuing criminal sanctions against homosexuality put its very existence at risk, by the end of 1971 the organisation had groups in Edinburgh, Glasgow, Aberdeen and St Andrews with a total of more than 200 members. In December of that year the *Scotsman* reported that the organisation's annual general meeting had endorsed the launching of a homosexual law reform campaign in conjunction with the Scottish National Council for Civil Liberties.[13]

SMG spent the next two years preparing a draft Bill to legalise homosexuality in Scotland and established good contacts with a group of influential politicians from both Houses of Parliament including Lords Boothby and Beaumont, and David Steel. A major breakthrough for the campaigners seemed to have been achieved in the summer of 1973 when the Scottish Lord Advocate issued a letter stating that there would be no prosecutions in Scotland for homosexual acts between consenting adults in private, and assuring homosexuals of police support in the event of blackmail or robbery. But the group's parliamentary sympathisers remained pessimistic and suggested that the gay lobby should be pressing more forcibly for new legislation to reduce the age of consent in England and Wales which in turn would help to bring about reform in Scotland. Following this advice SMG joined with CHE and NIGRA to produce a draft Sexual Offences Bill for the whole UK.

The next four years saw little concrete progress for the Scottish gay rights movement. Although the failure to prevent the anti-homosexual laws being included in the Scottish Consolidation Bill in 1976 was a disappointment, it did bring the issue to the attention of a number of sympathetic MPs including Labour's Robin Cook. The success of Lord Boothby's Bill in 1977 was another encouraging sign, but the reform still seemed to be as remote as ever and in the Autumn of 1979 the Scottish Homosexual Rights Group (as SMG was now known) told *Gay News* that, following correspondence between Robin Cook and the Scottish Office, they considered there was 'little likelihood of any Parliamentary moves in the near future'.[14] It was therefore clearly the Saunders judgement which provided the catalyst for the daring and unexpected initiative launched by an all-party group of MPs in June 1980. During Gay Pride Week, Robin Cook tabled an amendment to the Government's Criminal Justice (Scotland) Bill which would have the effect of extending the 1967 Sexual Offences Act to Scotland.

Opening the debate on 22 July Mr Cook used the Saunders case to highlight the urgent need for homosexual law reform in Scotland.[15] The continuing illegality of homosexual behaviour had undoubtedly been a factor influencing the findings of the Employment Tribunal and a continuation of this state of affairs would also impede future campaigns to end this type of discrimination. Although he personally supported an age of consent of 18, Mr Cook had retained the age of 21 in the amendment in order to avoid unnecessary controversy. His arguments placed the issue of gay law reform firmly in the sphere of civil liberties and linked them into the broader international context.

The House is given to developing a strong line in criticising the neglect of human rights in the Soviet Union. Those

criticisms are well deserved. However, in this instance the
state of our law is no better than that in the Soviet Union. It
would be more constructive to put our own house in order
first.

Although Liberal leader David Steel strongly supported the
move he made plain his dislike for setting the age of consent as high
as 21. From the back benches the indomitable Leo Abse expressed
his disappointment that the new clause carried over the 'compromises and blemishes' which he had been forced to put into the
1967 Act; he felt that its sponsors had been 'far too accommodating
to the prissy prudes who apparently oppose it'. He went on to make
a scathing attack on the 'untenable position' which the present Lord
Advocate and his predecessors had adopted with regard to the
existing law:

> Who does the Lord Advocate think he is – the Lord himself?
> – to hold over the issue of life and death, according to his
> whim, upon men who have a perfect right to live their lives
> with their own difficulties provided they do not impinge in
> any offensive way on the wider community?

He concluded that this situation was 'an affront to civil rights'.

Given the strength of the case for reform it was hardly surprising
that the few opponents of the measure had to fall back on time-honoured condemnations of homosexuality as undesirable and
dangerous. One Conservative MP condoned the prevailing policy
of the Lord Advocate on the hypocritical grounds of 'What the eye
does not see, the heart does not grieve over'. Harking back once
more to the philosophy that homosexuals could only be tolerated
so long as they remained out of the public sight, he claimed gay
men were pushing homosexuality down his throat and the throats
of his children by arguing openly for their rights:

> the gay society campaigns to convince us that if we are
> normal and heterosexual we are queer. Its members try to
> convince us that they are the normal gay people. Indeed the
> very use of the word 'gay' is an affront to the meaning of the
> word, and to ordinary, normal people.

Donald Dewar (Lab.) felt that gay activists had every justification
for such a strategy: 'If I were in that ludicrous legal limbo to which

we have consigned the gay community I would be in a strong campaigning mood myself.'

The Secretary of State for Scotland, George Younger, seemed concerned by the lack of opposition to the amendment and without giving his personal opinion did his best to indicate that the Government's neutrality meant that it disapproved of the proposal. He further felt obliged to ask his fellow MPs to consider whether there had been sufficient public debate on such a controversial subject. Another Labour MP pointed out that the Lord Advocate had taken his decision not to uphold the Scottish law against homosexuality 'with no public discussion, with no authority, without any debate'.

The clause was passed by a convincing majority of 203 votes to 80. Every single Scottish Conservative MP voted against the measure led by George Younger, his deputy Malcolm Rifkind (who four years earlier had been one of the principal speakers in favour of the reform), and fellow ministers, including Douglas Hurd.

According to the *Scotsman* it was the 'most significant victory in over a decade' for the Scottish gay community,[16] and even the *Glasgow Evening Times* gave its dour approval. However, the *Aberdeen Press and Journal* called it 'a shock decision that has crept up on Scotland almost unnoticed'. The *Sun* typically dubbed it the 'McGay's Charter'.[17]

The forces of repression, clearly caught off guard by the speed and scale of this victory, were quick to counter-attack. Within the week the Free Presbyterian Church of Scotland had written to the Lord Advocate protesting at the decision and calling on him to persuade the House of Lords to reverse it. On 27 August the director of the fundamentalist Christian organisation, the Nationwide Festival of Light, had a letter published in a number of Scottish newspapers which condemned this 'sudden and unexpected' attempt to change the law and warned of the shocking repercussions that the 1967 Act had already wrought south of the border:

the flaunting of homosexual behaviour is now so common in England that the intention of removing criminality from homosexual practices is being abused. In effect these practices are not being performed in private but publicly commended, to the offence of most decent people and the inevitable corruption of the young.[18]

It was this familiar appeal to the myth that all homosexuals are child molesters that led to the formation of a group called 'Parent

Concern' which bombarded the Scottish press with calls for greater protection for their children. They backed their case by quoting the headline 'MPs PASS "ORGY LAW"' which had appeared on the front page of *Gay News*.[19] This unnecessarily gratuitous heading was a reference to the fact that the law in Scotland would now be less restrictive than in England and Wales because the Cook amendment did not include the infamous 'privacy' clause from the 1967 Act which outlawed homosexual acts in public lavatories, or in situations where more than two people were present.

A few days before the Lords were due to debate the new clause, gay campaigners met the Lord Advocate and learned that he had been inundated by letters opposing reform, most of which quoted the *Gay News* report. He, too, had taken great exception to the way in which the paper had 'trivialized the matter' and was therefore backing a further amendment which would incorporate the 1967 Act's definition of 'privacy' into the Bill.[20]

During the debate on 21 October the self-righteous indignation of many of the noble speakers was not to be mollified by the last minute introduction of this 'fail-safe device'.[21] Harking back to the paranoic obsessions which MPs had expressed in the late 1950s regarding secret homosexual cabals in the Establishment, the Earl of Lauderdale insisted that the absence of the 'privacy' clause in the original Commons amendment was proof of a deliberate conspiracy.

> I suspect that behind the sincere intentions of Mr Cook there were other intentions that may have been less sincere and more obscure. It might even be described as a calculated con trick because the case was that this was to bring Scots law into line with the English.... But supposing the promoters had got away with this... 'orgy law', as *Gay News* called it... then the next proposition would have been to bring the English law down to the level of Scots law.

He then launched into a swingeing attack on the whole 'disagreeable subject' of homosexuality which put a new, pseudo-psychological slant on the well-worn theory of the condition being one that was spread by the temptation and seduction of youth:

> this practice is gratification for gratification's sake; socially it is without purpose; it produces no offspring; it demands no special commitment of the partner; it is especially toler-

ant of promiscuity. And since those who advocate this behaviour cannot multiply by procreation are they therefore to
be allowed to do so by recruitment, by public display, advertising, by soliciting the young?

One Peer claimed that the Scottish people had been denied the
opportunity to debate the whole distasteful matter; another harked
back to James Adair, the Wolfenden Report and the debates of the
1960s to justify his opposition; and one even called on the Government to fund medical research to find a cure for homosexuality!

In such a highly charged atmosphere Lord Boothby, as the
leading supporter of the Cook amendment, felt it expedient to
agree to the inclusion of the new 'privacy' clause, although he
stressed that it was unnecessary. A familiar group of peers including
Lord Beaumont, Lord Monson and the indomitable Lady Gaitskell
lent their usual support and although the debate had been dominated by their opponents ensured that the motion was carried by
59 votes to 48 (a very small majority in comparison to the overwhelming vote of 127 to 25 in favour of Lord Boothby's identical
Bill in 1977). Robin Cook's amendment was duly accepted as part
of the Criminal Justice (Scotland) Act.

SAVE ULSTER FROM SODOMY

Any expectations which this success might have raised within the
gay community in Northern Ireland with regard to its own campaign to get the 1967 Act extended to Ulster were quickly dashed
by a report in the *Belfast Telegraph* on 23 July 1980 that the Northern
Ireland Office considered it 'unlikely' that there would be an early
Commons vote on the issue. The Northern Ireland Secretary
confirmed this line in a written Commons answer a week later.[22]
After years of bitter controversy, broken promises and political
prevarication by both Labour and Conservative Governments, the
prospects for homosexual law reform in the troubled Province
seemed as remote as ever.

The conservative moral attitudes promulgated by both the Catholic and Protestant Churches coupled with the sectarian violence
which had undermined the political and social stability of the
Province since the late 1960s were undoubtedly factors which
prevented gay men establishing their own campaigning groups
until much later than their counterparts in the rest of the United

Kingdom. Although a few organisations modelled on the GLF appeared in the early 1970s they encountered considerable hostility and were unable to attract the same mass support as the mainland movement. The first gay rights campaigning group did not appear until 1974 when the Campaign for Homosexual Law Reform (CHLR) was set up with the sole aim of pressurising the British Government to extend the 1967 Act to Northern Ireland.

The campaigners were frustrated by the continuing suspension of Ulster's own Parliament at Stormont because of the sectarian troubles and angry at being ignored by Ministers at Westminster who now exercised extensive discretionary powers to implement Northern Ireland legislation. After a co-ordinated International Gay Pride Week protest on 27 June 1974 had yielded no response from Westminster the CHLR decided to prepare a submission to the European Court of Human Rights claiming that the existing state of the law was denying the basic human rights of gay men in Northern Ireland. During the following year the CHLR was wound up and its members formed the Northern Ireland Gay Rights Association (NIGRA) to work on the preparation and launch of the all-UK Gay Rights Bill in association with CHE and SMG.

In January 1976 the Royal Ulster Constabulary (RUC) drugs squad carried out a series of raids on the homes of gay men, concentrating on those who were involved with the gay law reform campaign. The magazine *Community Care* takes up the story:

> The secretary of the Homosexual Law Reform Committee was held for three hours and asked to sign a statement about his homosexual activities. The committee's files were taken away and have not been returned. Richard Kennedy, president of the Northern Ireland Gay Rights Association, whose files were also removed and have not been returned, was held for 16 hours of what he describes as 'hostile and very degrading interrogation'.[23]

Police found cannabis in Kennedy's house and he was subsequently charged with possession of the drug and given a suspended prison sentence.

Ironically, it was at the height of this crackdown that Northern Ireland Secretary Merlyn Rees announced that he would be reconsidering the homosexual laws by referring them to the Northern Ireland Standing Commission on Human Rights. However, shaken by the continuing police interference in their private lives, the leaders of NIGRA decided that the time had come to submit their case to the European Court of Human Rights. Since the Court would only accept submissions on behalf of individuals one of their members, Jeff Dudgeon, claimed that by refusing to legalise homosexual behaviour in Ulster the British Government was invading his privacy and discriminating against him in comparison to heterosexuals, thereby breaching Articles 8 and 14 of the European Convention of Human Rights. The case initially had to be considered by the European Human Rights Commission who would then refer it to the European Court for a judgment if they felt the complaint to be valid.

In the mean while, Jeff Dudgeon and other NIGRA members complained to the Chief Constable of the RUC about the activities of the drugs squad and subsequently found themselves arrested and questioned. By the middle of June, 23 gay men in Belfast had been arrested and released, and four were expecting to be charged. It was not until March of the following year that they were officially informed by the Attorney General's office that no charges would be brought against them.

In the same way that the witch-hunts on the mainland in the 1950s had the effect of bringing the subject of homosexuality out into the open, this spate of police activity made certain sections of the Northern Ireland community consider homosexual law reform for the first time. On 19 May 1976 the *Belfast Telegraph* argued that it was time for the Province to face up to the issue.

the point has come when, for the sake of common humanity, action should be taken.... There is more than enough suffering in this community to add to it by threatening people for being what they are.

In July 1977 the Northern Ireland Human Rights Commission recommended that homosexuality between consenting adults in private should be legalised in the Province[24] and the Government announced that it would issue a draft proposal to that effect.[25] Democratic Unionist Party (DUP) MPs unanimously condemned the move and Ian Paisley was one of the most vociferous in his disapproval:

The crime of sodomy is a crime against God and man and its practice is a terrible step to the total demoralisation of any country and must inevitably lead to the breakdown of all decency within the province.[26]

On 19 October the party launched its campaign to 'SAVE ULSTER FROM SODOMY' and called on the people of the Province to sign a petition against the proposal. Two Unionist MPs led a cavalcade of more than 60 cars to Stormont on 20 February 1978 to hand in their petition which they claimed had been signed by 70,000 people.

In mid March the European Commission announced that Jeff Dudgeon's case was considered admissible and that it would give a ruling in due course. This seemed to galvanise the Government to take action but despite the publication of the long-awaited draft 'Order in Council' on 26 July 1978 no further developments had occurred by the beginning of the following year. An article in the *Guardian* on 14 February 1979 claimed that the Northern Ireland Office were planning to introduce legislation within a fortnight because it needed to give some response to the European Commission. The next two weeks passed without event and at the beginning of March the paper revealed that the reform had been shelved as a sop to the Ulster Unionist MPs whose support was needed by the Government to prevent it being voted out of office.[27]

In the Commons on 8 March the Leader of the House, Michael Foot, was unable to tell an angry Leo Abse when the Government intended to proceed with the Northern Ireland reform, but refuted the MP's suggestion that the whole matter had become 'the victim of squalid inter-party discussion'.[28] A fortnight later *Gay News* published a Northern Ireland Office document which showed that the gay rights Order in Council had originally been scheduled to be placed before Parliament in April 1978![29] But before the end of the month the Callaghan Government had been forced into a general election and on 3 May 1979 Mrs Thatcher's administration took over at Westminster.

Within days of the new Government's arrival it informed the European Commission that it was not prepared to introduce the reform because the temporary circumstances of 'direct rule' in the province meant that the UK Government had

a special responsibility to ensure that the wishes of the people of Northern Ireland are fully taken into account before decisions are taken about matters on which people living there feel very strongly indeed.

It stressed the opposition of the 12 Ulster MPs, the objections which had been made by various religious organisations, including the Roman Catholic Church, and concluded that: 'The subject is a particularly sensitive and controversial one. It is reasonable therefore for the law to be less liberal than in England.'[30] It did, however, assure homosexuals in Northern Ireland that they would not be prosecuted for behaviour that was legal under English law. On 2 July the new Northern Ireland Secretary, Humphrey Atkins, confirmed in the Commons that the law would not be changed in the Province.[31]

JUSTICE IN A FOREIGN COURT

Although rumours began to leak out as early as April 1980 that Jeff Dudgeon had won his case, details of the European Commission's findings were not revealed until 19 September. The Commission had come to the unanimous conclusion that the law in Northern Ireland did interfere with the applicant's right to respect for his private life and that the UK Government was therefore guilty of breaching Article 8 of the European Convention.

> It would be quite contrary to this principle to allow a majority an unqualified right to impose its standards of private sexual morality on the whole of society.... Even if the majority of people in Northern Ireland disapproves of homosexual conduct on moral grounds, this does not mean that it is necessary to prohibit it in order to protect morals in a democratic society.[32]

As expected, the reaction to the judgement in Northern Ireland was distinctly hostile: in the opinion of the *Belfast News Letter* it was 'an intolerable intrusion and infringement of national sovereignty'.[33] In the House of Lords the Government had already made it clear it would not change its policy on the basis of the Commission's findings but would wait until their decision had been considered by the European Court itself.[34]

An imposing court of 21 judges (instead of the usual seven) was duly convened at Strasbourg on 23 April 1981 to consider its first ever gay rights case, and on 22 October by 15 votes to 4 it declared its ruling in favour of Mr Dudgeon. At a press conference NIGRA applauded this historic judgment but expressed its disappointment that the Court had followed the Commission in refusing to consider

Jeff Dudgeon's second complaint that he had been discriminated against in comparison to heterosexuals, contrary to Article 14 of the convention. It was particularly disturbed by the Court's reiteration of the Commission's view that there was

> the legitimate necessity in a democratic society for some degree of control over homosexual conduct, notably in order to provide safeguards against the exploitation and corruption of those who are especially vulnerable by reason, for example, of their youth.

Nevertheless, a delighted Jeff Dudgeon was hopeful that the end of the campaign was finally in sight: 'This result is binding.... The Government has been found guilty by the European Court of violating human rights. The question now is – when will they change the law?'[35]

Although the Northern Ireland Office now agreed to reconsider the law in the light of the European Court's ruling, four months passed before Ulster Secretary James Prior announced that the new draft Order in Council to implement the change would be published.[36] His decision may have been forced after Labour MP Robert Kilroy-Silk submitted an amendment to the Criminal Justice Bill to extend the 1967 Act to Ulster, which was only withdrawn after the Government gave its positive assurance that it would introduce a measure itself. Even before the Order appeared on 18 March the opposition's campaign was well under way, led this time by MP Enoch Powell who attacked the Strasbourg Court's methods of procedure and accused it of

> not acting as a court of law but as a sovereign legislature making laws at its own discretion.... I would sooner receive injustice in the Queen's courts than justice in a foreign court. And I hold that man or woman to be a scoundrel who goes abroad to a foreign court to have the judgments of the Queen's courts overturned.[37]

Ian Paisley and the DUP seemed to be keeping an uncharacteristically low profile, possibly because of the party's connections with the Kincora Boys Home which had recently become the centre of a scandal involving allegations of homosexuality and prostitution.

The Draft Order in Council was finally laid before Parliament in July but MPs had to wait until 25 October for their one and only chance to vote on the measure.[38] Discussion was considerably curtailed since legislation passed in this way may not be altered or amended during the one and a half hours which are allowed for debate. Secretary of State, James Prior outlined the details of the Order and admitted graciously that the decision of the European Court was 'the main reason' behind its introduction. And he affirmed proudly: 'This Government believe in fulfilling their international obligations.' Labour's Front Bench spokesman welcomed the updating of the law – a surprising change of heart which only seemed to have been brought about by two and a half years in opposition.

As expected, Ian Paisley was the first speaker to denounce the measure – principally on the grounds that opposition to it was virtually the only issue which united the warring Protestant and Catholic communities!

> I thought this House would encourage such unity, because
> I have heard it said often 'Why can you not get together?
> Why can you not agree on something?' Here is something
> on which they agree.

He went on to warn that the change in the law would lead to demands for the age of consent to be reduced to 14, putting young children at risk of homosexual corruption.

Leo Abse enjoyed teasing the opponents of reform for their irrational prejudices before going on to denounce the 'miserable saga of humbug and hypocrisy' which had forced the Government to 'grudgingly' present such 'an old and out-of-date provision' to Parliament. One of the most passionate supporters of the measure was Conservative MP Matthew Parris who explained that the brevity of his speech was not due to any lack of personal commitment to the cause 'but where I feel as deeply, strongly and personally as I do on this issue, argument altogether fails me. I support the measure with all my heart.' Experienced parliamentary observers, familiar with interpreting the subtleties of Conservative MPs' heavily coded speaking style, may well have recognised this as the first voluntary admission of homosexuality by an MP in the Commons chamber in the history of Parliament. However, it was not until several years after Mr Parris had left politics for a career in the media that he was explicitly to admit to being gay.

Mr Prior wound up the debate by calling on the House 'to bring about the long-overdue change in the law' and in the 'free vote' that followed he was supported by a unprecedented turnout of 22

Government Ministers, which included eight members of the Cabinet! It was hardly surprising that the Order was approved by the enormous majority of 168 votes to 21. The gay contingent in the Commons public gallery, which included Jeff Dudgeon and Richard Kennedy, greeted the outcome of the vote with cheers which resulted in the arrest of three of their number who were later released without being charged. In the House of Lords on the following afternoon every speaker backed the Order, which was finally approved without a vote being taken.[39]

In a press statement NIGRA welcomed the 'positive and immediate benefits' this victory would bring to gay men in Northern Ireland, although it recognised the 'vintage nature' of the 1967 Act. But for Jeff Dudgeon the whole business was not yet over. It was not until February of the following year that he was awarded a miserly £3,315 costs to cover the expenses of his six-year campaign. Writing in the Summer 1984 issue of the *Socialist* magazine he claimed that the Court's bureaucracy had been determined to punish him for his repeated efforts to force them to consider his complaint under Article 14. Consequently the Court turned down his claim for compensation for the distress and disruption caused by his arrest in 1976 on the grounds that the subsequent change in the law was adequate compensation, and reduced the repayment of his modest legal fees of £4,000 by one third on a technicality. The Government had apparently disputed these legal costs in a 30 page document, although they had themselves spent an estimated £500,000 in fighting the case.

While acknowledging the importance of the Strasbourg Court in securing the reform, Jeff Dudgeon had a warning for gay rights activists who might be planning to use this mechanism in future campaigns.

The knowledge that the European Court will eventually force change has given government unprecedented extra powers of delay and disinterest. It no longer needs to participate in standard democratic argument and discussion, rather it has exported its power. And necessary change is left to a process that is painfully slow, governed by lawyers and one which a government can prolong almost at will by shedding mounds of foreign office briefs and papers at every stage.

8

THE LESSONS WE SO TEDIOUSLY UNLEARNED: 1982-4

We are talking about policemen deliberately going not just to public lavatories, but to pubs and clubs where gay men are known to meet. Such behaviour can be explained only by saying that homosexual relations between consenting adults used to be illegal. However, that law has been changed, so it cannot be against the law for gay men to meet each other and decide to have a relationship.

Clare Short – House of Commons 14/5/84

WILL IT ALL END IN TIERS?

Significant though it was, the extension of the 1967 Act to Scotland and Northern Ireland was nevertheless only the first step along the road to full homosexual equality as far as the gay rights organisations were concerned. For them it was now clearly time to take stock of the situation and re-assess their strategy as it applied to both Parliament and grass roots opinion. The recent law reform campaign had highlighted their inadequate resources and funding which suggested that they had failed to mobilise widespread support within their own communities – if such support actually existed.

During the late 1970s and early 1980s developments within the gay community itself had led to a significant change in the attitudes of gay men towards the political initiatives of the national gay rights groups. As the largest of the three groups it was perhaps inevitable that CHE should be most directly affected by this trend. CHE had always suffered from a certain schizophrenia – although its overall aim was political, a large proportion of the gay men attracted by its network of local groups were primarily looking for initial social

155

contact and subsequent emotional and sexual involvement with their own kind. Unlike the radical GLF, local CHE groups did not automatically expect their membership to be transformed into gay activists, and this relaxed approach probably accounted for the organisation's rapid growth in the mid Seventies. However, once CHE members had found their confidence they often left their local group, attracted by the wider opportunities offered by the rapidly expanding gay commercial 'scene' of pubs, nightclubs and discos.

By the late Seventies most large towns had at least one pub or disco which welcomed gay men, and the major cities like London and Birmingham offered a rich and varied choice of night-life for the young and attractive, or affluent and professional, gay man looking for sex and excitement. In such an essentially hedonistic environment, which slavishly followed the trends and styles of the more overt and sexually promiscuous American commercial scene, it was easy to ignore the prejudice and inequality highlighted by the 'political activists'. After all, so long as sex and drugs and rock and roll were available without interference, what was the problem? The prevailing philosophy was: 'We're all right, Jack! We've never had it so good – so stop rocking the boat!'

As euphoria over the launch of the CHE Law Reform Bill in 1975 gave way to disillusionment with the Labour Government's intransigence and the failure of the law reform initiatives in 1977, the membership of CHE fell from its peak of 5,000 to fluctuate around the 3,000 – 4,000 mark for the remainder of the decade. The inevitable frustrations which this situation bred within the organisation from 1976 onwards led to internal disputes, personality clashes, resignations and increasing bureaucracy. In April 1977 Bernard Greaves, a former member of CHE's Executive Committee who had moved on to become director of the Liberal Party's gay rights education campaign, made some suggestions as to the direction that the organisation needed to take to regain its momentum.

> If CHE is to have more political bite it has to reorder its priorities and devote itself more to campaigning on specific issues on both a national and local level. I would like to see all of its executive committee members actively involved in campaigning all the time. Spreading yourself as widely as CHE does ensures that nobody takes any notice of you.[1]

However, the steady trickle of active members leaving to join the growing number of gay rights groups which had sprung up to campaign within specific areas continued; and as Gays Against the Nazis, Gay Rights at Work and the gay pressure groups within political parties, trade unions and professional organisations grew, CHE's membership increasingly took a downward turn. The organisation tried to respond to the criticisms and sought to redefine its role, as its Information Officer, Nigel Hart, explained to *Gay News*:

CHE should stop trying to maintain a monopoly on gay activism.... Instead, on a national... level, we should become the secretariat of the gay movement, liaising with gay groups working in other fields.... It is vital to the swift implementation of gay rights that the gay movement should be heard to speak with a single voice and I believe that that voice should be CHE's.[2]

But attempts to move in this direction with proposals for appointing a full time lobbyist and official spokesperson for the gay community merely caused further disagreements. Finally, a spate of resignations from the Executive Committee in the autumn of 1979 and spring of 1980, coupled with the looming prospect of bankruptcy, led the organisation to appoint a 'Special Commission' to find a solution to the crisis. The 14 page report presented to the annual CHE conference in August recognised that the increasing diversification within the gay movement and its fragmentation into special interest campaigning groups meant that CHE could no longer credibly claim to represent the whole gay community on all issues. Instead the organisation should offer liaison and support to these other groups, and concentrate its own efforts in areas relating more specifically to law reform. The report made 70 recommendations, nearly half of which related to a complex new organisational structure to pursue the law reform campaign.

Conference delegates, somewhat overwhelmed by this formidable document, decided instead to endorse a Minority Report put forward by Commission members Roy Burns and Peter Naughton. Under the headline 'WILL IT ALL END IN TIERS?' the Conference Gazette outlined their proposal for:

a radically changed, two tier CHE, in which a broadly-based commercially minded tier provides the financial backing for campaigning work, spearheaded by those with the energy, time and commitment to devote themselves to gay rights.

This plan for a slimmed-down campaigning group – still called CHE – funded by a new Gay Community Organisation (GCO) was phased in over the following two years. Unfortunately its implementation caused unforeseen upheavals at grass-roots level where local groups were expected to split their social and campaigning functions, which in some cases led to internal disputes and divisions. However, national CHE succeeded in establishing initial financial security by persuading a proportion of its former membership to provide funding for its work by becoming 'supporting members' of the revamped organisation.

The situation facing the new-look CHE was extremely daunting. The parliamentary lessons of the Scottish and Northern Ireland campaigns indicated that politicians were loath even to translate existing legal practice into statute law when homosexuality was involved. In addition the reformers faced a new threat of organised opposition from right-wing, fundamentalist Christian organisations like the Festival of Light which had helped to fuel a growing parliamentary backlash against further gay law reform. The extraordinary displays of hostility and indignation aroused by Lord Arran's attempt to reduce the age of consent in June 1977 and the omission of the 'privacy' clause in Robin Cook's amendment in July 1980 were a clear indication that any attempt to extend the rights of gay men beyond the bounds set by the 1967 Act would be fiercely resisted. As one of the seasoned gay activists asked by *Gay News* to give his views on the 1980 Gay Pride week, historian Jeffrey Weeks used the opportunity to predict some of the difficulties which might lay ahead for the gay movement in the coming decade as the social and political climate turned increasingly hostile.

In the first place we will see a halt in the forward momentum, and like a train grinding to an emergency halt, the shudders will shake us all. Confusion on aims and purpose is likely to reign. Secondly, a more authoritarian climate will make it difficult to be openly gay, and this will affect particularly people in exposed work conditions and young people just coming out. Nothing the gay movement on its own can do will turn the tide... the only way the gains of the 1970s can be held is by advancing in the 1980s on a wider radical front.[3]

NO. NO. NO!

The publication of the long-awaited Report of the Criminal Law Revision Committee (CLRC) on the age of consent in April 1981 had provided further evidence that attitudes were becoming increasingly intolerant in Whitehall as well as at Westminster. The Report reproduced the case made by the CLRC's policy advisory group two years earlier which rejected any further extension of individual sexual freedom and confirmed that the permissiveness reforms of the 1960s had gone far enough.[4] The age of consent for heterosexuals was therefore to remain at 16 and although the homosexual age of consent was acknowledged to be too high, parity with heterosexuals was considered 'wholly unacceptable to public opinion' although no proof of this contentious assertion in the way of opinion polls or public surveys was produced. The compromise age of 18 was recommended on the basis of a motley collection of arguments. Since the age of majority had been reduced to 18 in 1969, the homosexual age of consent should follow suit in accordance with 'the spirit of the Wolfenden Report'. Secondly, the majority of organisations submitting their opinions to the Committee had supported the age of 18. Thirdly,

> the removal of the prohibition by the criminal law of homosexual relations in private with young men aged 18–21, which in our opinion is no longer necessary for the protection of such men, would provide a more compassionate approach towards homosexuals in our society.

Although five women members of the Commitee had produced a minority report advocating 16 rather than 18, the rest of their colleagues defended the age being set higher on the grounds that 'the law would then be regarded as a factor in encouraging those young men who need protection and assistance to avoid homosexual relations while they are immature'. Despite closely argued submissions from CHE and several other civil liberties groups the acceptance of the principle of homosexual equality remained as remote as ever. Once again, as far as the Establishment was concerned, the gay rights lobby had failed to produce concrete evidence that the public approved of their proposals.

The media reaction to the CLRC Report further emphasised the extent to which opposition to gay rights was becoming stronger. Even before the Report was published some sections of the press had launched an all-out attack on its modest proposals. 'FURY OVER SHAKE-UP IN SEX LAW' was the front page headline in the *Daily Express* on 6 April, which devoted almost its entire 'exclusive' to the opinions of those opposed to any reduction in the gay age of consent. Tory MP Nicholas Winterton was reported to have said: 'Its appalling that such a proposal is even being considered. I will not tolerate recommendations that encourage youngsters to indulge in unnatural relationships.' Anti-pornography campaigner (and self-styled expert in all matters sexual and moral) Mary Whitehouse commented:

> The period of adolescence in men is more extended than in women and can very well go as high as 21. For that reason I think a move like that would be a mistake.

The *Sun* added its voice to the clamour by saying 'No, no, no!' to the proposal:

> There is today an increasing tolerance of homosexuals. Yet their path is still lonely and difficult. It often leads to ostracism and not infrequently tragedy. *We think it is in the youngsters' own interests to wait until they understand themselves a little better.*[5]

Strong backing for the CLRC line was noticeable only by its absence. On 10 April the *Morning Star* was the only national daily to give coverage to the reactions of the gay community, and in particular to the young gays whose lives would be most directly affected by the recommendation. It quoted from a statement issued by the Joint Council for Gay Teenagers which condemned the CLRC for refusing to recommend an equal age of consent of 16 for both homosexuals and heterosexuals.

> If emotional or biological immaturity is to be used as an argument, then all male sexual activity under 18 should be banned. A man who is old enough to die for his country is old enough to be able to decide who to sleep with.[6]

The Police Federation weighed into the dispute by issuing a strong denunciation of the recommendation which deplored

> the way in which official thinking on this subject appears to be surrendering to the pressure groups who try and persuade society that homosexual conduct is perfectly normal.

The existing law is, in itself, a liberalizing measure and the Police Federation believes it goes far enough.[7]

Many local newspapers around the country enthusiastically fell in line with this overwhelming display of reactionary zeal. The *Northern Echo* in Darlington claimed that 'a majority view' was being expressed by the Police Federation,[8] while the *Lancashire Evening Post* described homosexuality as a 'handicap' and concluded: 'The law will do as it is'.[9] In an editorial entitled 'A CASE FOR RESTRAINT – STILL', the *South Wales Echo* described the committee's proposal as contrary to 'the prevailing view of society' and suggested a simple remedy which a parent might reasonably adopt to protect his own child:

Most fathers know quite well just how insecure and vulnerable an 18-year-old boy can be and it is a fair indication of the current attitudes in our society that such a father would be likely to take issue with, and possibly punch quite properly on the nose, an older man who introduced his son to homosexuality.[10]

Over the following few weeks the correspondence columns in both the national and local press were swamped with letters from gay men, some of whom were under 21, denouncing these displays of anti-gay prejudice. Appalled by the leading article in the *South Wales Echo* (quoted above) which he claimed condoned violence against homosexuals, one courageous gay teenager gave a rare public insight to the private misery which was being heaped upon young gay men by the existing state of the law.

I am a 19-year-old homosexual and I have been an open homosexual for two years. I knew I was homosexual long before this, but it was attitudes such as those expressed in the article which prevented me from seeking help until I was 17. Instead, I sank into a state of depression which lasted almost two years. Eventually my parents helped me to have the courage to accept my homosexuality. They are caring, loving Christian parents, something you are obviously not.[11]

A few months later this prevailing Establishment determination to prevent any further extension of gay rights took a distinctly menacing turn for the worse when the Government took over another private prosecution which had been brought by the ever-zealous Mary Whitehouse, which accused theatre director Michael Bogdanov of 'procuring an act of gross indecency between two males' for presenting his production of Howard Brenton's controversial play *The Romans in Britain* at the National Theatre. This outrageous attempt to misuse one of the most iniquitous clauses in the 1967 Act was based on the fact that one scene in the play involved actors *simulating* buggery! The case got as far as the Old Bailey before it was thrown out by three judges, but Mr Bogdanov was released with a warning and the legal costs of £20,000 were paid out of public funds.

A MATTER FOR 'POLITICAL EVANGELISATION'

The Conservative Government once again made clear its intention to resist any attempts at gay law reform by defeating an attempt to repeal the section of the 1967 Act relating to men in the services during the passage of the Armed Forces Bill in May 1981.[12] There were, however, encouraging signs that the Labour Party was now giving serious consideration to the issue. In February 1981 MP Tony Benn had called on the party and the trade unions to take a lead in campaigning for full legal equality for homosexuals and one month later Labour issued a discussion document which argued that equal rights for gay people should be seen as part of the party's broader campaign for civil rights. A survey of MPs' attitudes compiled by Gay Lobby and CHE's Law Reform Committee confirmed that there were a significant number of Labour MPs who might back this pro-gay stance. According to their figures 111 Labour MPs were sympathetic to further changes in the 1967 Act, along with 65 Conservatives and 7 Liberals. Some 30 Labour MPs were opposed to any alteration of the law, along with 113 Tories; 66 Conservative and 22 Labour Members remained non committal, while the opinions of the remaining 136 MPs were unknown.[13]

One leading Labour politician who decided to make his views known on the subject was the recently elected Leader of the Greater London Council (GLC), Ken Livingstone. Speaking to the Harrow Gay Unity Group on 17 August 1981 he announced his firm support for homosexual equality and declared that the GLC would work actively to combat all forms of discrimination against gay men and women. He promised that applications for financial support by gay organisations would be looked upon sympathetically and that the Labour Group would consider how gay issues could be integrated into its education policy for London's schools. Most of Fleet Street reported Mr Livingstone's commitment to gay rights with a detached disapproval: on 19 August the *Daily Express* took exception to his promise of financial aid to gay groups which the paper claimed was against the wishes of the Londoners who had voted Labour to power; the *Daily Telegraph*'s leader on 20 August reiterated its support for the 1967 Act but suspected that the politician might be using the matter for political advantage and voiced its disapproval of the idea that 'one's sexuality should be a matter for political evangelization'.

A survey of more than 2,000 *Gay News* readers in October 1981 showed the political allegiances of a cross-section of gay men: 25 per cent would vote Labour; 24 per cent for the Liberal Party; 23 per cent for the Conservatives; and a remarkably high 21 per cent for the recently formed SDP.[14] Gay Lobby subsequently reported that 22 of the 30 SDP MPs were either fully supportive of, or sympathetic towards, an extension of gay rights.[15] In the same month a National Opinion Poll on current public attitudes towards homosexuality found that 63 per cent of respondents thought that homosexual relations between consenting adults should be legal, 25 per cent disagreed and 12 per cent had no opinion on the matter. This was in spite of the fact that 46 per cent believed there were more homosexuals than 25 years ago. While 49 per cent believed that homosexuals should be allowed in the armed forces (against 41 per cent who thought they shouldn't), there were clear majorities who disapproved of homosexuals working as prison officers (67 per cent), junior school teachers (66 per cent) or doctors (50 per cent).

Although these figures showed that the proportion of people supporting the legalisation of homosexuality had remained fairly stable over the previous two decades (63 per cent in 1965 and 58 per cent in 1977), the percentage opposed to it had dropped from 36 per cent in 1965 to 22 per cent in 1977, only to record a small but significant rise of 3 per cent over the next four years. This confirmed the trend of increasing public sympathy towards homosexuality which had been observed by Michael Schofield and others in the late 1970s, although it was disturbing to note that a number of people who had previously held no strong opinion of the matter now seemed to disapprove of the changes made in the 1967 Act.

In an article in the *Guardian* on 21 June 1982 celebrating the tenth anniversary of *Gay News*, its editor Andrew Lumsden drew attention to the increasing dichotomy he had noticed over the previous decade between this greater public tolerance and the entrenched Establishment prejudices against it.

It's incomparably a better country in which to be gay or come out as gay than in 1972.... There's now an acceptance of the reality of gay people, and that we're not heterosexual with an unfortunate failing.... The great conservative institutions, the legislature, the judiciary and the press are the exceptions to this improved climate. They haven't changed.

Almost exactly a month later this latter point was clearly illustrated when Home Secretary William Whitelaw announced in the Commons that the Queen's personal bodyguard Commander Michael Trestrail would be resigning from his post after the *Sun* newspaper had exposed his 12 year relationship with a male prostitute.[16] The tabloids had a field day with the story as the following selection of front page headlines from 20 July shows:

DISGRACED. NEW PALACE SCANDAL OVER SEX SECRET OF QUEEN'S POLICEMAN – *Star*

SHAMED. QUEEN'S TOP COP RESIGNS OVER AFFAIR WITH A MAN – *Sun*

SCANDAL OF THE MAN WHO GUARDED THE QUEEN – *Daily Express*

In an article in *The Times* on 28 July entitled 'THE LAW THAT FAILED TO LIBERATE GAYS' Leo Abse drew attention to the injustice of a situation in which a man could be hounded from his job although he had not been guilty of any crime or breach of security. The MP went on to castigate Mr Whitelaw for having

in 15 seconds put back the clock 15 years.... A Home Secretary had confirmed ancient prejudices by substituting public pillory for criminal penalties, and homosexuals would have had confirmed their often paranoid belief in the hostility of the heterosexual world.

That paranoia must have seemed even more justifiable when the London newspaper *Capital Gay* revealed on 3 October that the police had raided a private party in West London where it was alleged that homosexual acts were taking place which were not 'in private'. The host, Martin Johnson, and 37 of his guests were arrested and held overnight at a local police station. Two months later they were informed that no charges would be brought against them. As a result of this incident Mr Johnson announced that he would be preparing a submission to the European Court of Human Rights to have the privacy clause in the 1967 Act repealed.

This incident took place against a background of growing concern within the gay community and other groups such as the National Council for Civil Liberties (NCCL) over the Government's intention to extend police powers of arrest in its new Police and Criminal Evidence Bill. In the *Guardian* on 7 March 1983, solicitor Paul Crane described the Police and Criminal Evidence Bill's proposed new power of arrest for 'an affront to public decency' as 'a recipe for harassment' against the gay community. He went on to give a comprehensive overview of the ways in which the limited freedom granted to gay men by the 1967 Act was already being circumscribed by judicial decisions and police methods. He quoted a case where three men had been convicted for having sex together in breach of the privacy clause in the 1967 Act; and noted that convictions for homosexual importuning had increased by a staggering 247 per cent – from 488 in 1977 to 1,208 in 1980. He concluded:

> At best the legal position of gay men's sexual relationships or contacts is uncertain and unclear in many circumstances. At worst the Act and associated legislation have become effective tools for prosecutions, and large numbers of gay men of all ages remain 'sexual outlaws'.

Mrs Thatcher's announcement of a June general election meant that the Bill would not reach the statute book before Parliament was dissolved and the gay rights campaigners switched their attentions instead to ascertaining the attitudes of prospective parliamentary candidates and their parties to gay issues. Although the Liberal Party confirmed its continuing support for homosexual equality the newly formed SDP had no firm policy on the matter, and neither of the other two main parties mentioned the matter in their respective manifestos. Many gay activists had been deeply disappointed when the Labour Party had backed away from accepting equal rights for gays in its 'Labour Programme 1982' policy statement which proposed an age of consent of 18. In the party's 'Campaign Document' for the election this had been reduced to the promise that homosexuals were unfairly treated and that they would be protected from unfair discrimination.

The extent of the Labour leadership's genuine support for the cause had already been the subject of considerable concern after their campaign to prevent Peter Tatchell from standing as official Labour candidate in the Bermondsey by-election in February. In his book *The Battle for Bermondsey*, Mr Tatchell makes it clear that this hostility sprang less from his homosexuality than from the bitter internal struggle between the left and right wings of the party which had surfaced in the aftermath of its overwhelming election defeat in 1979.[17] His left-wing brand of community politics was more unacceptable to the party hierarchy than his sexuality, but both these issues were seized upon and linked together by the tabloid press who subsequently mounted a merciless smear campaign against him. It was this, he alleges, in association with the gutter tactics adopted by some local Liberals, as well as the 'Real Labour' candidate who stood against him, which contributed to his devastating defeat. Labour's 12,000 majority of 1979 was turned into a 10,000 majority for the Liberal candidate Simon Hughes.

Fleet Street pilloried Tatchell throughout the campaign for being Australian, homosexual, left wing and emigrating to Britain to avoid being conscripted to fight in the Vietnam war. Such vicious character assassination disturbed many people including Conservative MP Matthew Parris who called for an end to it in an article in *The Times* on 19 February entitled 'Stop Being Beastly to Tatchell'. And two days before polling day an all party group of MPs tabled a Commons motion expressing 'disgust at sections of the press, television and radio in their treatment of the Southwark-Bermonsey by-election and their character assassination and smear tactics'.

As a result of this persistent harassment Peter Tatchell was forced to leave his job, and for more than a year was subjected to a stream of obscene phone calls, hate mail, death threats, and physical and verbal abuse. *Gay News* dubbed Bermondsey: 'the most homophobic by-election of our times'.[18] The media had proved that the homosexual preferences of a political candidate could be used as a devastating propaganda weapon to undermine fatally support for the Labour Party. It was a lesson which was obviously not lost on certain Conservative politicians, who would apply it in the future to further their electoral advantage.

In the light of this unprecedented orgy of gay-bashing by certain sections of the popular press the collapse of *Gay News* on 16 April came as a profound shock since it deprived the gay community of its only national newspaper. The paper had suffered a series of financial and organisational upheavals since it had been sold by its original owner and editor Denis Lemon to Robert Palmer, and its sudden closure was accompanied by considerable acrimony and bitterness. However, the title was soon sold on, and by August the *New Gay News* was on sale. But its place had already been usurped by Alex McKenna's revamped *Him Monthly* magazine which had captured the old *Gay News'* readership and, having established itself as the heir to the newspaper, duly renamed itself *Gay Times*.

AN AFFRONT TO PUBLIC DECENCY

Mrs Thatcher won another landslide victory in the June general election and the resulting shake-up in her Cabinet saw William Whitelaw replaced as Home Secretary by Leon Brittan. The re-introduction of the Police and Criminal Evidence Bill by Mr Brittan on 27 October 1983 confirmed that although the faces might have changed the policies certainly hadn't: there had been some cosmetic alterations to the Bill but the controversial 'public decency' clause remained intact. Once the new-look measure had safely passed its Second Reading the new Home Secretary turned his attention to Jo Richardson's Sex Equality Private Member's Bill which aimed, amongst other things, to outlaw discrimination in employment on the grounds of homosexuality. Mr Brittan was joined by an impressive array of senior Ministers, including Douglas Hurd, Chancellor Nigel Lawson and Education Secretary Sir Keith Joseph, who helped to ensure that the Bill was decisively defeated by 198 votes to 118.[19]

Mr Hurd was already playing a leading role in piloting the Police and Criminal Evidence Bill through its marathon Committee Stage. When the clause allowing arrests on the grounds of 'an affront to public decency' was discussed on 31 January 1984, Labour members of the Committee launched an all out attack to defeat the proposal. Robin Corbett was extremely worried by evidence he had received of 'pretty police' tactics used by the Metropolitan Police which involved attractive, casually dressed policemen being sent into gay pubs to lure gay men into approaching them.

A publication called *Capital Gay* has made an allegation

about the arrest of 25 men last summer in the Earl's Court area, charged with importuning. It alleges that it was actually a plain clothes policeman who made the advances. Such events seem to have occurred among those frequenting the Coleherne pub in Old Brompton Road. It appears that the plain clothes officers were so well known in the pub that they were known to regulars as the Beverley Sisters.

Shadow Home Secretary Gerald Kaufman announced that he had written to the Home Secretary and Sir Kenneth Newman, the Commissioner of the Metropolitan Police, demanding an investigation into these claims. Gerald Bermingham was very concerned that the term 'public decency' had no strict definition in law and would be open to wide interpretation, thus making the proposed offence 'a recipe for arbitrary arrest'.

Mr Hurd reassured the Committee that entrapment of victims was not permitted by Home Office guidelines which stated that 'no member of the police force shall counsel, incite or procure the commission of a crime'. He rejected the arguments of the Opposition, suggesting that they were attempting to pre-empt the findings of the Criminal Law Revision Committee which was still studying the law relating to importuning. (It is worth noting that the Home Office had defeated an attempt two years earlier by Labour's Robert Kilroy-Silk to extend the amendment which abolished imprisonment for female importuning to males during the passage of the Criminal Justice Bill.) When a vote was forced on Robin Corbett's amendment MPs split along party lines and defeated it by 11 votes to 7.

Over the following months there seemed to be a noticeable increase in police activity directed against the gay community in London. In February a young gay couple were arrested for kissing in Oxford Street and were subsequently fined £100 for 'insulting behaviour likely to cause a breach of the peace' and bound over for a year. Two more arrests for similar incidents were reported later in the year. On Sunday 11 March no less than 50 police officers descended on The Bell gay pub in Camden to investigate an alleged infringement of licensing laws. It was against this background that the raid by the Customs and Excise on London's highly successful – and only – gay community bookshop 'Gay's the Word' took place on 10 April. The shop, which had just fought off an attempt by the police to have it classified as a sex shop, was invaded by Customs and Excise Officers who proceeded to confiscate over 800 books (30 per cent of its total stock) on the grounds that they were imported titles from America which might be 'indecent or obscene'. Many of these titles were readily available in British editions and included works by such well-known authors as Rita Mae Brown and Truman Capote.

Even more disturbing were the simultaneous raids on the homes of two of the shop's directors and its manager which resulted in prolonged questioning, refusal of permission to contact solicitors and the seizure of 'business data' – including certain items which were outside Customs' jurisdiction. It was later revealed that the shop's telephone, along with those of CHE and several other gay organisations, had mysteriously ceased to operate during the period of the raid. Shortly afterwards, Lavender Menace, Scotland's gay bookshop, was raided by the police who confiscated a number of titles for examination by the Procurator Fiscal. Fleet Street treated the incident with a deafening silence which resulted in an impassioned letter in the *Guardian* on 30 April calling on the paper to take notice of this and other cases, which the writer claimed were evidence of a concerted attack on the civil liberties of the gay community.

> These are not just incidents; they are part of a long and sordid history of persecution and discrimination which most gay people thought was coming to an end.... Police harassment tells us once more the lessons we so tediously unlearned: gays ought to feel guilty, ashamed, ought to keep quiet and invisible; gays ought not to be able to read a book freely, or write one, and ought not to be able to organise and meet together.... Our rights are being systematically taken from us, most importantly our right to life with dignity and self-respect.

ACCEPTABLE PUBLIC CONDUCT

The Gay's the Word case and these other incidents of police interference were detailed by Labour's Chris Smith during the debate on the Report Stage of the Police and Criminal Evidence Bill on 14 May.[20] Dissatisfied by the Home Office's reassurances about police use of *agents provocateurs*, Liberal MP Jim Wallace had tabled a clause to amend the 1956 Sexual Offences Act under which prosecutions for importuning were carried out. He proposed that arrests for this offence should only be carried out by a uniformed policeman, and that the arresting officer's evidence should be corroborated by another person, other than a policeman, who had been offended by the behaviour.

Mr Wallace argued that police resources would be better used to combat the continuing rise in serious crime, rather than wasted in the entrapment of homosexuals in public lavatories for behaviour which had usually offended no one except the police. Often the only victim of such a crime was the person arrested. He felt certain that public opinion was becoming increasingly disapproving of this sort of police behaviour and quoted from an editorial which had appeared in the *Scotsman* that very morning:

> Liberalization of the law against homosexual acts in private has been followed by a rise in the number of men charged with homosexual behaviour in public. Just as in the era before homosexual law reform the blackmailer was generally regarded with greater detestation than his homosexual victim, in today's different moral climate the police *agent provocateur* might be more generally disliked than the homosexual whom he arrests.[21]

He felt that these *agent provocateur* tactics were further undermining relations between the police and the gay community.

> There have been debates in the House and in the country on the importance of the damaging effects of police behaviour in times past on their relations with certain racial communities. That has received widespread public attention, but what has not been so much discussed is the serious feeling within the gay community against what its members feel has been a number of years of police oppression.

The majority of speakers from both sides of the House not only offered firm support for the amendment, but also showed considerable sympathy towards the increasing concern of gay people about police behaviour towards them.

Chris Smith was particularly worried about police practices in London which seemed to be part of a 'concerted policy' against the gay community. Gerald Kaufman agreed, and strongly denounced the practice of sending 'pretty police' into gay pubs and clubs to entrap and arrest gay men. He went on to attack the underlying

legal assumptions which continued to uphold the idea that homosexuality was still unacceptable outside the strict definition of
privacy set in 1967.

> we are now looking at something that has been built around
> the Sexual Offences Act and not at a context in which
> homosexual relationships are regarded, in and of them-
> selves, as criminal offences. Yet the assumption and
> consequences of such arrests is to punish them as such. The
> disposition to have a homosexual relationship is turned into
> a criminal tendency. That is not what the law requires or
> what Parliament has asked the police to do.... What kind of
> affront to or offence against public decency... is committed
> by one homosexual towards another in a place where homo-
> sexual people gather to meet one another? In that context
> an offence against public decency cannot in logic, as distinct
> from what is technically within the law, be taking place.

Ignoring the evidence that the vast majority of importuning
cases involved consenting adult males Tony Marlow (Con.) wasted
no time in rallying his fellow Tory backbenchers with an increasingly familiar call to save the nation's children from corruption. He
demanded to know if Mr Kaufman was satisfied that children would
be 'sufficiently protected' from being approached in public lavatories if the new clause were adopted. His colleague Peter Bruinvels
pressed home the same point even more forcefully. In putting
forward the Government's objections Home Office Minister David
Mellor further amplified this emotive and irrational fear. Although
he agreed that the police should not spend a disproportionate
amount of their time dealing with such offences he was certain that
plain clothes officers were essential in preventing this particular
type of 'public nuisance'.

> I believe that is the price that we are entitled to expect to
> extract so that the law may be properly enforced, and the
> public may have confidence they can use a particular facility,
> or that their children can use it without the danger of their
> children being molested.

However, when Clare Short (Lab.) challenged his implicit assumption that most homosexuals were inclined to molest children, Mr
Mellor quickly conceded that this particular problem did apply
equally to heterosexuals.

The Minister went on to claim that Mr Wallace's proposal would restrict the enforcement of the law against importuning and would therefore be 'counter-productive and against the public interest'. He assured MPs that the Government 'deplored' the use of entrapment techniques and as a result of discussions Sir Kenneth Newman had agreed 'to make some amendments to the rules to point out even more clearly that officers deployed on plain clothes duty should never act as *agents provocateurs*'. Despite the unprecedented display of support for the new clause the Government whips ensured that it was defeated by a majority of 60 votes.

On the very same day as the debate, the news broke that MP Dr Keith Hampson had resigned as Parliamentary Private Secretary to Defence Minister Michael Heseltine after being arrested in a gay strip club in Soho. He was supposed to have committed an indecent assault on a plain clothes police officer who was there carrying out 'routine duties'. Although the incident had taken place two weeks earlier the MP had not yet been charged with the offence. Naturally press interest suddenly became focused on this whole area of police activity. There was some confusion over the details of the incident: according to the *Sunday Mirror* the police had denied that officers acted as decoys, but on the same day the *Observer* reported that their inside sources claimed the decision to use *agents provocateurs* had been taken at a very high level.[22]

Whatever the truth of the matter *Gay Times* noted that Fleet Street's commentators were 'unanimously favourable in their support for an end to entrapment' – this sort of behaviour had clearly upset the English notion of fair play.[23] The *Daily Telegraph* was outraged:

> The presence of officers in plain clothes of a fancy sort, drawing on and encouraging sexual approach which would be an offence is inexcusable and should be no part of British practice.

Even the *Sun* castigated the police for wasting manpower in this way: 'the real crime that worries the public is out on the streets. For most people safety on public transport and in their homes comes before private morals'. According to the *Standard*, Ken Livingstone thought it 'absolutely monstrous' that police officers were 'wasting their time standing around gay bars waiting for someone to pinch their bums'. Linda Lee-Potter summed up the general feeling in the *Daily Mail*:

If the destruction of Dr Keith Hampson MP's career results in ending the vendetta against homosexuals which the police have been conducting for years, possibly one iota of good will emerge from this sad and sorry case.[24]

But unfortunately no such positive results emerged. On 18 May *Capital Gay* called the Government's promises to re-consider police procedures 'THE BIG CON'. Scotland Yard had apparently denied that there were any plans to tighten up the rules and suggested there had been 'a bit of a misunderstanding'. And a week later the paper revealed that a new clause had been slipped into the Police Bill which classified 'indecent assault which constitutes an act of gross indecency' – which included one man simply touching another's genitals in a public lavatory – as a 'serious arrestable offence'.[25] Anyone suspected of such an offence could be subjected to an intimate body search and be detained by the police for four days without access to a lawyer. The amendment had been accepted by the Commons without debate or a vote at 2.15 a.m. on 16 May. According to CHE's Peter Ashman the inclusion of such a relatively minor crime in this new category was totally inappropriate. There were hopes that the House of Lords might defeat this new clause and attempt to reinstate the amendment banning 'pretty police' tactics.

Despite strong representations from several Peers during the Committee and Report Stages of the Bill in the Lords the Government refused to reconsider the matter.[26] A last ditch attempt by Alf Dubs (Lab.) to stop gay men from being convicted for importuning on the sole evidence of a policeman was defeated when the Bill returned for its final Reading in the Commons.[27] However, the pressure which had been brought to bear on the Home Office had resulted in a drastic reduction in the number of arrests for importuning in Earls Court, which had fallen from 117 in 1982 to 12 in 1984 according to figures provided by David Mellor. While re-affirming the Government's opposition to the amendment he did confirm that new orders forbidding entrapment had been issued to the Metropolitan Police. Gerald Kaufman refused to accept this unsatisfactory position: 'We say clearly and unequivocally that a change in the law is needed. We shall continue to press for that change.'

Less than a week later, on 10 November 1984, 1,000 demonstrators attended a rally at Rugby in Warwickshire to protest at the decision by the town's Conservative council to remove a clause forbidding job discrimination on the grounds of sexual orientation from their equal opportunities employment policy. Guest speaker Chris Smith MP went on stage and calmly announced: 'My name's Chris Smith, I'm the Labour MP for Islington South and Finsbury and I'm gay.'[28] In doing so he became the first sitting MP in the history of the House of Commons to voluntarily admit to being homosexual.

Of course, the line of MPs whose homosexual inclinations had only been revealed as a result of public indiscretions was a depressing one that stretched back over three decades. Chris Smith's public acknowledgement of his sexuality provided a clear marker of how much parliamentary and public attitudes had changed in the 30 years since Sir John Wolfenden's Committee had assembled for its first meeting. Whereas the merest hint of homosexual scandal automatically spelt political disaster and social ostracism in the 1950s for William Field and Ian Harvey, by the 1980s Labour MPs George Morton and Dr Roger Thomas continued to sit in the Commons with the support of their constituency parties in spite of convictions for homosexual importuning. In a profile of Chris Smith for *Gay News* Andrew Lumsden reported that there was at least one other MP who was prepared openly to speak up on gay issues, but he was not prepared to admit that he was gay in public interviews until he had won at least two further elections. Despite Mr Smith's emphatic assertion that he did not expect other gay MPs to follow his example, he hoped that his action had inevitably made it easier for them to do likewise.

The MP was front page news in his local paper, the *Islington Gazette*, which gave him a fair platform to explain his unexpected announcement; but otherwise media reaction was limited to a few congratulatory comments in the *New Statesman* and the *Observer*. By 'coming out' in this way Chris Smith had completely flummoxed the media, and in particular the national tabloids who had been deprived of a sensational exposé. He had made it impossible for the press to launch a campaign of innuendo and smears of the type which had destroyed Jeremy Thorpe's political career and led to Peter Tatchell's defeat in Bermondsey.

In an article in the *New Socialist* in January 1985 he acknowledged the fact that the cause of gay rights would only be advanced if more gay public figures had the courage to follow his example.

the form of oppression from which most gay and lesbian people suffer is one that forces them to hide their true sexuality and affections. It forces them in many ways to be untrue to themselves and to the people around them. One of the things I felt strongly in standing up and saying in public that I was gay, was that honesty and openness are the major weapons that people can use against that form of oppression. The more people who do that, the better. But it's very hard to do, and I still feel constrained in many other ways.

But an omen of the reception which Chris Smith and others who chose to make a public statement of homosexuality might have to face from an overwhelmingly anti-gay press was provided by *The Times* on 21 November 1984. A leader article made an indirect reference to the openly gay MP in a viciously homophobic piece which used fears about the Aids epidemic spreading through blood transfusions as an excuse to attack the whole cause of gay liberation. Demanding that all blood donors should be subject to 'strict questioning' to ensure the 'rigorous exclusion' of active homosexuals the paper suggested that the Department of Health and Social Security (DHSS) should consider methods adopted in Australia where anyone knowingly donating contaminated blood now faced a two-year prison sentence.

The infection's origins and means of propagation excites repugnance, moral and physical, at promiscuous male homosexuality – conduct which, tolerable in private circumstances, has with the advent of gay liberation become advertised, even glorified as acceptable public conduct, even a proud badge for public men to wear.

9

BEING DEFINED BY OUR COCKS: 1984–6

One of the most regrettable aspects of the development of Aids has been the tendency in some quarters for those who suffer from the disease to be treated as pariah figures. This may in part be due to ignorance and to fear of infection; it may also be related to the social stigma which may still attach to homosexuality. It is profoundly to be hoped that such attitudes towards victims of this disease will change and that they will be accorded all the care they need – care which needs to embrace not only them but their loved ones.

Baroness Cox – House of Lords 18/3/85

A DOUBLE-EDGED ATTACK

There is no doubt that the anti-gay band-wagon was picking up speed long before the first media-manufactured scare brought the Aids epidemic to the forefront of public consciousness in February 1985. However, the appearance of this sexually transmitted and ultimately fatal virus was to offer a powerful weapon which the moralists of the right and their political allies were to use with considerable effect against the cause of gay rights. Of course, the gay community had already been living under the growing personal threat of the killer disease for the previous two years, during which time repeated pleas to the Government for an acknowledgement that there was a fatal virus at large were simply ignored.

The first British case of the rare cancer Kaposi's sarcoma (KS), which was later to be recognised as one of the opportunistic infections associated with Aids, was reported in the *Lancet* in December 1981. That the magazine *Doctor* should be one of the first publications to report that an unusually large number of cases of

KS had been found among American gay men was only to be expected, but to use it as an excuse to print a short but vicious item entitled 'Nothing Gay about This Epidemic' was unforgivable. This piece owed more to unabashed bigotry than medical opinion and was spiteful, mocking and inflammatory.

> The common usage of that pretty little adjective 'gay' as a euphemism has now become the sad name for a mysterious virus that turns harmless germs into killers.... Perhaps there should be a Government health warning: Gays can kill.[1]

If the medical press was going to condone such blatantly homophobic remarks, then it was inevitable that their less scrupulous colleagues in Fleet Street were going to have a field day. However, the general coverage over the following year was minimal: in the same month as the *Doctor* article *The Times* referred to the phenomenon as the 'gay syndrome' and *Time Out* later described it as the 'Scourge of the Gays'[2] but the reports simply concentrated on the spread of the virus in America. Coverage by the gay press was more comprehensive but equally irregular, and took much the same line.

In November 1982 the gay community in Britain made their first positive response to the Aids threat by setting up a charity to raise money for research and to persuade gay men that the disease was no longer confined to America. It was named the Terrence Higgins Trust (THT) in memory of the first gay man in Britain known to have died from Aids. One of the founders of the Trust told *Capital Gay* 'There is no money coming from the public purse. We have got to finance this ourselves.'[3]

One month later *Gay News* reported that the BBC was making a documentary about the spread of the disease in America to be shown the following year, and warned:

> British gay men had better prepare themselves for some major shocks in the months ahead. They will be under a double-edged attack from both disease and media coverage if recent American experience is repeated here.[4]

This prediction was proved to be startlingly accurate: on 26 April 1983, the morning after the Horizon programme 'The Killer in the Village' had been transmitted, virtually all the national daily newspapers commented on the matter – many for the first time. Several took the opportunity to adopt a disapproving moral stance which implicitly suggested that the gay men affected had brought this terrible fate on themselves by indulging in perverted sexual practices. Under the headline 'AIDS: THE PRICE OF PROMISCUITY?' the *Daily Telegraph* couldn't resist quoting the view that the epidemic might be 'a supernatural gesture by a disapproving almighty'; the *Mail* predictably followed suit.

But in the *Evening Standard* Lucy Hughes-Hallet railed against this smug reaction.

> There is a streak of very nasty puritanism underlying the public fascination with AIDS, a sense of re-assurance that those of us who don't dare indulge ourselves as the frequenters of New York's East Village do are not just timid, but also sensible, a mean satisfaction that they're not getting away with it after all.

The Times agreed that it was 'Everyone's problem': 'you have a situation which ought to induce careful thought well beyond the confines of the gay community.... The DHSS had better wise up on this, and fast.'

Unfortunately there were already ominous signs that the Department of Health was determined to ignore the whole business. On 13 March a spokesman had told the *Sunday Mirror* that no steps were being taken to ban American blood or blood products despite experts' fears that these might be contaminated with the Aids virus. Whereas before the Horizon documentary this story had been virtually ignored by the rest of the newspapers, when the *Mail on Sunday* made the same allegation on 1 May under the front page headline 'HOSPITALS USING KILLER BLOOD' the first panic began. While the disease had been restricted to homosexuals the press had only mentioned it in passing, but now that there was evidence that the disease could be spread to the rest of the community through blood transfusions and the use of blood-related products by haemophiliacs there was suddenly great concern. According to the *Telegraph* the next day the Department of Health had admitted that there were suspicions that the virus might be passed by blood transfusions but that 'the evidence was too slight at present to justify immediate action'.

It was *Doctor* magazine which, once again, provided the platform for the views of another rampant homophobe by printing an article which laid the blame for the crisis firmly at the door of the gay community and argued that homosexuals had brought the disaster upon themselves. A distinction was made between them and the 'innocent' victims which they were now putting at risk (a distinction which was quickly adopted by the popular press).

> Venereal disease has always been nature's quiet hint that she would really like us to be monogamous. With AIDS – fatal, incurable, vilely mysterious – nature has stopped hinting and started screaming the house down.... But what about the innocents, particularly children, who are being infected by the lifestyle of others?[5]

These unhelpful and unjustified attacks merely served to encourage the gay community's own efforts to organise a series of practical initiatives to tackle the growing problem. Gay Switchboard set up the first public seminar on Aids on 21 May 1983 with funding provided by the Government-backed Health Education Council. The meeting agreed that voluntary bodies were not going to be able to fight the disease alone and several leading doctors appealed for Government funding for research. In *Capital Gay* on 3 June columnist Brian Kennedy pointed out that Government money would only be forthcoming if considerable pressure were put on grant-giving bodies like the Medical Research Council, and warned that the gay movement would have to accept that the THT would never be able to raise the enormous sums required for adequate research.

> Their activities will be called 'too political', there will be opposition to public money being spent on gays.... Some of that opposition will be from outside, as we expect, but some such arguments have already been voiced from within our own gay 'community': that gay people are not deserving of public money, that if gay people want something they should pay for it directly, rather than via taxes and rates. Let me labour a very clear point. If we expect donations and benefits to pay for AIDS research then it will simply not happen.

In that same month *Gay Times* carried a series of articles about Aids, one of which reported on the debate raging in America over promiscuity and the gay lifestyle, and noted the absence of this controversy in Britain. A THT spokesman confirmed that the threat of Aids was forcing gay men to be less promiscuous: 'In America... monogamy is the most fashionable thing since the mini-skirt.' The magazine was contemptuous of the extreme reactions of some sections of the American gay press which it claimed had turned the Aids crisis into 'an obtuse gay rights problem'. However, it admitted that the low key approach which had been adopted by the British gay community could be contributing to the alarming amount of ignorance which still persisted in the medical establishment.

A MENACE TO ALL SOCIETY

The ignorance of the medical profession offered an ideal excuse for the Government to continue pretending that the problem did not exist. In the House of Lords on 14 July 1983 Lord Glenarthur confirmed that 14 cases of Aids had been reported to the Communicable Diseases Surveillance Centre (CSDS). The only new initiative he announced was the setting up of a Medical Research Council working party to consider and co-ordinate research into the disease; he also promised a half-hearted gesture over blood donations which was clearly designed as a sop to growing public concern.

> There is no conclusive evidence AIDS is transmitted by blood or blood products but the department is considering publishing a leaflet indicating circumstances in which blood donations should be avoided.[6]

The *Mail on Sunday* returned to the attack on 2 October with its coverage of the 'scandalous and unnecessary death' of a 58 year old hæmophiliac, described as 'the first non-homosexual in Britain to die because of Aids', and demanded to know: 'Must another innocent man die before action is taken?' A lurid 'special report' on the 'gay plague' in the *Sun* on 11 November chronicled the distress of the haemophiliac's widow:

> After Peter died I saw my husband's name linked with what was called the Gay Plague. It was disgusting.... It is vital to realise that other people apart from homosexuals can be destroyed by this disease.

The message was clear: readers should not waste their sympathy on homosexual victims who had brought the disease upon themselves. An interview with a gay man suffering from Aids preached the new puritan gospel advocated by the *Sun*.

> I suppose I have paid the penalty for the way I used to live.

I wasn't fussy about who I had sex with – I saw it all and did it all. In a way I see AIDS as a sort of message to homosexuals to act more responsibly. Now I have stopped partying and I am a better person.

The first meagre grants totalling £250,000 over three years were handed out by the Medical Research Council in April 1984 and at the end of that month French and American scientists announced that they had isolated the Aids virus which became known as HTLV III. Doctors immediately began working to produce a test which would be able to detect the virus in blood, but a cure was still considered a long way off.

In November 1984 the death of a third British haemophiliac and the news that three babies in Australia had caught the disease from blood donated by an infected homosexual donor led to another spate of sensational headlines. *The Times* led the rest of the Fleet Street pack in demanding that gay men should be banned from giving blood in the notorious leader article which not only attacked openly gay figures (like MP Chris Smith) but questioned the right of the gay community to exist in the public domain.[7] A few weeks later the *Sun* called gay men with the Aids virus 'walking time bombs' and described those who passed their infection to others by donating blood as 'a menace to all society'.[8] The Government made the usual reassuring noises, promising that British blood products would be heat-treated to kill the Aids virus by the spring of 1985 and that the country would be self-sufficient in those products by December 1986.

In January 1985 a report from the Royal College of Nursing estimated that if the Aids epidemic continued to spread at its current rate more than one million people would be infected with the deadly virus by the end of the decade. The popular press eagerly seized upon this frightening prediction as an excuse to launch into another round of sensational speculation designed to whip up public fear and thereby to force an apparently complacent Government into acknowledging that Aids presented a real threat to the heterosexual population and that positive action now needed to be taken. The political temperature was turned up another notch when Jill Knight, Chairman of the Commons Health Committee, insisted that 'steps must be taken as quickly as possible to protect the general public' and joined a growing number of MPs who were demanding that Aids should be classified as a 'notifiable' disease.[9]

According to a Health Department spokesman this would mean: 'we could take legal steps to keep the patient in hospital, possibly in sterile conditions, or to prevent him from giving blood transfusions.'[10] No one explained how this extraordinary policy might be policed, or how the NHS would be able to fund the beds and nursing facilities for the growing number of people whom they would be obliged to restrain in hospitals.

Without regard for these practicalities or the civil liberties implications of such a move, a number of national and provincial newspapers immediately jumped on this new bandwagon. Of course, the fact that the vast majority of Aids sufferers were gay men may have accounted for the enthusiasm with which these alarmist measures were being promoted. This led other journalists to offer even more extreme solutions; in the *Sunday Telegraph* on 20 January, Auberon Waugh disingenuously wondered why

> nobody has mentioned what might seem the most obvious way of cutting down this figure [of 1 million by 1990] – by repealing the Sexual Offences Act of 1967 and making sodomy a criminal offence once again.

Other newspapers like the *Colchester Evening Gazette* delved back into the past to exhume a theory of divine displeasure which would have done a medieval theologian proud.

> It is surely no coincidence that the spread of this curse has followed the homosexual liberation and promiscuity that we have fostered. Could it be that a force far higher and far more powerful than well-meaning mortals is now making judgement on the way of the world we have been entrusted with?[11]

John Smith in the *Sunday People* was one of the few columnists to warn against this sort of homophobic backlash, offering in its place a simple and constructive solution:

> It's time the Government came out of the closet on this growing problem and went on TV with a series of public service messages explaining just what AIDS is, how you can catch it, and how you can avoid it.[12]

This sort of rational solution was cheerfully ignored in Fleet Street, where the tabloids were locked into a vicious circulation war in which Aids was providing ideal ammunition, as the coverage of the death of a prison chaplain at the end of the month proved. Under the headline 'GAY PLAGUE KILLS PRIEST' the *Sun* claimed that nurses had worn special protective clothing when approaching the dying man and laboratory staff had refused to handle his blood samples; when he died his body was immediately placed in a plastic bag and deep-frozen, and a pathologist would not carry out a post-mortem examination on it. The local medical officer considered it 'likely' that the dead man was homosexual but confirmed that attempts to trace his contacts had been called off because 'If anyone has the disease there's nothing anyone can do for them'.[13] The other national tabloids reported the story in equally lurid terms.

Having implied that Aids was as infectious and deadly as the bubonic plague the popular press then avidly charted the wave of hysteria it had unleashed. Their banner headlines showed how gays were being made the principal scapegoats by a terrified public. Prisoners in the gaol which had been visited by the dead chaplain barricaded themselves in their cells and demanded Aids tests, and prison officers flatly refused to accept prisoners transferred from gaols where there were suspected Aids cases. A gay couple was banned from their local working men's club because other members feared they might catch Aids from the drinking glasses used by them; a taxi firm stopped picking up fares from gay clubs and pubs; parishioners all over the country refused to take communion in case they could pick up the virus from chalices; and firemen were advised by their union to stop giving mouth-to-mouth resuscitation in order to avoid the risk of infection.

Determined to leave no stone unturned in its crusade to bring the truth about this catastrophe to its avid readers, the *Sun* ran an article on the views of a vicar who claimed Aids was the wrath of God. The Reverend revealed that he would shoot his own son if he caught the virus – which was described as 'the modern Black Death'. In case the message was too sophisticated for *Sun* readers to grasp there was a picture of a vicar aiming a shot-gun at a young man's head.[14] CHE complained to the Press Council that the article was at best irresponsible and alarmist, and at worst could encourage violence against those suffering from the disease. The Press Council considered the matter for over a year and finally rejected the complaint on the grounds that the paper had simply chosen 'a dramatic way to focus attention on the danger of Aids'!

POPULIST PRESSURE

The Department of Health's first reaction to this rising panic was to issue a statement from the Government's Chief Health Officer, Sir Donald Acheson, which advised homosexuals to stop being promiscuous if they wanted to avoid catching and spreading the virus. Hardly surprisingly, this had little effect on curbing the growing public alarm. It was certainly not enough to impress political opinion and on 8 February an all-party group of 50 MPs signed a Commons motion calling on the Government to make some positive moves to tackle the issue. Faced with these pressures Health Minister Kenneth Clarke confirmed that he was considering making Aids a notifiable disease. This declaration naturally gave a considerable boost to the advocates of that policy. But on the same day in the Commons it was revealed that the Aids Advisory Committee (which had been hastily set up by the DHSS) had already told the Government that there were 'no clinical grounds' for making the disease notifiable.[15] Medical experts were instead urging ministers to launch a health education campaign to inform the public about the virus, and the ways in which it could be transmitted.[16]

By the end of the following week the majority of Fleet Street dailies were demanding that Aids be made notifiable, led by *The Times* which warned gay men that the limited freedom granted to them by the 1967 Act would be put at risk unless they showed a greater sense of responsibility. An unashamedly homophobic editorial resurrected the familiar view that homosexuals were fifth columnists indulging in dangerous sexual practices which threatened the very fabric of society.

> This disease is capable not only of physical harm but also of dissolving the trust on which social life is built, the trust which allows us to separate and tolerate private conduct, even of an immoral and exotic kind, from the public business of society.[17]

Although the *Daily Mail* agreed that Aids should be made notifiable it castigated the Government for creating a 'TIDE OF FEAR' by its failure to respond to the problem over the previous three years, and in an uncharacteristic display of concern warned of the dangers of an anti-gay backlash: 'Making AIDS a notifiable disease must not be an excuse for a witch hunt against homosexuals but part of a campaign to stop it spreading.'[18] It was unfortunate that the *Mail* had not made this rather obvious connection a few weeks earlier when it was eagerly splashing stories about the 'gay plague' across its front pages in competition with all the other tabloids.

It was hardly surprising that few newspapers bothered to report on the views and reactions of the gay community to the epidemic; the *Observer* article 'ANATOMY OF A PANIC' was a rare example – quoting the opinions of an Aids counsellor at a London hospital:

> The effect on the gay community has been devastating. Apart from their own alarm about picking up the disease... public reaction has made homosexuals feel increasingly oppressed.... We are getting all sorts of stories about gays being sent home from work and about people who cannot get workmen to go to their houses because they might pick up Aids there.... Many of these people already suffer feelings of guilt because they have homosexual tendencies. In the end this can turn into self-loathing, and some have even attempted suicide.[19]

Although the gay community was at its most vulnerable in the face of such an unprecedented wave of discrimination it was still prepared to fight its own corner. *Capital Gay* launched a furious attack on the Government's proposal to make the disease notifiable in a blistering editorial entitled 'FOUR WASTED YEARS'. The paper called on the Department of Health to answer charges of gross negligence over its handling of the epidemic, and warned that the Government was being panicked into ignoring the opinion of its own experts for reasons of 'political expediency'. The paper concluded: 'So long as Aids remained "a bug that killed faggots" it was of no interest to Government or Fleet Street.'[20]

Anxious to be seen to be doing something positive Kenneth Clarke duly announced in the Commons on 20 February that although he would not make Aids a notifiable disease, 'reserve powers' would be introduced to allow Health Authorities to detain Aids patients in hospital if they were in 'a dangerously infectious condition'.[21] Since Aids was primarily passed through sexual contact or blood products, and was therefore not highly infectious, this policy made very little sense. Aids expert Dr Ian Weller told *Capital Gay* 'I think it's a political move to keep people quiet... a sort of half-way house.' According to a spokesman for the New York State Health Department similar powers had not been considered

PEERS, QUEERS, AND COMMONS

necessary by health officials in America despite the fact that nearly 8,000 cases of the disease had been recorded there – compared to 132 cases in Britain.[22] In his regular Aids column in *Capital Gay* on 19 April Julian Meldrum commented:

> The biggest flaw in this legislation is that it blames people who are ill for transmitting the disease.... Laws which single out people with Aids for special attention as sources of infection have negative educational value. Education, not compulsion, should be the order of the day.

More than a year later it was revealed that the move to make the disease notifiable had only been blocked by the threat of 'high level resignations at the DHSS'.[23]

While the Minister continued to insist there was no need for extra funding for the treatment of Aids a member of his newly appointed Standing Advisory Committee on Aids (which did not include a single representative from the gay community) estimated that the cost of patient care by the end of the year could be £6 million.[24] The sterling work of the pathetically underfunded THT was acknowledged by several Peers during a lack-lustre debate on Aids in the House of Lords on 18 March 1985.[25] All the speakers approached the matter with informed concern and most called on the Government to provide extra resources to tackle the rapidly growing problem. Several, including Baroness Cox, were particularly worried that Aids was being used as an excuse for 'gay bashing'. The Government's only practical response was to announce a grant of £15,000 to the Haemophilia Society and a miserly £25,000 for the THT.

The news that film star Rock Hudson was dying from Aids brought the disease back to the front pages of the tabloids in July, but this time in a directly personal and human way. It was hard to tell whether the public was more shocked by the tragedy of seeing one of its most popular and attractive screen idols reduced to a shrunken and emaciated skeleton or by the fact that this apotheosis of heterosexual masculinity had been revealed to be homosexual. According to Randy Shilts in his book *And the Band Played On*[26] Hudson's death was the turning point in the fight to get the Reagan administration to acknowledge the seriousness of the Aids epidemic and take concrete measures – a 48 per cent increase in research funding was requested by the White House bringing the sum committed for the 1985/6 financial year up to $126.3m. Unfortunately the British Government did not follow this example, and despite pleas from medical experts very little new money was being made available. On 25 August the *News of the World* ran the headline 'MINISTER KILLED BY AIDS' and claimed that the death of bachelor Lord Avon was 'Britain's most sensational Aids tragedy'. The next morning the *Sun* took up the story and asserted that the peer was 'well known as a homosexual by Whitehall and Westminster officials'. Having noted the fact that the former Minister was a close personal friend of the Prime Minister, *Capital Gay* expressed the hope that his death might persuade the Government to take the Aids epidemic more seriously.[27]

The news that a 29 year old Aids sufferer had been detained in a Manchester hospital on 14 September under the 'reserve powers' granted to health authorities back in February was clearly not the sort of positive action that was being sought. There was an immediate storm of protest from the gay community: in the *News of the World* a spokesman for the local Aids Line condemned the move:

> It's wrong to criminalise a man who went to hospital. A lot of people will be discouraged from going for treatment. The decision creates panic and anxiety in the community at large.[28]

The Terrence Higgins Trust appealed to the High Court and the order was rescinded ten days later.

THEIR RIGHT TO BELONG
TO THE HUMAN RACE

A Cabinet reshuffle in the same month had brought Barney Hayhoe from the Treasury (where he had been presiding over the prosecution of Gay's the Word Bookshop) to the Department of Health. The new Minister indicated that he had personally decided to make Aids a priority and on 26 September he announced an extra £1 million to provide Aids treatment and counselling in the Thames region. 'Not before time' commented the *Daily Star* the next morning, expressing its concern that a similar amount of money had not been allocated for research work.[29] In a letter to the *Evening Standard* Peter Tatchell dismissed the sum as 'too little, too late', noting that Britain's total funding had reached a mere £2.5m in comparison to $109m committed by the American Government.[30] Although *Capital Gay* columnist Julian Meldrum agreed that the money provided was totally inadequate, he felt that by promising public funding and setting up new committees to co-ordinate research and discuss policies on Aids the Government was implicitly committing itself to future action. He highlighted the need to tackle discrimination against those suffering with Aids in prisons, schools, housing, life insurance and mortgages, and employment. He argued that the gay community should be pressing for reform of the sexual offences laws which the police might use against gay men in order to 'protect young people from Aids'.[31]

Gay men who were unconvinced by this latter argument must, however, have been given cause for thought by the revelation that a group of Conservative MPs were working behind the scenes at Westminster to persuade the Government to close down gay pubs and clubs to curb the spread of Aids. Their leader, the outspoken backbencher Geoffrey Dickens, had already set up a meeting with the Health Minster. He told *Capital Gay*:

> I haven't got it in for gays. It doesn't matter to me what your members do. I may not like it and I may not understand why they do it but it doesn't matter.... I just want to stop this disease from spreading.[32]

In an article in *Capital Gay* on 13 December 1985 entitled 'ECHOES FROM THE 1930s' *Guardian* correspondent Nicholas de Jongh argued that politicians like Geoffrey Dickens would not be able to make such inflammatory and dangerous suggestions if the ground had not been so well prepared by the unremittingly homophobic coverage of Aids in the tabloids, and particularly the recriminalisation arguments being pedalled by a few right-wing Fleet Street columnists.

> Their undertones are ominous. Those who are different will be tolerated as long as they keep quiet and do not jeopardise the security or existence of the majority. Aids, when charac-terised falsely as a 'gay plague' threatens that majority and steps, therefore, may have to be taken to control that dan-gerous minority. So too the porcine self-publicist Geoffrey Dickens clambers over these journalistic backs to tell *Capital Gay* readers that he wishes to see gay social life brought to a halt. 'You have no need to worry. You people are certainly under no threat from me', he soothes. Where last, or most notoriously, was that cry heard this century, if not in the

earliest phase of the Hitler regime, when the first forebodings of the Jews needed to be pacified?

On 2 December 1985 Social Services Secretary Norman Fowler announced an extra £6.3 million to combat the spread of Aids – £2.5 million of which was set aside for a national information campaign. Six haemophiliac centres were given £270,000, but the Terrence Higgins Trust received no extra funding to expand its work in the gay community.[33] *Capital Gay* pointed out that the Government was now spending £275 for each of the estimated 1,000 haemophiliacs who were HTLV III antibody positive, as opposed to £1.75 per head through the THT for the estimated 20,000 gay men who were similarly infected.[34] The Trust's Chairman, Tony Whitehead, considered the whole package inadequate to deal with the growing crisis in all sections of the community. He described it as 'an unhappy compromise between real health needs and political expediency' and criticised the Government for totally ignoring gay men. Andrew Lumsden in the *New Statesman* accused the Government of deliberate 'denigration' of the Trust and drew attention to the fact that donations from the lesbian and gay community had matched the Trust's original £35,000 grant penny for penny.[35]

Plans for the much-heralded Government education campaign had already been in preparation for some time, but an article in *Hospital Doctor* in September reported that the new Health Minister had already rejected the use of sexually frank language and wanted to aim more at 'reassuring the public, rather than scaring them off sex for life', although his advisers, including Dr Acheson, were warning against pandering to moral squeamishness on the matter.[36] The banning of a Horizon programme on Aids in January 1986 which looked at the connection between Aids and male homosexual practices using some graphic language and descriptions suggested that those advocating a direct approach were in for a hard fight. *The Economist* unequivocally told the Government on 1 February 1986 that plain talking was essential if its campaigns were to succeed and warned: 'RETICENCE IS DANGEROUS':

These campaigns will cause great offence. Puritans will denounce them as indecent, libertarians as an invasion of privacy, fiscal conservatives as a waste of public money. All these groups will have to be offended.

However, according to the findings of a Gallup poll in the *Daily*

Telegraph on 12 March 56 per cent of people interviewed were willing to pay extra taxes to help find a cure for Aids (33 per cent were not), while 53 per cent thought that the Government would be spending more money on research if the disease did not affect mainly homosexual men (28 per cent disagreed). More disturbing was the degree of public ignorance: 36 per cent believed the virus could be caught by kissing, 25 per cent by sharing a drinking glass, 20 per cent by being sneezed on and 19 per cent from sitting on a toilet seat. Although given that these sorts of distortions and misconceptions had been peddled by the popular press it was perhaps surprising that these figures were not higher.

After a postponement of a week – allegedly because of continuing disagreement over the precise wording of the adverts – the 'DON'T AID AIDS' campaign was finally launched on 16 March 1986 with full page adverts in the national press. Tony Whitehead told *Capital Gay* on 21 March that he was disappointed that the language used had not been more direct. According to the *Observer* Ministers had vetoed the explicit campaign at the last minute; Barney Hayhoe defended the decision on the grounds that: 'We had to get a sense of balance. We did not want to create a backlash against minority groups.'[37] Of course, this sudden concern for minority groups did not extend to providing them with adequate funding. On 19 April it was announced that the THT would be given £100,000 to expand its work – only half the amount it had requested. *Capital Gay* accused the DHSS of treating the Trust, which was the country's most experienced and longest established Aids charity, 'as little more than a fringe group'.[38]

In the mean while Larry Kramer's play *The Normal Heart* had arrived in London.[39] This harrowing drama was a powerful and uncompromising account of the struggles of America's first Aids organisation to persuade the authorities and the gay community of the dangers posed by the mysterious and deadly virus, based on the author's experiences as a founder member of Gay Men's Health Crisis. Kramer used the play to question the whole ethos of gay liberation which, for the majority of his countrymen, meant a lifestyle based on multiple casual sexual encounters. Many American gays felt bewildered and betrayed by this attack, which seemed to undermine the very basis of their sexual identity:

MICKEY: I've spent fifteen years of my life fighting for our right to be free and make love whenever, wherever.... And you're telling me that all those years of what being gay stood for is wrong... and I'm a murderer. We have been so oppressed! Don't you remember how it was? Can't you see how important it is for us to love openly, without hiding and without guilt?

Through his main character Ned Weeks, Kramer argued that gay men could only throw off their guilt and fear and master their own fate by acknowledging that indiscriminate promiscuity was spreading the virus. But in order to do this they would have to find new ways of defining their homosexual identity.

NED: The only way we'll have real pride is when we demand recognition of a culture that isn't just sexual. It's all there – all through history we've been there; but we have to claim it, and identify who was in it, and articulate what's in our minds and hearts and all our creative contributions to this earth. And until we do that, and until we organise ourselves block by neighbourhood by city by state into a united visible community that fights back, we're doomed. That's how I want to be defined: as one of the men who fought the war. Being defined by our cocks is literally killing us. Must we all be reduced to becoming our own murderers?

In *The Times* on 28 April Bernard Levin accepted Kramer's premise that homosexuals still needed to assert themselves against discrimination and prejudice but argued that it was dangerous and inappropriate for them to claim a separate identity which set them apart from the heterosexual majority. By taking this path gays would merely be 'exchanging one kind of ghetto for another'. He suggested that since Aids was an indiscriminate killer of both homosexuals and heterosexuals alike perhaps the time had come to dispense with the whole idea of using those terms. A *Guardian* article entitled 'THE FLIP-SIDE OF GAY LIB' had posed equally disturbing questions along the same lines a year earlier.

Is there a gay ethos? What is its useful input to an overwhelmingly heterosexual society? To what extent do gays want a separate existence? Do they have goals different from straights?... It seems no longer sufficient to regard gays as conspiratorial purveyors of an equally conspiratorial, fatal disease in the mid-eighties. That is an outworn metaphor.

There needs to be a new one and gays should contribute to
its promotion, though they are in a bleak position to do so.[40]

Unfortunately the prospect of the gay community being able to
address itself to this sort of philosophical reappraisal at a time when
it was facing the twin challenge of a fatal sexually transmitted
disease and an unprecedented level of homophobic hysteria was
slim indeed. While an unscrupulous press hounded gay men as
convenient scapegoats it was inevitable that many would either be
driven back into the ghetto to seek protection and support, or
simply slam their closet doors firmly shut on an increasingly hostile
heterosexual world. This persecution might have been expected to
encourage greater solidarity within the gay movement, but any
such tendency was undermined by the fact that Aids had transformed sex from being the one thing which all gay men had in
common to a dangerous act carrying the risk of death.

In fact, the crisis had revealed the vulnerability of the British gay
community which, in turning its back on CHE's attempt to build a
united national mass movement with effective political clout, had
opted instead to dissipate its energies in sectional interests and
confine itself to the political margins. Although the gay organisations had responded quickly and responsibly to the Aids epidemic
it was not surprising that they tended to concentrate on a pragmatic
and personal approach to the disease. Although the gay press gave
the matter comprehensive coverage – and was repeatedly criticised
for doing so by a minority of its readers – there was very little
discussion of the wider implications of the disease in terms of private
morality and gay pride, issues which were tearing apart the American gay community. The THT's demands for Government funding
seemed to provoke more controversy than its 'safe sex' campaign
which was recommending gay men to cut down on the number of
sexual partners.

At the beginning of July the annual Gay Pride march and festival
took place in London and, as usual, most of the press chose to ignore
the event. However, on 8 July the recently launched *Today* newspaper carried a perceptive editorial which recognised that this
public demonstration of gay solidarity had assumed a new importance in the wake of the Aids backlash. It acknowledged that simply
by being openly gay the participants were showing 'a special kind
of bravery'.

They came from all over Britain to show that they refused

to be victims or to be seen as public health threats, and to assert their right to belong to the human race. Most important of all they marched to remind us that an appalling disease has unwittingly been brought into our society, and to encourage us all to find a cure. AIDS does not discriminate when it chooses its victims. Nor do the men who walked through the rain to help find an answer to it.

IRRESISTIBLE DEMANDS

In November 1986 the Thatcher Government finally decided to take positive action on the Aids crisis and appointed a Cabinet Committee to be headed by the Deputy Prime Minister, William Whitelaw. This sudden change of heart followed a new wave of media coverage which had been sparked off by several television programmes on Aids. 'This Week' carried out a live poll of their audience and discovered that the majority were in favour of mass screening of the entire population and legal restrictions on homosexual behaviour. The tabloids eagerly seized on these results to reiterate their demands for Aids to be made notifiable, and gave new prominence to those advocating forced quarantine of victims and the recriminalisation of homosexual acts. Since the Government had ignored this type of pressure for the previous three years its new initiative may perhaps have been connected with rumours that 1987 was being considered as a general election year. The fact that recent opinion polls had indicated that the Conservative Party were seen as 'uncaring' at a time when the majority of voters identified Aids as one of the major problems facing the country may possibly have been another relevant factor in the political equation. Outbursts by some local Conservative activists on the subject had undoubtedly contributed to this perception. In particular, the comments of Bill Brownhill, Conservative leader of South Staffordshire council, received widespread media coverage on national radio, television and in the national press. After viewing an educational film on Aids the councillor had remarked:

Those bunch of queers that legalise filth in homosexuality have a lot to answer for and I hope they are proud of what they have done.... As a cure I would put 90 per cent of queers in the ruddy gas chamber.[41]

A Harris Poll published in the *Observer* in November showed that

66 per cent of the public did not believe the Government was doing enough to warn people about the dangers of Aids.[42] It was therefore no great shock to learn that the outcome of the first meeting of the Cabinet Committee was the announcement of yet another public education campaign. A 'forceful' £5m publicity drive would be followed by a leaflet drop to every home in the country to promote the slogan 'AIDS: DON'T DIE OF IGNORANCE'. Confident its Fleet Street critics would be silenced by this news the Government permitted the Commons to stage its first debate on the matter on 21 November 1986. This was a dull and uninspiring affair since it had been unanimously agreed that the issue was too serious to be subjected to the indignities of party political wrangling.[43] In fact, the occasion was principally used by Mr Fowler as a launching pad for his advertising campaign, which had now been allocated a £20m budget.

The new Aids adverts duly appeared in the press and were splashed over 1,500 hoardings throughout the country. Television and cinema adverts with their sophisticated state-of-the-art images of exploding volcanoes and incandescent icebergs were not unveiled until January 1987 and were universally condemned as uninformative and irrelevant. A Marplan opinion poll in the *Guardian* on 13 February found that although 71 per cent of people had read the Government's Aids leaflet, 82 per cent thought that the publicity campaign was having little or no effect on the spread of the disease and 44 per cent felt that it was not explicit enough. Ministers now decided that the time had come for a more direct approach and a month later the British public found themselves unable to turn on their radio or switch on the television without being subjected to in-depth discussions on intimate sexual behaviour, and practical demonstrations of how to unroll condoms over wooden phalluses. In that one week there was probably more explicit coverage and graphic illustration of sexual practices – both homo and hetero – than there had ever been in the entire history of British broadcasting!

From the very beginning the Aids threat had presented an uncomfortable challenge to the Thatcher administration. A commitment to individualism, the free market economy, the reduction of public spending and increased privatisation mitigated against the allocation of state funding to tackle a disease linked with minority sexual practices. As the *Daily Telegraph* wrily observed:

It is ironical that it should have fallen to a Government temperamentally so opposed to the state's meddling in people's lives to deal with the scourge of AIDS.... The Government's aims are about as intrusive as it is possible for a state to be – no less than to influence its citizens' attitudes towards sex, thereby inducing a radical change in their sexual habits.[44]

A Government flirting with the fundamentalist Christian lobby, extolling the sanctity of the family and welcoming the demise of the permissive society was naturally going to be hard pressed to respond sympathetically to an epidemic primarily affecting a deviant sexual minority and apparently spread by casual promiscuity through anal intercourse. Therefore, so long as the statistics continued to suggest that Aids was confined to the gay community, the British Government was content to sit back, ignore repeated warnings about the dangers of its spread and await developments.

The remarkable degree of sexual frankness which had been tolerated in the media without provoking the usual puritan backlash by the spring of 1987 was an impressive achievement for the Thatcher Government. Of course, by ignoring calls for intervention for so long and allowing the media to whip up the public into a state of panic it had demonstrated its characteristic unwillingness to become embroiled in this sort of matter. So when the administration did finally act it was able to claim to be responding to overwhelming public pressure. Having taken on the thankless task of saving the nation, it then had to weigh up the political consequences of doing so. The Cabinet committee was fully aware of the inherent dangers of the situation and adopted its 'softly-softly' approach accordingly. As one of its senior members explained to the *Guardian*:

Just as it would have been unthinkable to fit children with gas masks until the Second World War made it acceptable, so steps to stop Aids spreading could be tolerated only if public opinion was mobilised beforehand.[45]

The news of this calculated policy of prudery must have been a great comfort to the thousands of people who were infected with the Aids virus as a result of it. As one leading Aids specialist put it:

The Government had plenty of time to act.... It did not, until now, because of a fear of losing votes. This has meant that people have needlessly lost their lives.[46]

Despite the Government's undoubted success, in purely political terms, in handling the crisis it did not escape criticism from some of its own supporters. In the *Mail on Sunday* on 21 December 1986 Julie Burchill warned that some Conservatives believed that this 'laissez-faire attitude' to Aids could be an electoral liability because it was totally out of step with the mood of the country.

> From woman with the whip to lady with the lamp; AIDS will see to it that Mrs Thatcher is remembered as the Johnny Appleseed of the Perm Soc, graciously scattering needles and cut-price condoms in her wake.

There was certainly considerable disappointment from the Christian right wing of the party that the advertising campaign had not been used as an opportunity to launch a crusade against perversion and permissiveness. The fundamentalist brigade, having benefited from the sudden tabloid interest in a return to traditional morality, were quick to take up the challenge which the Government seemed determined to avoid. In the *Daily Mail* the Archbishop of York made his bid for the leadership of this new crusade with an outspoken attack on local authorities who advocated 'gay studies' in schools which he claimed would encourage the spread of Aids.[47]

A few weeks later another contender emerged in the person of the Chief Constable of Manchester, James Anderton who told a conference on Aids that the disease was 'a self-inflicted scourge' which homosexuals had brought on themselves by indulging in sodomy and other 'obnoxious practices'. He claimed that homosexuals, prostitutes and promiscuous people were 'swirling about in a human cesspit of their own making'.[48] Anderton's rantings were eagerly seized upon by most of the tabloids. The *Sun* gave the 'top copper' three cheers for blaming gays for spreading Aids:

> Their defiling act of love is not only unnatural. In today's Aids-hit world it is LETHAL.... What Britain needs is more men like James Anderton – and fewer gay terrorists holding the decent members of society to ransom.[49]

The *Standard* praised the Chief Constable for 'articulating a deep-rooted feeling in Britain' and a telephone poll by LBC radio showed

74 per cent in favour of his views.[50] According to an editorial in the *Sunday Telegraph* Mr Anderton was talking more sense than all the Government propaganda; while in the *Sunday Mirror* under the headline 'WHEN BEING GAY SHOULD BE A CRIME' the proudly homophobic George Gale repeated his demand that Aids should be made notifiable and for 'buggery' to be made a criminal offence.[51]

Determined not to be left out the Church of England issued a report urging the Government to promote chastity as a way of controlling the spread of Aids, and suggested that condoms should be more freely available – provided they were not used to encourage promiscuity.[52] On the other hand Cardinal Basil Hume, as leader of Britain's Roman Catholic Church, called the promotion of condoms 'a counsel of despair' and described Aids as 'a moral Chernobyl'.[53] Although neither Church commented specifically on the homosexual aspect of the problem, the Vatican had only recently condemned all forms of homosexual behaviour as 'morally irregular' and 'alien to order', while the Archbishop of Canterbury had described homosexuality as 'a handicap' which could never be accepted by the Christian community as an equally valid alternative to heterosexual behaviour.[54]

In this heady atmosphere of moral re-armament Dr Michael Fitzpatrick, a London GP, and gay activist Don Milligan were engaged in writing a small pamphlet entitled 'The Truth About the Aids Panic' which was published in February 1987.[55] Firstly the authors dismissed the claim that the Aids epidemic was an immediate risk to the heterosexual population and claimed that the Government had used fears generated around the disease to deliberately create a 'moral panic'.

> We do not regard the Aids scare as a conspiracy, but something much more insidious. It reflects the concern of a threatened establishment to strengthen its grip over society by seizing any opportunity to promote the values of conformity and discipline.

According to Messrs Fitzpatrick and Milligan, the Thatcher administration had played upon the fear created by the deadly virus to distract people from other more fundamental political issues and also to bolster its drive for 'family values'.

So long as people are anxiously calculating their chances of being HIV positive, thinking about how to practise sex safely and weighing up the pros and cons of condoms, their minds are kept safely away from unemployment, welfare cuts, declining wages, racism and war.

They went on to argue convincingly that the best way to contain the spread of the virus among gay men was to remove the stigma from homosexuality which forced so many repressed homosexuals into clandestine sexual behaviour which put them most at risk of contracting and passing on Aids. The pamphlet threw down a real challenge to the gay movement which it accused of preaching the Government's gospel of safe sex, thereby accepting the view that promiscuity was responsible for spreading the virus. The call for a fundamental re-evaluation of tactics was passionate and unequivocal.

How tragic that, while working overtime to ensure that its members die peacefully, the gay movement has given up the fight for day-to-day freedom and dignity. Indeed by endorsing the safe sex campaign, it has given its approval to the continuing suppression of gay rights.... It is the *oppression of homosexuals* that allows HIV to spread among gay men. Hence the way to stop the spread of Aids is neither to pretend that it is a threat to heterosexuals, nor to make futile exhortations to gays, but rather to challenge *every* act of discrimination or harassment directed against homosexuals.

10

LIKE A TURKEY VOTING FOR CHRISTMAS: 1986–7

One of the characteristics of our time is that we have for several decades past been emancipating minorities who claimed they were disadvantaged. Are they grateful? Not a bit.... We emancipate homosexuals and they condemn heterosexism as chauvinist sexism, male oppression, and so on. They will push us off the pavement if we give them a chance. I am, in their jargon, a homophobe, a heterosexist exploitationist. The whole vocabulary of the loony Left is let loose in a wild confusion of Marxism, Trotskyism, anarchism and homosexual terminology.

Lord Halsbury – House of Lords 18/12/86

VALUELESS VALUES

Aids could not have made a more timely arrival on the British political scene for the tiny but vociferous minority of right-wing Christian moralists, who had been given unprecedented opportunities to air their views in the corridors of power since 1979. Their influence had grown stronger after the 1983 election with the emergence of a small and strident group of MPs, like Peter Bruinvels and Vivian Bendall, who were committed to upholding decent family values by campaigning against permissiveness. In the same way that the Wilson Government in the 1960s encouraged backbenchers to introduce social reforms on such issues as abortion, homosexuality and censorship, the Thatcher administration lent its support to a succession of Private Member's Bills which aimed to place new constraints in these same areas.

John Corrie's Abortion Bill met with fierce opposition and was duly talked out in 1980, but later in that same Parliament the

Indecent Displays Bill passed successfully into law with the Government's tacit approval. In the aftermath of the landslide Conservative victory of June 1983 backbencher Graham Bright successfully piloted his Video Recordings Bill through the Commons. This imposed a draconian system of censorship on all video recordings in order to prevent children from seeing 'video nasties'. In the spring of 1986 Winston Churchill's Bill which aimed to protect children from sex and violence on television by extending the Obscene Publications Act to all forms of public broadcasting received its Second Reading by a considerable majority, its success undoubtedly boosted by the personal support of the Prime Minister. Opposition rallied when a closer inspection of the measure revealed that obscenity was to be defined by a 'laundry list' of prohibited acts. The Arts Establishment rose as one to condemn the Bill which was savaged in Committee and duly defeated. Less than a year later Conservative backbencher Gerald Howarth had introduced a new Bill along similar lines.

As well as encouraging these specific initiatives aimed at narrowing personal and sexual freedom of choice, the Government itself sponsored a number of public order measures including the Police and Criminal Evidence Act and the Public Order Act which were attacked by civil liberties groups on the grounds that they imposed new restrictions on the rights of the individual citizen. In addition, there were a number of court cases which had disturbing implications for gay rights. The trials of several members of the Paedophile Information Exchange (PIE), including the group's Chairman Tom O'Carroll, were used by the popular press as an excuse to give an airing to all the old myths about homosexuals being child molesters. The case awakened fears within the gay community that similar legal moves might be made against other unpopular sexual minority groups.

Even more disturbing was the indictment of the eight directors and assistant manager of Gay's the Word Bookshop in November 1984 on charges relating to 'conspiracy to import indecent and obscene material'. Customs and Excise had impounded 144 titles imported from America (including a book about Aids) in a series of raids. The case caused considerable concern throughout the literary community; there was a storm of protest from MPs, the NCCL, authors, publishers and booksellers. An article in the *Bookseller* on 22 September had already pointed out that by using the wide-ranging and ill-defined Customs and Excise laws instead of the

Obscene Publications Act the authorities had the two advantages of easier conviction and the avoidance of setting a legal precedent should the case be lost. Since many of the seized titles were already available in British editions gay activists suspected that the Customs were deliberately attempting to restrict the availability of gay books and publications.

In June 1984 Treasury Minister Barney Hayhoe had assured MPs that the guidelines covering seizures were 'non-discriminatory on the grounds of sex and sexuality'[1] and in October he insisted that the Customs did not distinguish 'between presumed homosexual material and other material'.[2] However, at the Committal proceedings against Gay's the Word in June 1985 one Customs officer admitted that he had intercepted books bound for the shop because he associated it with homosexuals and certain homosexual practices with obscenity; another thought that he might have detained a book 'because it had the name of a homosexual author on the cover'; and a third told the court that all books with descriptions of homosexual acts had to be submitted to headquarters. Several officers said that they had been given no training as to legal definitions of indecency and obscenity and admitted that they could not remember looking inside certain books before seizing them. Despite five days of this extraordinary testimony the defendants were duly committed for a full Crown Court trial.[3] Later that year the directors of Millivres Ltd – publishers of *Gay Times* and several male pin-up magazines such as *Zipper* and *Mister* – were found guilty of sending 'indecent material through the post' in contravention of the Post Office Act and fined over £5,000. This was in spite of the fact that the police agreed that the magazines would not lead to charges under the Obscene Publications Act!

The first concrete proof that the Conservative Party as a whole was moving to embrace the moral re-armament cause came during their Annual Conference in October 1985. One of the platform speakers was loudly cheered when she coined the new political slogan: 'If you want a queer for a neighbour, vote Labour'. Less than a month later Tory party chairman Norman Tebbit used the Disraeli Memorial Lecture as an opportunity to launch a swingeing attack on the 'valueless values of the permissive society' and drag his party on to the backlash band-wagon. He predicted a general revulsion against the sexual liberation of the 1960s which he claimed had contributed to a massive increase in violence and crime.

I know that at the front of that campaign for a return to traditional values of decency and order will be the Conservative Party; for we understand as does no other party that the defence of freedom involves a defence of values which makes freedom possible without its degeneration into violence.[4]

Mr Tebbit further expounded his new philosophy from a church pulpit in the spring of the following year, arguing that national standards had been debased by the 'anything-goes society' and that 'the poisoned legacy of the permissive society' could only be overcome by the restoration of order and personal responsibility.

Legislation on capital punishment, homosexuality, abortion, censorship and divorce – some of it good, some of it bad, but all of it applauded as progressive – ushered in in quick succession an overwhelming impression that there were not only going to be no legal constraints, but there was no need to have any constraints at all.

He made little attempt to disguise his view that the decriminalisation of homosexuality was one of the 'bad' pieces of legislation: 'Tolerence of sexual deviation has generated demands for deviance to be treated as the norm.... Love of the sinner has slipped into love of the sin.'[5] A *Guardian* editorial the next morning suggested that the Tory chairman was 'testing the political temperature' to see if moral re-armament was likely to be an electoral asset, and accused him of coming close to being 'outright anti-gay'.[6]

BUILDING THE NEW JERUSALEM

As the Conservative Party shifted appreciatively towards a repressive moral stance with a specifically anti-gay bias, the Labour Party had moved from the unsympathetic attitudes of the late 1970s to a firmer commitment to full legal equality for lesbians and gay men. This transformation seemed to have taken place largely as a result of many gay activists turning their attentions away from the direct lobbying of Parliament in the late 1970s and concentrating their efforts instead at the grass-roots level in local Labour groups and trade union branches. The election of the Thatcher Government in 1979, which to many campaigners signalled an effective end to further reform in the immediate future, was undoubtedly a significant factor in this process. The increasing fragmentation of the gay rights movement and the re-structuring of CHE inevitably accelerated this trend. Anna Durrell of CHE later described their initial impact within the Labour movement:

> At one point, of course, we'd given up on the Labour Party....
> But then we started re-joining at constituency level, thousands of us – look at the London Labour branches. I'd say in many, up to 50% are gay. Sexuality wasn't a particular issue until we brought it up.[7]

It was Ken Livingstone's decision in 1981 to commit the Labour-controlled GLC to fight discrimination against gay men and lesbians that enabled the cause of gay rights to take a quantum leap. A Gay Working Party had been established in 1982 and a wide range of initiatives was implemented in the areas of employment, housing, law enforcement and arts and recreation. By 1984 nearly £300,000 in grants had been allocated to gay and lesbian groups, and £750,000 had been paid out to establish the London Lesbian and Gay Centre. A report presented by Ken Livingstone on 16 October concluded by reaffirming the GLC's continuing commitment to gay rights as part of its general anti-discrimination policy. The document was passed by an overwhelming majority; the only vote against came from a Conservative councillor – the rest of the Tory group had abstained.

This degree of accord demonstrated the enormous progress that had been made towards silencing the vehement opposition towards pro-gay policies. This was in marked contrast to the fierce controversy which had been whipped up by the Conservatives in the early days, as one Councillor later remembered;

> They engineered debates with a focus on grants to gay organisations... the Tories were extraordinary, the level of cruelty was beyond belief. One Tory member encapsulated the policy as 'buggery on the rates'.[8]

These clashes had been reported with great relish by Fleet Street, where the grants to gay groups were cited as yet another example of the unparalleled profligacy of Red Ken's 'loony left' administration. Since the reduction of public expenditure had been the principal plank of the Tory manifesto in 1979 and 1983, local government spending was identified as a prime target for cuts and a series of severe rate capping measures were introduced to impose strict spending limits. As a justification for this policy Labour councils were cast as fiscal bandits holding rate payers to ransom in order to finance extravagant and unnecessary policies, but the popularity and success of the GLC continually undermined these arguments, and in the aftermath of the 1983 election legislation was introduced to abolish it and other Labour-controlled metropolitan councils. As opposition to this decision grew, the Tory tabloids and the local press in London mounted a hysterical propaganda war against Labour town halls, using support for gay groups as proof of left-wing infiltration. In spite of the media vendetta, and encouraged by the example being set at County Hall, other London boroughs with Labour councils began to introduce policies to outlaw discrimination against the gay community and by the autumn of 1985 at least 10 of the 32 boroughs guaranteed equal opportunities for gays and lesbians in employment and housing. Islington Council had even appointed an openly gay councillor, Bob Crossman, as its Deputy Mayor. Labour councils in Manchester, Southampton and Birmingham were taking similar steps.

This burgeoning grass-roots support for gay rights was clearly responsible for the unexpected success of a gay rights motion at the TUC conference on the 6 September 1985. This 'spectacular triumph', as *Capital Gay* described it,[9] paved the way for another equally significant victory at the Labour Party Conference on 4 October, when a motion calling for full legal equality for gay men and lesbians was approved by a majority of nearly 600,000 votes. This was a remarkable achievement in the light of the fact that Conference had never discussed the matter of gay rights before. In moving the resolution, delegate Sarah Roelofs made an impassioned plea to her party to attack heterosexism within its own ranks.

> An ex-Labour MP said to me that we should be building the new Jerusalem and not Sodom and Gomorrah. I want no part in your Jerusalem unless you include us.

She was one of several speakers who used the platform to make public declaration of their lesbian and gay pride. Although the party hierarchy unsuccessfully attempted to persuade the conference to refer the matter back to the National Executive Committee for further consideration, MP Jo Richardson promised delegates that:

> The next Labour Government will outlaw discrimination in

jobs, in housing and in other areas and promote equal opportunities policies.... The Labour Government will also take a strong line with the police to prevent them from harassing, intimidating and seeking to entrap lesbians and gay men.

In October 1985 the doomed GLC published a Charter for Gay and Lesbian Rights entitled 'Changing the World' which examined the ways in which society's inherent heterosexism (the assumption that only heterosexual behaviour is normal and natural and homosexuality is therefore abnormal and unnatural), lay at the heart of the continuing oppression of the gay community.[10] This rather Utopian document went on to make 142 recommendations as to how this discrimination could be identified and eliminated. Relaunching the Charter at the newly opened London Lesbian and Gay Centre in February 1986 Ken Livingstone promised that the gay community would receive its share of the GLC's £25m 'forward funding' which had been set aside to assist voluntary groups after abolition.

An editorial in the *Express* on 3 February entitled 'Squander mania' argued that the funding of gay groups and other 'exotic' bodies by the GLC and the Metropolitian Councils vindicated the Government's decision to abolish 'these Labour-controlled money-shredding machines'. However, in *Capital Gay* Chris Smith felt that the destruction of the GLC was a bitter blow for the gay community. He suggested that making lesbian and gay rights an openly discussed and publicly supported political issue was the Council's greatest achievement. By unashamedly advocating those policies Ken Livingstone had blazed a trail which other politicians had been prepared to follow.[11] In an interview in *Gay Times* Ken Livingstone agreed with this analysis, but expressed his concern that GLC funding had fuelled complacency and thereby contributed to the downturn in gay activism which had taken place since the late 1970s. He felt that the demise of the GLC would make the gay community stand on its own feet once again.

> Whilst in the short term it'll be traumatic, it'll force people to build up alternative support and campaign in different ways.... Abolishing the GLC doesn't mean the ideas and campaigns go away, they just shift to a different area.[12]

As public opposition to the abolition of the GLC had grown, the

Government had been forced to mount a fierce rearguard action. Grants to the gay community were seized upon as yet another example of the misuse of public funds – an argument which conveniently ignored the fact that gay men and lesbians were ratepayers too. But this right-wing propaganda campaign linking gay rights with the so-called 'loony left' of the Labour Party took a new and more sinister turn after the Labour Conference vote. The *Sunday Telegraph* on 6 October 1985 dragged the issue further into the party political battleground in an article which propounded the dangerous notion that Labour local authorities who pursued pro-gay policies were thereby encouraging the spread of Aids. This argument was pressed home by George Gale in the *Daily Express*, attacking Lambeth Council's plans to send its staff on 'anti-hetero-sexism' courses.

> The cost of this Lambeth lunacy must be to encourage homosexuality, and with it, often the risk of death through AIDS. Lambeth thus comes out the most lunatic: for it is using ratepayers' money to help kill off those it supports.[13]

A letter in the *Western Daily Press* even questioned that gays should be entitled to any civil rights.

> So, the Labour Party Conference has passed a resolution defending the rights of homosexuals. What rights? The right to inflict AIDS upon the innocent. The right to compel us all that this unhealthy, unwholesome, unnatural practice is an acceptable part of civilised life?[14]

THE VALUE OF FAMILY LIFE

In the spring of 1986 new ingredients were added to this already potent cocktail of prejudice and politics. In the run-up to the first local elections since the abolition of the GLC, issues concerning gay rights were once again subjected to the full glare of the political spotlight. Education was a particularly sensitive issue for the Government in view of the long-running teachers' pay dispute which had disrupted schools throughout the country, and Labour's control of the Inner London Education Authority (ILEA) which was to be elected directly for the first time. To distract from these issues, the emotive subject of sex education was chosen as the basis for a new smear campaign by the tabloids.

Several London councils' pledges to fight heterosexism in education and to promote positive images of homosexuality were pilloried in the Tory tabloids. Then a week before polling day the *Islington Gazette* splashed a story over its front page which claimed that a storm of protest had been sparked off by 'a gay school book' called *Jenny Lives with Eric and Martin* which showed pictures of a naked homosexual couple in bed with a five-year-old girl.[15] The truth of the matter was that the book was recommended by the ILEA as an aid for teachers in individual cases where they deemed it necessary, but had never been stocked in schools, but this fact was conveniently ignored in the fracas that followed. The *Sunday Mirror* was outraged by the news.

The idea that homosexuals form an oppressed minority is nonsense. The notion that they are entitled to propagate their peculiar practices at the public expense is preposterous. Yet they are contriving to do so. They are now insinuating their sexist propaganda into some of our schools.[16]

Two days later the *Sun* had the effrontery to claim the story as an 'Exclusive' under the front page headline 'VILE BOOK IN SCHOOL' and went on to state that parents and teachers were trying to prevent this 'shocking' publication being made available to junior schools.[17] The *Today* newspaper's coverage was headed 'SCANDAL OF GAY PORN BOOKS READ IN SCHOOLS' on 7 May; then, on the morning of the election, the paper published a checklist of spending on 'militant campaigns' which included grants from Labour boroughs for lesbian and gay projects and called on voters to expel Labour extremists from the town halls. Of course, no attempt was made to quantify the amount of money being 'wasted' on the gay grants. Assuming that 5 per cent of rate payers were lesbian and gay then it might be argued that the same proportion of council funds could reasonably be appropriated for spending on their needs. But, of course, not one of the boroughs was spending anywhere near that proportion of its income on their gay citizens.

Given this barrage of propaganda Labour's subsequent gains in both the local and ILEA elections were considerable achievements. *Capital Gay* noted that the party increased its majorities in three of the boroughs openly committed to gay rights, but admitted that there was some evidence that the combined weight of the *Islington*

Gazette's smear campaign about the sex education book and the anti-gay tactics employed by some SDP canvassers (who had asked voters how they felt about having a gay mayor and a gay MP) may have contributed to the reduction of Labour's majority in that borough.[18]

Unfortunately, the fact that the homophobic line had not deterred voters from backing the Labour Party in most areas only served to encourage the Conservatives to even greater efforts. This was made easier by the fact that the Government's new Education Bill was in the process of passing through Parliament. In the House of Lords a number of peers claimed that sex education which accepted homosexuality as a valid alternative to heterosexuality was not only undermining family life and encouraging divorce, but was somehow linked with the increase in rapes, attacks on children and sexual crime in general.[19] Several peers repeatedly tried to persuade the Government to accept amendments instructing local authorities to provide sex education only in the context of Christian morality and family life, and many referred to the book *Jenny Lives with Eric and Martin* to bolster their arguments, including Baroness Cox who commented: 'I cannot imagine how on earth in this age of Aids we can be contemplating promoting gay issues in the curriculum. I think that it beggars all description.'

Education Minister Kenneth Baker duly introduced a new clause into the Bill requiring local authorities to ensure that sex education would encourage pupils 'to have due regard to moral considerations and the value of family life'. The *Daily Telegraph* approved of the move which it regarded as an integral part of Norman Tebbit's 'campaign for moral revival'; and in the *Express* the amendment was describe as a 'bombshell' which had shaken the foundations of the permissive society![20] However, during the Bill's Committee stage the 'moral values' clause came in for considerable criticism. In the mean while a group of right-wing fundamentalist MPs led by Peter Bruinvels began lobbying for parents to be given the right to withdraw their children from sex education lessons altogether.

An attempt was made to pacify this puritan lobby by issuing new guidelines to teachers advising that sex education should be presented 'in the context of family life, loving relationships, and of respect for others'. It advised that homosexuality should be treated 'objectively and seriously', although teachers were asked to bear in mind that while there has been a marked shift away from the general condemnation of homosexuality, many individuals and groups within society hold sincerely to the view that it is morally objectionable.[21]

The *Daily Express* warned local Labour councillors to heed this advice:

in view of the clear statistical link between Aids and homosexual behaviour, how can it be right for Labour councils to use public money to justify such practices? Labour used to work for the New Jerusalem. Now it seems intent on building the new Sodom.[22]

On the following day in the House of Lords the Education spokesman, Lord Swinton, made it clear that the Government certainly did not consider Haringey and Ealing Councils' plans to present 'positive images' of homosexuality in schools to be at all appropriate.[23] He described their proposals as 'pretty horrific' but did, however, admit that there had been a 'number of rather exaggerated press reports' on the matter. As a result of the publicity surrounding the Education Bill the London boroughs with pro-gay education policies now found themselves at the centre of fierce local controversies which were further stirred up by the local media.

In an answer to a parliamentary question on 2 December 1986 the Prime Minister gave her first public hint that she sympathised with the view that Aids meant that homosexuality should be discouraged: 'I think that much of the behaviour that has been going on will be totally unacceptable for many and varied reasons.'[24] Reading the runes of this statement by their leader undoubtedly encouraged a number of Conservative backbenchers to use a Commons debate on Local Government a few days later to launch another vicious attack on the pro-gay London boroughs.[25] Kenneth Hind (Con.) introduced his motion by drawing attention to Ealing's plans to operate an equal opportunities policy to recruit gay teachers. The expressions he used were disturbingly similar to those adopted by Leo Abse and his supporters 20 years before:

I have great sympathy for these people. They have difficulties. They must discipline themselves. I warn the House that parents throughout the country will be anxious about their children being taught by teachers of gay orientation, who are deliberately encouraged to come into our schools.

A similar line was pursued by Government Minister Rhodes Boyson:

> The family is the normal unit. To have anything else is anti-life and the end of life... I do not want anyone to be persecuted but children are being brought up with the presumption that the family is not the normal way of life.

Labour's front bench spokesman Jack Straw made a spirited defence of these policies and accused Tory MPs of using the debate as 'an excuse for prejudice and bigotry to run amok'.

> Do Conservative Members believe that we should do nothing to try and end discrimination against gays and lesbians?... Only one hon. Member... has felt strong enough to say that he is gay. I believe he has gained the respect of us all. Until more hon. Members feel sufficiently confident to say that, the prejudice, bigotry and discrimination against gays and lesbians will continue.... Millions of our fellow citizens are gay or lesbians, and it is right that they should be able to play a full and outgoing part in society.

A fortnight later the House of Lords sank to new levels of intolerance in a debate which in terms of reactionary hysteria equalled the homosexual law reform debates of the 1950s.[26] Lord Halsbury, proud veteran of the 1977 campaign to defeat Lord Arran's Bill to reduce the age of consent, introduced a Bill to 'restrain local authorities from promoting homosexuality as an acceptable family relationship', which aimed to give parents the right to sue councils providing financial or other assistance to 'positive images' policies. Offering their virtually unanimous support for the proposal, speakers from all sides of the House vied with each other to denounce the heretical notion that homosexuality and heterosexuality were equally valid.

Amid criticism that the ecclesiastical benches were not backing the measure, several peers took it upon themselves to give spiritual guidance to the nation. According to one:

> Homosexuality clearly is not what God intended for human beings. Therefore I deplore any attempt to promote it by public money as an acceptable family relationship. I deplore it even more if public money is used to indoctrinate children with it.

The ex-Lord Chancellor, Lord Denning, went further; after reading the Old Testament story of Sodom and Gomorrah he suggested a modern re-write which equated the sins of the Cities of the Plain with the pro-gay policies of the London Borough of Haringey:

'But the councillors of the Borough of Haringey were gay, and corrupted the children of the Borough exceedingly.' And I would like to add on after this Bill, 'The Lord destroyed these councillors.'

Lord Graham of Edmonton was the Bill's sole opponent, claiming that it would inhibit open discussion within schools and mitigate against greater understanding of the nature of sexual orientation which was badly needed. However, the Government's spokesman strongly advised against the measure, arguing that the attempt to outlaw abuses by a small minority of councils using imprecise terminology would be open to wide legal dispute and harmful misinterpretation which could damage the teaching of homosexuality in schools in a balanced and factual manner. But the overwhelming support for Lord Halsbury ensured that his Bill was given a Second Reading without a vote being taken. The measure subsequently passed through its committee stage[27] where its drafting was 'improved' and it returned to be given a Third Reading.[28] The Bill was introduced into a thinly attended House of Commons in May 1987 by Tory backbencher Jill Knight, but was scuppered after Labour forced a vote proving that there were too few MPs to form a quorum. Shortly afterwards Mrs Thatcher told the Commons that she supported the objectives of the Bill: 'I think it was a great pity that it did not complete its passage through the House.'[29]

A SAD SIGN OF THE TIMES

In the Spring of 1987 election speculation was growing, and as the political parties hastened to polish up their respective manifestos it became clear that gay rights was going to be played up as an election issue for the first time. The Alliance Manifesto committed a Liberal/SDP Government to introducing a Bill of Rights to protect the civil rights of citizens regardless of their sexual orientation; proposed laws to outlaw discrimination against gays in employment; and contained a promise to equip the NHS to deal effectively with the Aids epidemic. Despite David Steel's excellent track record of active support for campaigns on gay issues, the Liberal leader had revealed in January 1986 that he would personally prefer to treat gay equality as a matter of individual conscience and would therefore encourage free votes on such issues by providing more time for Private Member's Bills. Although he agreed that the homosexual age of consent should be 16 he felt that current political realities meant that it would be better to compromise on a reduction to 18.[30]

The SDP leader, Dr David Owen, had previously told *Gay Times* in April 1986 that his party's principal aim was to create 'an open, classless and more equal society which rejects prejudices based on sex, race, colour and religion', but admitted that the proposal to include 'sexual orientation' in this definition had been rejected by his party. This somewhat ambivalent support for gay rights within the Alliance was even more marked among the grass roots of their parties. The Alliance 'Action Programme for the Districts' for 1987 had only committed its councils to ensuring that gay organisations had access to facilities and grants on a 'non-discriminatory basis'.

In September 1986 the Labour Party Conference had passed a motion to outlaw discrimination against the gay community by a 79 per cent majority, which automatically committed the party's National Executive to consider it for inclusion in the party Manifesto. When Labour's Election Manifesto duly appeared in May 1987 the section on 'Enhancing Rights, Increasing Freedoms' promised that a future Labour Government would 'take steps to ensure that homosexuals are not discriminated against' without providing details of how this would be achieved. Although this was not the uncompromising commitment some had hoped for, it decisively disproved claims made in March 1987 that Labour was about to renege on its gay rights policy when the *Sun* had leaked a private letter from Neil Kinnock's press officer which discussed Labour's defeat at a recent by-election and commented that 'the lesbian and gay rights issue is costing us dear amongst pensioners'.[31] In *Capital Gay* on 13 March the Labour leader's private office confirmed that Mr Kinnock firmly supported the party's policy on gay rights.

The Conservatives were the only national political party in the election without a commitment to furthering gay equality. The issue was only referred to indirectly in their manifesto in the section dealing with education which included a promise to ban 'sexual propaganda' from the classroom. In March 1987 Tory backbencher Geoffrey Dickens had appeared on the BBC programme 'The Heart of the Matter' to argue the case for the recriminalisation of homosexual activity as a measure to prevent the spread of Aids.

What we should be saying is: 'Look, I'm afraid this sort of behaviour is totally unacceptable. You're putting your nation at risk by your behaviour. We're not going to have this in the future. And that's why we're legislating to make this a crime once again.'

Asked if under his proposal two known adult homosexuals sharing accommodation would be liable to be raided by the police, the MP answered 'Oh, absolutely'[32]. It was therefore no real surprise to find the Conservative election campaign featuring attacks on Labour's pro-gay policies. In a Party Political Broadcast on television at the beginning of May Norman Tebbit ridiculed London Labour councils for their policies designed to promote equal rights for women, ethnic minorities and the gay community. Shortly afterwards an election poster appeared featuring the book *Young, Gay and Proud* under the headline 'IS THIS LABOUR'S IDEA OF A COMPREHENSIVE EDUCATION?'.

Cold comfort was offered in the June issue of *Gay Times* which reported that the Prime Minister's Private Office had given an assurance that the Government had 'no intention of introducing legislation to repeal the Sexual Offences Act of 1967', but it was also stated that no legal protection against the discrimination of gay men and lesbians would be considered. The magazine's editorial condemned the Tory's exploitation of anti-gay prejudice which it described as 'a sad sign of the times', but also suggested that it was equally unfortunate that the other parties had fought shy of making strong public declarations in support of gay rights and gloomily concluded that: 'one might be forgiven for thinking that no political party can be trusted to adopt a sensible attitude towards gay men and lesbians'. *Capital Gay* offered its readers more positive advice; it drew attention to the Conservative's repeated attacks on gay rights and duly recommended:

> The choice is between voting Labour, or voting tactically for the Alliance to show Mrs Thatcher the back door to Number Ten. For it is clear that a gay voting Conservative is like a turkey voting for Christmas.[33]

The *National Gay* was even more direct: 'Get Her Out' it shouted from its front page, and *Gay Scotland* and Manchester's *Gay Life* echoed the same sentiment.

Evidence that the gay community was as politically divided as the rest of the electorate was provided in a poll carried out by *Capital Gay* at a number of London gay venues in May of the previous year. In a sample of more than 600 people, 33.5 per cent said they would vote Conservative, 33 per cent for Labour and 19 per cent for the Liberal/SDP Alliance.[34] This split had been reflected in correspondence columns of the gay press throughout 1986 and into 1987 as supporters of each of the main parties launched increasingly bitter attacks on the motives and policies of their rivals. Despite this sectional controversy, a successful attempt was made in October 1986 to unite gay activists of all political persuasions behind a new Legislation for Lesbian and Gay Rights Campaign (LLGRC) with the sole aim of producing a comprehensive Gay Rights Bill to put before Parliament. But when hundreds of delegates from gay organisations around the UK arrived to attend the LLGRC's long-awaited Conference on 23 May 1987 to hammer out the details of the Bill in the shadow of the forthcoming general election, they were disillusioned and angered as initial accord degenerated into chaos and acrimony.

Ken Livingstone's pledge at the opening session of the conference that the Labour Party would give full backing to gay rights drew a storm of applause. Mr Livingstone went on to promise:

We will take your legislation and place it on the floor of the House of Commons after June 11. We will keep bringing it back until the legislation you have drafted is carried as a law and we see full equality for lesbians and gay men.

However, the workshops following the main session which were intended to produce draft sections for the Bill were disrupted by political in-fighting and consequently there were virtually no concrete proposals available for the final session. According to *Capital Gay*'s report:

For three hours the proceedings at the Camden Centre resembled a rowdy student union meeting rather than a serious political conference. Speakers were heckled, jeered and some delegates left in despair... the meeting continued to be disrupted by the far left groups and the aggressive caucus of black lesbians and gay men who sat at the front of the conference chamber.[35]

The conference duly agreed that seven self-appointed caucuses claiming to represent minority groups such as disabled lesbians and

'I'm Free' by Franklin. © Rex Features/News International. First appeared in the *Sun*, 26 May 1987.

gays, young lesbians and gays, elderly gays, and so on should be given an automatic power of veto over all future actions of the campaign. With this complete negation of democratic procedure it was hardly surprising that the conference's only achievement was to pass two resolutions: one calling on all political parties to 'repeal discriminatory legislation' against gay men and lesbians and the other declaring the intention of continuing the campaign to prepare a draft Bill.

With polling day only a fortnight away the rampantly Tory newspapers seized avidly on Mr Livingstone's remarks to launch a further attack on Labour's policies. The *Sun* led the pack with a large article entitled 'LABOUR ROCKED BY KEN'S GAY CHARTER' accompanied by a picture showing 'Red Ken' in conversation with 'failed former Labour candidate' Peter Tatchell.[36] Its coarse cartoonist made a pathetic attempt to satirise the story with camp

TV star, John Inman, arriving outside 10 Downing Street where Ken Livingstone stands with a banner reading 'Labour Gay Rights Campaign' and another figure holds a second banner reading 'A Gay for Premier (see p.215).[37] KEN DISPLAYS GAY ABANDON' was splashed on the front of the *Sunday Telegraph* on 24 May, but presumably for maximum tactical effect the *Daily Mail* waited until 6 June before reporting the story on its front page under the headline 'THE LEFT'S PLAN FOR GAY CHARTER'. This was not the worst on offer; the *News of the World* had really scraped the bottom of the barrel on 17 May by running a double page spread with one story headlined 'MY LOVE FOR GAY LABOUR BOSS', exposing the 'bizarre gay love triangle' of 'Labour's election campaign supremo' Peter Mandelson, alongside another piece about the resignation of Tory MP Harvey Proctor who was to face indecency charges for spanking young men.

It is most unlikely that this vicious gay bashing campaign was of any significance in helping Margaret Thatcher pull off her political hat-trick on 11 June 1987, and remain in power with a majority of more than 100 MPs. The only good news for the gay law reform campaign was that Chris Smith had retained his parliamentary seat, actually doubling his modest majority at a time when there was an overall swing away from Labour in London. This was a historic victory which finally destroyed the myth that an openly gay politician is unelectable. In his acceptance speech Mr Smith thanked those who had voted him back to Westminster.

> The people of Islington South and Finsbury have demonstrated something today and it is the first time that any constituency has done so.... They have shown that they prefer principles to prejudice and that they prefer honesty to bigotry.[38]

The newly elected MP went on to express his fears about the future of all civil liberties during the third term of Thatcherism, and these were echoed by other gay activists. The Labour Campaign for Lesbian and Gay Rights predicted that the attack on pro-gay local councils would intensify.

> We have to defend 'positive images' in schools because fundamentally we are dealing with the question of whether homosexuality is to be seen as desirable or whether it is to be undesirable and simply to be tolerated but not accepted.[39]

And a spokesman for CHE ominously summed up: 'Anti-gay legislation is a very dangerous prospect.... There is trouble brewing and our situation may become very much worse.'[40]

11

A SMELL OF WEIMAR: 1987-8

The proponents of this clause have been saying... that there is only one form of relationship, one form of sexuality and one form of lifestyle that is acceptable. That sexuality will be endorsed, approved, applauded and given enhanced legal status, and everything else will become second-class. It is a view which refuses to recognise the difference, the diversity and the very richness of human life and human society. It is intolerant, immature and undemocratic, and... it is profoundly immoral.

Chris Smith – House of Commons 9/3/88

WHETHER TO BE POPULAR OR PRINCIPLED?

It was the Prime Minister herself who signalled the main assault on the gay rights policies of Labour councils by pouring scorn on the very notion of gay equality in her closing speech to the Conservative Party Conference in October 1987. She declared: 'Children who need to be taught to respect traditional values are being taught that they have an inalienable right to be gay.' On 8 December, apparently with the Prime Minister's personal blessing,[1] backbench MP David Wilshire introduced a revised version of the Halsbury proposals (drawn up by Jill Knight) as a late amendment on the final day of the Committee stage of the Local Government Bill.[2] The amendment stated that a local authority should not

promote homosexuality or publish material for the promotion of homosexuality;... promote the teaching in any maintained school of the acceptability of homosexuality as

218

a pretended family relationship by the publication of such material or otherwise.

Furthermore, councils were forbidden to give 'financial or other assistance' to any person engaged in these activities.

Local Government Minister Michael Howard welcomed the proposal because he

did not believe that it was any part of a local authority's duty to encourage youngsters to believe that homosexuality is on an equal footing with a heterosexual way of life.

But he introduced an additional clause which ensured that nothing in the amendment should 'prohibit the doing of anything for the purpose of treating or preventing disease'. He and Mr Wilshire went to great lengths to insist that they did not want to discriminate against homosexuals. Liberal spokesman Simon Hughes and Labour's Jack Cunningham seemed somewhat taken by surprise – although both expressed reservations about the proposal they agreed that their parties would not force a vote since they accepted that homosexuals should not receive special privileges. Bernie Grant (Lab.) was the only speaker vehemently to oppose the measure, although several MPs insisted that the definitions of 'promote' and 'pretended' should be clarified when the Bill returned to the Commons for its Report stage and made it clear that if the Government refused to do this, they would introduce amendments to that effect.

A *Guardian* editorial on the following morning suggested that there was 'no more unpopular group of people in this country today than homosexuals', quoting a 1986 Social Attitudes Survey that had revealed nearly 70 per cent of people believed homosexual relationships to be mostly or always wrong. It accused the Conservatives of using this fact as an excuse to become the 'anti-gay party', and called on Labour to oppose the motion:

The Government claims to be against the persecution of minorities and against state indoctrination. The new ban is both. The Government's opponents must therefore decide whether to be popular or principled.[3]

However, Julie Burchill in the *Mail on Sunday* took Labour to task for its cowardice:

The party's decision to back the proposal is not only cynical and dishonest, but a bad tactic. Didn't Labour keep telling us during the last election that the idea of Loony Left Councils was a politically-motivated myth of the Murdoch Press? Now, it would seem the tabloids were telling the truth all the time. The party, in its electoral anxiety, is accepting a piece of legislation totally devoid of logic.[4]

The *New Statesman*, on the other hand, praised Labour's front bench

for not walking blindly into a Tory trap. Instead of a vainglorious, but ideologically pure, charge at the guns, Labour decided to fight a rearguard guerilla action. In the current climate... these tactics are correct.[5]

Meanwhile, the rest of the national press gave its seal of approval to the proposal, claiming that parents and teachers were relieved and grateful to the Government. The *Express* raised the spectre of Aids to justify its support for the move in its editorial on 9 December.

At the best of times, growing children face enough emotional difficulties without being further confused by the insidious claims of adults who prefer unnatural sexual relations. But these are not the best of times. Homosexuals are the group hardest hit by AIDS and most involved in its spread. More than ever, no one should be allowed to do or say anything that could tip youngsters towards homosexuality.

Naturally enough, it was the *Daily Telegraph* that waded in to defend the Government from the criticism that had been levelled at it by the *Guardian*.

The fact that a government responds to decent people scandalised by the excesses of some proselytising homosexuals does not make it vote-grabbingly 'anti-gay' and disqualify it as the agent of the public good.[6]

On the day before the new clause was due to be debated on the floor of the Commons, Chris Smith told the *Guardian* that he believed his party had made a 'tactical error' in not voting against it in committee. The same article reported that more than 700 lesbians and gays had descended on Parliament to lobby MPs, their mood was described as 'sober' as many were afraid of the potential effects of the iniquitous measure – which it was claimed could stop all grants to gay organisations and counselling services, and prevent local authorites from licensing gay clubs, pubs and discos. There was disappointment and confusion at Labour's initial refusal to oppose the Clause; but there was also anger at the news that *Capital Gay* had been the subject of an arson attack over the previous weekend. The Organisation for Lesbian and Gay Action (OLGA), which was co-ordinating the lobby, had called the Clause 'an act of frightened, restrictive bigots', while gay councillor Bob Crossman labelled it 'moral fascism'.

During the Third Reading of the Local Government Bill on 15 December Jack Cunningham proposed an amendment which would permit local authorities to continue to undertake activities which discouraged discrimination against homosexuals or protected their civil rights; Simon Hughes moved a second amendment which would allow sex education in which 'an awareness of different sexual orientations may be taught'.[7] Local government Minister Michael Howard rejected these attempts to restrict the Clause as 'a Trojan horse' which would undermine its effectiveness. Conservative MPs were duly whipped through the lobbies and both amendments were defeated. Several of their number enjoyed the opportunity to parade their homophobic prejudices; the Clause's sponsor David Wilshire posed the question: 'If it is right to encourage homosexuality then why is it not right to encourage racial hatred?' Asked if he thought the two were equivalent the MP replied that both were 'equally wrong'. When fellow Tory backbencher Elaine Kellet Bowman was challenged to repeat an alleged remark she had made that the arson attack on *Capital Gay* was a good thing, she answered: 'I am quite prepared to say that there should be an intolerance of evil.'

Dame Jill Knight, prime mover behind the Clause, was pressed time and again by Labour MPs to cite specific examples of local authorities encouraging children to be homosexual, but other than listing certain authorities and stating 'There is overwhelming evidence, not least in the strong objections of parents in those local authorities, of what has been done to their children', she did not provide any names of particular schools or individuals who had been affected. Rushing to her rescue Mr Wilshire insisted that the notorious *Jenny Lives with Eric and Martin* was stocked in an ILEA teachers' centre. Chris Smith immediately jumped on the opportunity to dispute the stories printed by the press about the book, which he argued 'was never put in front of a pupil or used in a classroom in an ILEA school'. Clive Soley (Lab.) backed him up with the assertion that the newspaper coverage was 'known to be and had been found to be lies'.

Ken Livingstone (Lab.) quoted the appalling statistics provided in a study by the London Gay Teenage Group which revealed the difficulties experienced by many gay teenagers under the existing law.

> at school 25% of young homosexuals felt isolated, 21% suffered verbal abuse, 12% were beaten up and... the most horrific statistic was that one in five of those young lesbians and gay men attempted to commit suicide because of the anguish, loneliness and despair that they felt.

He expressed his concern that the proposed restrictions would make it even harder for gay teenagers to seek the support they so badly needed.

The Minister was not moved by these considerations; in fact he identified lesbian and gay youth groups, along with phone lines and social facilities as being 'precisely the sort of activities against which the Clause is directed'. Mr Howard also dismissed claims that the Clause would affect the licensing of gay premises or stop teachers from giving unbiased counselling on homosexuality. MPs were not impressed by such assurances, which Ken Livingstone dismissed as 'totally irrelevant. What the Minister thinks will not matter. It is what the judges think that matters.'

THE PRICE OF TOLERANCE

When it was announced that the amendments had been defeated, the gay men and lesbians in the public gallery, who had repeatedly been threatened with expulsion by the Speaker for cheering opposition MPs and booing Tories during the debate, now erupted in angry shouts of protest. 'SCREAMING GAYS BRING COMMONS TO A HALT' was the *Sun*'s front page headline on the following day which reported that the Speaker had been forced to suspend the sitting for five minutes while the public gallery was cleared. Paul Johnson in the *Daily Mail* described the demonstrators as 'squealing sodomites' and MPs who had attacked the clause as 'Labour's fascist Left'.[8] Right-wing Tory MP Terry Dicks called the protesters a 'ragbag rent-a-mob' and thundered:

These homosexuals should take their handbags and lipsticks elsewhere – not into the mother of parliaments. Their behaviour was disgraceful, and God help any of them who taught such filth to my grandchild in school.[9]

The gay community was not to be intimidated by these sort of threats, but many were rightly extremely worried by the overt homophobia which had been unleashed. For those with long memories, like veteran reform campaigner Antony Grey, this latest threat to gay rights had parallels with persecution in pre-war Germany; he quoted the views of his friend the late Charlotte Wolff who had lived in Berlin in the 1930s and had told him that there was 'a smell of Weimar' about Britain in the 1980s. But, said Mr Grey: 'There's not a smell anymore, there's an absolute stench.'[10] In an article entitled 'BRING ON THE GAYSTAPO', Bernard Levin came to the same conclusion.

This country seems to be in the grip of a galloping frenzy of hate, where homosexuals are concerned, that will soon, if it is not checked, lead to something like a pogrom. I have not sensed such a tide sweeping away tolerance, reason and decency since long before the 'Arran Act'... indeed, I believe the present rush to judgement is actually worse than in the old days.... Are we really to go back to a time when homosexuals were not simply embarrassed or reluctant to disclose their sexual nature, but *afraid* to? Well, if we are not to return to such conditions we should start speaking up; if the price of liberty is eternal vigilence, the price of tolerance is enough voices saying No all at once.[11]

On 9 January 1988 between 8,000 and 10,000 lesbians and gay men raised their collective voice to oppose the Clause in a demonstration march through London arranged by OLGA, and timed to foreshadow the debate which was due to take place in the Lords on the following Monday. American lesbian comedienne and gay rights activist Robin Tyler whipped up the crowd with her passionate denouncement of the proposed legislation.

I am here to promote homosexuality, and to do what they say we must not do.... How dare they think we are going back in the closet. The closet does not stand for privacy, it stands for prison. This is not a movement about crotch politics, or a movement about sexuality. This is a movement about lifestyles and about choices. This is a movement about the right to love.[12]

Other speakers included Chris Smith MP; lesbian council leader Linda Bellos; and actor Michael Cashman, better known as the gay character Colin in 'Eastenders', who read out a letter of support signed by most of the regular cast of the BBC series. A few of the demonstrators were not satisfied with expressing their opposition verbally and attempted to force their way into Downing Street as the march passed. Mounted police took immediate action and 32 people were arrested and later charged. The media played up this incident, and there was even an item on the ITN News. Press coverage was extensive, if largely unsympathetic: the *News of the World* described the incident as 'a brawl' and the *Sunday Times* article was headlined 'GAY RIGHTS MARCHERS IN BATTLE WITH POLICE'.[13]

Their Lordships' discussion of Clause 28 (as it had now become) in the Second Reading debate on 11 January[14] was brief, but Labour's spokesman Lord McIntosh of Haringey gave notice that he intended to re-introduce the amendments originally put forward in the Commons. He went on to point out the strong reservations which had been proffered by the Government's spokesman when rejecting the Halsbury Bill back in 1986 and announced his own personal intention to oppose the Clause. Most speakers objected to the vagueness of the definitions contained in it, and were concerned that it would create an anti-gay backlash. The Bishop of Manchester warned that politicians 'should be aware of the terrible dangers of encouraging prejudice in any form'; Lord Peston slated it for being 'almost unique in its combination of illiberality and nonsense', and Baroness Blackstone was certain that it would

> be interpreted as a signal that homosexuals are second class citizens involved in unacceptable relationships. Some of those who support the clause are on record as actually wanting to recriminalise homosexuality. We are on a slippery slope of intolerance and censorship.

The proponents of the Clause trotted out the familiar old prejudices to back their dubious case. According to Lord Boyd-Carpenter homosexuality was 'a real evil'.

The promotion of the idea in schools that homosexuality is

a way of life of equal merit to the more normal habits and standards of our fellow countrymen is most dangerous.

The stale old examples of 'wicked' Labour boroughs corrupting young children were spiced up with claims, by the likes of Baroness Cox, that 'children as young as 2 years old have access to gay and lesbian books', and that other explicit homosexual material was being foisted on schoolchildren. The battlelines had been drawn, and the struggle would begin in earnest during the Committee stage at the beginning of February.

In the mean time opposition to the new legislation was now being voiced well beyond the boundaries of the lesbian and gay community. In *The Times* on 12 January columnist Ben Pimlott expressed his concern that the Clause could be used to proscribe future literary and artistic endeavours. In the *New Statesman*, Harriett Gilbert listed the enormous contribution made by gay and lesbian artists to contemporary British culture and predicted that Clause 28 would drive the country towards a 'cultural Dark Ages'.[15] The Arts Council of Great Britain stepped into the fray on 23 January to announce that it had sought legal advice on the wording of the Clause and been advised that local authorities would be permitted 'to censor free speech and curtail the freedom of the artist'. The Council had therefore submitted a re-drafting of the Clause to the Government which it was assured would prevent such appalling censorship. The Association of Art Historians added its voice to the clamour, and it was also announced that a 'Stop Clause 28 Arts Lobby' had been launched to fight the legislation. At the Olivier awards on 24 January, eminent Shakespearean actor Ian McKellen used the opportunity of his acceptance speech for the 'Best Actor' award to warn of the danger to the Arts which Clause 28 represented. The next day he joined a dazzling array of celebrities from all areas of the Arts who gathered on the stage of the Playhouse in London to lobby Peers to vote against the Clause. An editorial in *The Times* on the following morning agreed with the concern of the Arts Establishment but dismissed certain of their claims as 'silly' and 'hysterical'.[16]

Sadly, on that same day the press was full of reports of a Harris poll which had been conducted for London Weekend Television's 'Weekend World' programme to accompany a debate on Clause 28 featuring MP Chris Smith and right-wing journalist Paul Johnson. This survey confirmed that the sustained anti-gay rhetoric of the press since the onset of Aids had taken a heavy toll on public opinion. Only 48 per cent of respondants believed that homosexual relations between consenting adults should be legal compared to 61 per cent who had supported that view in a March 1985 Gallop poll; and the number disagreeing had risen from 27 per cent in 1985 to a disturbing 43 per cent. Furthermore 83 per cent agreed that councils should not teach that homosexuality was 'on a par' with heterosexuality, with two out of three harbouring the belief that such teaching would encourage teenagers to become homosexual. Three out of four objected to the funding of gay meeting places by local authorities, and 52 per cent thought councils shouldn't subsidise counselling for gays. A massive 68 per cent disapproved of homosexuals displaying affection in public and 55 per cent believed that gay and lesbian magazines should not be on public sale. Just over 20 per cent agreed that the risk of Aids was their main reason for regarding homosexual relations as less 'valid'.[17] The *Daily Mail* revelled in this news and smugly predicted that the findings would 'give the Bill's backers a major weapon in the battle to have it accepted untouched'.[18]

Despite this apparent setback, rumours were rife that the Government was preparing to alter Clause 28 to mollify its critics in the Lords. On 29 January the Secretary of State for the Environment, Nicholas Ridley, tabled two minor amendments to the wording, but dismissed the mounting criticism by the Arts lobby as 'misguided'. The Chairman of the Arts Council was 'deeply disappointed' that the Government had ignored their proposed re-drafting and expressed the view that 'the clause remains a major threat to the Arts'; a spokesman for the National Council of Voluntary Organisations representing the country's voluntary sector described the changes as 'totally inadequate'. And at a conference in Edinburgh on that same evening, Labour leader Neil Kinnock launched a major attack on Clause 28 which he described as a

> pink triangle clause produced and supported by a bunch of bigots.... It is crude in its concept, slanderous in its drafting, vicious in its purpose. It is an assault on the civil rights of thought and expression of everyone.[19]

On 1 February, the day that the House of Lords was due to consider Clause 28, a full page advert appeared in the *Independent* which had been signed by 281 leading public figures from politics, the arts, show business, the judiciary, the Church and the academic world. It drew attention to 'A SENSE OF ALARM' felt by the signatories with regard to the wording of the Clause which, they argued, had no fixed or clear legal meaning.

> We are worried that an unthinking intolerance is being more confidently expressed in some quarters. We are anxious lest some people search among the imprecise terms of this Clause for new means of discrimination. And we fear that others are seeing in all the surrounding circumstances a signal for renewed hatred.... We ask their Lordships to look carefully at the Clause, with our anxieties in mind.

Thanks to the rising tide of concern that this declaration had so effectively demonstrated the Government found itself on the defensive as the Clause entered its Committee stage.

PLAYING HUMPTY-DUMPTY

The House of Lords needed two days to consider the numerous amendments intended to define more clearly the scope of Clause 28.[20] When opponents of the measure cited the widespread public opposition to it, Tory peers, as predicted, slung back the Harris opinion poll findings in reply. Viscount Falkland introduced the Arts Council amendment which left the phrase 'pretended family relationship' intact, but forbade a local authority from representing homosexuality as 'more acceptable' than heterosexuality and exempted material which 'serves, or may serve, a literary, artistic, scientific or educational purpose'. This was defeated by 166 votes to 111, demonstrating an extraordinarily high turnout for this debate. The alterations proposed by the Minister, which forbade councils 'intentionally' to promote homosexuality and stated that a court should 'draw inferences as to the intention of the local authority as it sees fit', were almost universally condemned as irrelevant, and were therefore accepted without a vote.

All other amendments were blocked by the Government spokesman Lord Caithness who repeatedly asserted that the changes he was proposing were sufficient to meet the misgivings over the wording of the Clause. Despite getting confused and contradicting himself over the way in which court cases might be initiated the Minister continued to maintain that all cultural and educational activities would be acceptable providing the local authority was not using them to promote homosexuality. The only concession which he offered was to re-consider the wording of the phrase 'pretended family relationship' which Baroness Cox, one of the Clause's most enthusiastic supporters, had described as 'inadequate' to cover the range of 'pornographic' homosexual material recommended in schools by certain local councils. But by the end of more than eight hours of debate there was still no definition of the terms 'intentionally' or 'promote' which one peer, as a lawyer, assured his colleagues were 'impossibly imprecise'. Baroness Seear quite rightly observed: 'the Minister is playing Humpty-Dumpty, is he not? "Words mean what I want them to mean" said Humpty-Dumpty, "neither more nor less".'

When it was finally announced that Clause 28 had been passed by a resounding majority of 202 votes to 122 (Tory Peers having once again been subject to the Whips) the chamber was disrupted as three women abseiled down from the public gallery on ropes to shouts of 'Lesbians are angry!' and 'It's our lives you're dealing with'. After being escorted from the Chamber and held in cells for several hours they were finally released. One of the women later told *Capital Gay*: 'Being quiet has not done any good. I think it's time we took a more militant line.'[21] The tabloids naturally had a field day: 'LESBIANS INVADE THE LORDS' screamed the front page of the *Daily Express* on 3 February; while the *Standard* reported that the 'tarzan lesbians' had vowed to continue their campaign against the Clause. An editorial in the *Independent* dismissed the Clause as 'irrelevant and offensive',[22] while Ian McKellen, who had sat through the entire debate, told the *Guardian* that he was 'deeply disappointed' by the decision and condemned the Minster's 'derisory contribution' to the discussion.[23] The Arts critic of *The Times* on 4 February argued that the resounding majority in favour of the Clause proved that

> we have clearly returned to a pre-Wolfenden era of gay-bashing.... All we need is for a budding Senator McCarthy to start on the far left, and we shall have got back, if not to Victorian values, then at least to the long-lamented witch-hunts and blackmail charters of the 1950s.

Three days before the Lords were due to debate the Clause further, the *Independent* reported that campaigners were claiming a 'modest victory' at the news that another amendment had been put forward by the Government. In an attempt to head off further criticism the section banning authorities from giving grants to organisations or individuals had now been deleted.[24] This ploy cut no ice with opposition Peers who sat up until long gone midnight on 16 February to complete the Report Stage of the Clause. Wearily they struggled with the finer semantic points of the disputed wording, as they waded through what one speaker described as a 'cats cradle of amendments'.[25] The Minister waffled on about 'adjectival phrases' replacing 'adverbial phrases' in an attempt to justify his window-dressing alterations, but again resisted all-comers who proposed any significant changing of the phraseology used. The debate contained one remarkable personal revelation from the Labour Peer, Lord Rea.

> I was brought up by two women, one of them was my mother, in an actual family relationship. There was no pretence there.... It was a good family and I maintain that there is nothing intrinsically wrong with a homosexual couple bringing up a child. I consider that I had as rich and happy a childhood as most children who are reared by heterosexual couples, and far better than many I see in my daily practice as a doctor.

The weekend after Clause 28 had been voted through to its next stage in the Lords an anti-clause rally was held in Manchester, organised by the Northwest Campaign for Gay and Lesbian Equality and supported by the local Labour Council, which attracted a crowd estimated to be between 13,000 and 20,000 strong. MPs and councillors were joined by a plethora of well known TV personalities and pop stars. Michael Cashman told the crowd: 'Gay men and lesbians are ordinary people made extraordinary by society's obsession with what we do in bed.' And in fighting spirit, fellow actor Ian McKellen called on everyone to take positive action:

> We must all be out and about, in the streets, in the class-rooms, talking to our friends and our families, promoting homosexuality, until the whole country realises that this law is an unnatural act and it must be made illegal.[26]

The *Daily Express* drew attention to this speech in its editorial on the following Monday.

> We should be thankful to Mr McKellen for his honesty. No one can now claim that lessons projecting homosexuality as just another 'lifestyle' are not meant to promote it...

McKellen's words amply demonstrate that Clause 28 comes not a moment too soon.[27]

When the Clause (now renumbered 29 due to other changes in the Bill) returned for its Third Reading in the Lords on 29 February Lord McIntosh argued that the amendments to it had severely limited its scope and would ensure that many of the feared restrictions could no longer be imposed.[28] However, he maintained it was still 'an abuse of the legislative procedure... and ought not to be allowed'. Lord Houghton accused the Government of being pushed into this legislation by their 'militant tendancy' which he termed neo-Fascist. The Earl of Caithness swiftly passed over the matter, merely claiming that the terms of the Clause were now 'clearly set out, so that there is no question of legitimate services being adversely affected'.

When the Clause returned to the Commons on 9 March (now, once again, renumbered as 28) opposition MPs launched a final blistering attack on its provisions and tried to amend it further.[29] Jack Cunningham led the charge:

> everyone's right to information, and the arts, the rights of minorities, the way in which a free society is tolerant of diversity, the way in which a free society organises itself, the way in which minorities are protected in a free and plural democratic society are at the heart of our objections to the provisions of clause 28.

He accused the Government of supporting the proposals for 'the basest and most contemptible political motives' and pledged that a future Labour Government would remove it from the statute book. Tony Benn (Lab.) took the opportunity of reading the 1986 Labour Conference resolution on lesbian and gay rights which committed his party to repeal all laws discriminating against the lesbian and gay community. He hoped that this strong statement would make it clear to those frightened by the introduction of the Clause that there were plenty of people who disagreed with the principles behind it.

Liberal spokesman, Simon Hughes, read out letters from his gay and lesbian constituents who recounted the appalling prejudice many of them encountered in their everyday lives. He went on to address the 'moral' aspects of the Clause.

Many people believe that it is hypocritical of the Govern-

" I SAID YOUR DAD WOULDN'T TAKE THE NEWS SO WELL, RODNEY ! "

'I said your dad wouldn't take the news so well,
Rodney!' by Franklin. © Rex Features/News International.
First appeared in the *Sun*, 9 March 1988.

ment to seek to legislate for morality as they define it when...
the poor become poorer, the rich become relatively richer,
the people who depend on social security will have less
chance of obtaining it and when, for many, opportunity in
our society will be reduced because they are not favoured
by the capitalist market-led Government.

There was even dissent from the Government's own back benches.
Robin Squire condemned the Clause, drawing attention to a cartoon which had appeared in the *Sun* on that very morning showing
an effeminate youth strung up from a lamp-post by his father for
revealing his homosexuality (see above). Mr Squire noted that a
cartoon depicting a racial or religious minority in similar circumstances would have caused justifiable outrage. Fellow Tory Andrew
Rowe revealed that he had changed his mind since the previous

debate and would now be voting against the Clause. He was one of only three Tory MPs who were to defy the Whips.

Needless to say, most of the speeches from the Tory benches were in support of the measure. Having been repeatedly pressured to produce concrete evidence of her claims that parents had been abused for opposing gay rights policies in schools Jill Knight turned instead to a shrill denunciation of the tactics of the opponents of her precious clause. She claimed that her car had been vandalised and she and her secretary subjected to 'pornographic telephone calls' in the early hours of the morning. Nicholas Fairburn treated the House to a wonderful display of pseudo-psychological clap-trap.

> In male homosexuality – homos in Greek meaning 'the same' and homo in Latin meaning 'man' – there is a perversion of the human function. It is using the excretory anus and rectum with a reproductive organ... anyone who comprehends the deep libidinal and psychological origins of male and female homosexuality should understand that it is a major and unnatural perversion.

With questionable sincerity Geoffrey Dickens assured the 'homosexual fraternity' that he would stand shoulder to shoulder with them against queer bashers if only they would stop flaunting their sexuality 'and thrusting it down other people's throats'. The Minister wound up the debate with a low key speech asserting that the amendments to the Clause would ensure that the fears expressed by many of its opponents were unfounded.

> Let me make it plain that it is no part of our intention in supporting this clause to affect the civil rights of any person. We are talking about the use of public money to give preferential treatment to certain people, activities and tendencies.

So, despite the fact that those speaking against the Clause had so clearly won the argument, when the vote was taken their amendments were defeated by 254 to 201 votes and the Clause went on to become Section 28 of the Local Government Bill.

And so it was all over bar the shouting – and there was plenty of that on 30 April when 30,000 people gathered in London for the largest anti-clause protest march to date, attended by the familiar posse of pop stars, media personalities and politicians. It was a defiant gesture accompanied by angry commitments that the struggle would continue, and confirming that the lesbian and gay community was prepared to fight for its civil liberties to the bitter end. On 23 May, the day before the legislation came into force, four lesbians invaded the BBC's Six o'Clock News to register their protest. Newscaster Sue Lawley retained her cool as her colleague Nicholas Witchell sat on one of the women to restrain her. This outrageous occurrence resulted in widespread news coverage on all channels that night and front page headlines in many of the tabloids the next morning. 'BEEB MAN SITS ON LESBIANS' shrieked the *Sun*, while the *Star* led with 'LOONY LEZZIES AT-TACK TV SUE'.[30] One of the women told the *Pink Paper*: 'This is just the beginning.... When we're through they'll be wishing they'd never heard of Clause 28.'[31]

There had already been disturbing reports that some authorities were imposing restrictions in anticipation of the new law; East Sussex had banned a booklet funded by the Home Office from its schools because it contained a reference to the London Lesbian and Gay Centre, and Strathclyde Regional Council had warned colleges not to provide money to gay organisations through student unions. However, on the weekend before the new Section 28 came into force there were several indications that it was 'a legal non-starter'; a senior QC informed the Association of London Authorities: 'It is open to serious doubt whether it will render unlawful many decisions or actions presently lawful.'[32] Manchester City Council had been advised that its grant of £150,000 to the city's lesbian and gay centre was perfectly legal because it was considered a welfare provision. Furthermore, on 25 May the Department of Education sent a circular to all schools advising teachers and school governors that their decisions regarding sex education and curriculum policies were not affected by the new restrictions on local authorities. It went on to state categorically that: 'It will not prevent the objective discussion of homosexuality in the classroom, nor the counselling of pupils concerned about their sexuality.' According to the *Sunday Times*, gay activists were convinced that the supporters of the legislation had scored an 'own goal' and commented: 'Putting clause 28 through parliament was one of the greatest promotions of homosexuality we have ever seen.'[33]

A PIECE OF RED MEAT

Summing up the campaign against Clause 28, which had taken up more than 25 hours of parliamentary debate over three months, *Capital Gay* concluded:

> we have seen the coming of age of the gay and lesbian move-ment. Well-known figures, previously quiet about their sexuality have come out fighting, we have found support from across the political spectrum; ordinary homosexuals have written protest letters and taken to the streets in the biggest ever lesbian and gay demonstrations, the media coverage has been massive (and often sympathetic), and the visibility of our community has rarely, if ever, been greater.[34]

The battle against Clause 28 was indeed a watershed in the struggle for gay equality. In fact, it could be argued that the gay and lesbian community in Britain had finally been faced with their own equivalent of the Stonewall riot. There had been an unpre-cedented display of gay and lesbian solidarity in protesting against the Clause, the fragmented campaigning groups had come together to co-ordinate their response and had organised a series of highly effective parliamentary lobbies, backed up by large-scale public protests. Such had been the success of the Arts Lobby that Ian McKellen had been invited to meet privately with both Michael Howard and Baroness Cox to discuss the matter. Senior sources in the Conservative Party had told him that the Government was embarrassed by the fuss and was doing everything to ameliorate the impact of the legislation. The Whips' office told the actor that the Clause was 'a piece of red meat which we have to throw to our wolves every now and then to keep them quiet'.[35] An ex-Minister informed McKellen that Mrs Thatcher didn't object to individual homosexuals but to groups of them, and therefore Clause 28 was her way of 'privatising homosexuality' and ensuring that public money could not be used to promote it.[36]

Whatever the truth behind the introduction of the Clause, in parliamentary terms it also marked a fundamental turning point in the story of gay law reform. This was the first successful attempt since 1967 by those opposed to homosexuality to place further restrictions on its public manifestations. It was clear from the very beginning that the legislation stemmed from a growing reaction against the emergence of a recognisable and unapologetic gay community. Repeatedly during the debates it was argued that a minority of gay extremists had brought this legislation on themselves by strident public demands for equality. According to Labour's Lord Mason:

> the bigots and militants of the homosexual groups have assisted this backlash against themselves.... The majority of homosexuals will not be affected. They will go on quietly and unashamedly living in their own way.

Lord Halsbury reinforced this dubious distinction by reading out a letter from one of the respectable majority of 'ordinary' homosexuals.

> 'I want to say how fed up I am with my fellow homosexuals. They have brought it upon themselves, their unpopularity. They are too promiscuous, too aggressive and exhibitionist. I cannot stand the sight of them. I wish they would keep themselves to themselves.'

This feeling that the overt demands for gay rights had alienated public sympathy was also voiced by some of those opposed to the Clause.

Even journalist Polly Toynbee accepted this view, offering a disappointingly simplistic analysis of its causes. In an article in the *Guardian* she claimed that sexual proclivity alone did not create a homogeneous grouping and therefore dismissed the concept of a 'gay community' as a 'myth' nurtured by left-wing activists. She proceeded to berate gay campaigning organisations for allowing their cause to be 'kidnapped by the far left', arguing that CHE's success in the 1970s was due to its refusal to allay itself to any one political party, and concluded with an appeal to

> moderate non-political people... to get back into these organisations, seize them from the extremists, remove them from the grip of the left-wing authorities and start to campaign effectively.[37]

One might argue that the growing anti-gay stance of the Government over the previous five years in response to Labour's positive support for gay equality had brought about such a political polarisation on the issue that the lesbian and gay community had little choice but to accept the policies of the left. Letters attacking Ms Toynbee's arguments poured in over the next few days; one from the editor of *Capital Gay* wanted to know if she was 'equally happy to blame the Jews for provoking Nazism and women for provoking rape?'[38]

Of course, this was precisely the line that had been taken by the *Sun*, using the excuse of the murder of newspaper boy Stuart Gough by a 'cruel, vicious and demented homosexual' to print an inflammatory leading article entitled 'WHEN THE GAYS HAVE TO SHUT UP'. It claimed that homosexuals were no longer campaigning for equal rights but wanted to be accepted as superior to heterosexuals, and continued with the warning:

> *They are risking a terrible backlash*. The mass of people have no great sympathy or understanding for homosexuals. They want them to be left alone. But more important, they want the homosexuals to leave THEM alone. That especially applies to their children. No one, in reason, can blame the homosexual community for what happened to Stuart Gough, any more than a reasonable woman could blame all heterosexual men for an act of rape or murder. But people are not always reasoning. Homosexuals have achieved equality. They have public understanding and they have the law's protection. *They would be wise to leave it at that*.[39]

In the *Financial Times*, John Lloyd considered this kind of knee-jerk response to the gay rights issue in a broader context. He suggested that the weakening of liberal tolerance had been caused by a reluctance on the part of the British public to abandon its archaic view that homosexuality was some form of sickness, combined with a refusal to face up to the radical re-definition of gender roles which had been presented by the GLF and was being demonstrated more openly in the public domain with the emergence of a distinctive gay sub-culture and lifestyle.

> That part of gay liberation which proselytises for a new sexual order, and which sometimes conflates the call for an assured minority status with that for overturning *all* assumed statuses, presents society with a giant agenda and thus provokes great ill will. It irritates prejudice, traditionalism and even liberalism.... Yet it is at least, in a free society, worth a thought or two.[40]

Regardless of its antecedents, there is no disputing the fact that Clause 28 placed the principle that homosexuality was socially undesirable and inherently inferior to heterosexuality on the statute book in an explicit form for the first time. In banning councils from 'intentionally promoting' homosexuality that interpretation was implicit, although the Government tried to argue that a simple financial issue was a stake: local authorities were abusing their statutory powers by using ratepayers' money for the purposes of 'social engineering'. But in the section dealing with education policy, which forbade teachers from presenting homosexuality as 'a pretended family relationship', this discriminatory rationale could not be disguised. However, such a blatant attempt to consign gay and lesbian relationships to second-class status meant that politicians opposing Clause 28 had a unique opportunity to challenge the myths and distortions about homosexuality which the popular press had implanted and nurtured in the public consciousness for more than four decades, and which lay at the heart of this legislation. As a result, for the first time, Parliament faced up to the real issue at the centre of the gay rights debate: whether homosexuality should be recognised as an alternative lifestyle which had equal validity to heterosexuality.

ACCEPTING AND
CELEBRATING DIVERSITY

Religious proscriptions against homosexual acts, which had for so long underpinned all resistance to gay law reform, were a relatively rare feature of the debates. However, on the few occasions they did surface, they were given short shrift by the likes of Lord Peston who dismissed them with the comment:

It does not seem to me that the view that one has to take... should be what is determined by either Christian or Jewish teaching specifically in its original or primitive form. Some of us believe that in the past 2,000 years there have been some developments in human thought and human moral values and therefore are not ashamed to take a different view.

The two notions behind the education section of the Clause – that the heterosexual nuclear family was the only acceptable form of relationship and that homosexual relationships were therefore inferior; and the idea of young people being diverted from their natural heterosexual leanings by the 'promotion' of homosexuality

– both came in for repeated hammerings. The former thesis was challenged by Allan Roberts, who demanded to know how a 'normal' family would be defined.

Are single parents, step-parents, heterosexual couples living together, married couples without children, single sexually active heterosexuals and celibates normal? Is what the majority does normal? Most people who get married, get divorced. Is that normal?

In the Upper House, Lord Rea, who admitted to being raised by a lesbian couple, put the fuss over the notorious book *Jenny Lives with Eric and Martin* into perspective by pointing out that

the small girl was actually a lot safer in bed with two gay men than some small girls are in the same bed with their own heterosexual father. The paediatricians of Cleveland may have been a bit trigger happy in diagnosing childhood sexual abuse. But... in the great majority of cases the guilty parent is living in a heterosexual relationship.

Lord Gifford contended:

Millions of our fellow citizens are gay men and lesbian women who make family relationships full of the mixture of affection, compatibility and sexual feeling and respect which make up any enduring love relationship. Those are family relationships as much as any between husband and wife.

And Lord Kilbracken pointed out a further absurdity adduced by the wording of the Clause.

will we not be faced with the illogicality that it is meritorious to counsel a heterosexual person to be monogamous and faithful but that to counsel a homosexual to eliminate promiscuity and stick to one partner may be seen as promotion of homosexuality and thus be illegal?

The latter pernicious and familiar claim that young people could be tempted into homosexuality, argued with such gusto by Jill Knight and her cohorts, was tackled head on by Lord Gifford.

People do not become gay through persuasion, reading books or through seduction. Their sexual orientation is fixed in early childhood so that a young person will discover at an early age when sexual feelings begin to develop that he or she is gay.

Therefore, observed Lord Hutchinson, 'One cannot promote a propensity'. Simon Hughes made the identical point in the Commons, and Mark Fisher insisted that

> Gays and lesbians no more choose how they feel than heterosexuals choose heterosexuality. This is not a logical choice that people make; this is something people feel.... If promotion were effective, everyone would be heterosexual because the overwhelming mass of material in our culture, media, advertising and family lives promotes heterosexuality.

But David Wilshire claimed there was no objective evidence to support this argument and insisted that 'until it is proved that somebody's sexuality cannot be changed, we must assume that it can be, just in case'. With all the talk from the sponsors of the Clause about the protection of children, Ken Livingstone wanted to know how it would help young gay men and lesbians. In his view it would simply 'open the way to a load of homophobia and litigious fanatics trying to prevent honest and open discussion of people's real sexuality', thereby leaving gay and lesbian teenagers, who already faced considerable hostility from heterosexual society, without essential counselling and other support.

On the second section of Clause 28, regarding the matter of expenditure by local authorities on promoting homosexuality the Government and its supporters time and again failed to provide any concrete examples which could not be refuted by the opposition. Jill Knight was accused of being 'extremely economic with the truth' with regard to her claims by one Labour MP, which another dismissed as 'scare stories and fantasies'. Jack Cunningham put forward the fundamental principle that since 10 per cent of the adult population was acknowledged to be gay and lesbian, 'It is not an abuse for a local authority to devote – as some do quite properly – relatively small resource allocations to meet the legitimate needs of those minorities.' It was left to Lord Willis to produce actual figures to show how little money was being splashed out by such reputedly profligate authorities as Camden and Haringey. In 1987–8 the former spent £133,000 on the lesbian and gay community out of its budget of £138m – a mere 0.096 per cent; the

latter's £127,000 contribution to gay and lesbian projects stood at
0.06 per cent of its 1987–8 budget of £204m. 'Is that wild and
extravagant considering the number of homosexuals in the community?', he demanded to know.

No argument put forward by the supporters of the Clause was
left unchallenged. Joan Lestor observed that while nobody made
complaints about the popular and degrading stereotyping of gay
men and lesbians,

> the moment a local authority or group of people challenge
> that stereotyping and says, 'Hold on a minute, homosexuals
> are not like that. Lesbians are not like that.... Let us present
> people in a positive way as individuals, making a contribu-
> tion to society' – as we all are – they are told, 'My God, you
> are promoting homosexuality. You are saying it is a good
> thing and something that everyone should emulate.'

Although the invidious claims about the 'aggressive proselytising' of gay campaigners were quashed by Jack Cunningham, his
comments drew attention to the terrible weakness of the legal
position of the gay and lesbian community in relation to other
minorities. He insisted that it was

> an important principle of equality before the law, for mi-
> norities to seek to advance their own lawful interests.... Just
> as the Sex Discrimination Act 1986 and the Race Relations
> Act 1976 make it less acceptable to discriminate against
> women and ethnic minorities, this clause will have the
> reverse effect and will make it more respectable to discrimi-
> nate against gay and lesbian people.

For the first time, every politician opposed to Clause 28 had framed
their arguments in the context of gay rights being a matter of basic
civil liberties. In fact, Lord Gifford, who had represented Geoff
Dudgeon in his successful fight to force the British Government to
extend the 1967 Act to Northern Ireland, suggested that the
legislation might well breach several articles of the European Convention on Human Rights.

A few MPs even argued that such a commitment to gay equality
had to be built on an acknowledgement of a much wider range of
sexual expression. As Simon Hughes put it:

> A civilised society should recognise that it has a duty to

legislate... for freedom to choose for all. Adults must be allowed to make their own choices and, provided they do not do harm to others, they must be free to do so without fear of being victimised.

Chris Smith, still standing proudly as the only openly gay MP, took the argument a stage further in suggesting that the individual's right to sexual choice was vital to the health of Britain's increasingly pluralistic society.

true morality and true decency mean accepting and celebrating diversity and being tolerant of the fact that everyone, no matter who or what he is, is entitled to live and lead his own life.

12

AN AIR OF HOPE
AND WILLINGNESS

Into the 1990s

We live in an age of doubt. Many moral certainties of
Victorian times and the orthodox Christian traditions of
earlier generations are being questioned, openly challenged
and quite often publicly flouted. Everyone should approach
moral questions with humility. The Greeks gave us an
injunction – 'Know thyself'.... How many people can claim
truthfully to have attained full self-knowledge? The road to
self-knowledge often takes us through stony places.
Sir Brandon Rhys Williams – House of Commons 8/5/87

THE MORAL AGENDA

In the summer of 1988 there was little evidence of the lesbian and
gay community conducting a post-mortem into the Clause 28
campaign, although an interesting discussion between a mixed bag
of gay and lesbian activists did appear in the June issue of *Marxism
Today*. Former Tory MP Matthew Parris argued that the battle over
the Clause had demonstrated the breakdown in the traditional
political consensus in Britain.

There was a liberal establishment that would have come to
the aid of the gay and lesbian community in far more certain
terms in the 60s and even the early 70s than appeared to be
the case this time.

Angela Cooper felt that this was because a decade of Thatcherism
had made the new generation much more selfish, the old political
constituencies had therefore disintegrated forcing the gay movement out on to the streets. Jeffrey Weeks observed: 'People are now
making decisions on sexuality which may undermine their tradi-

tional party loyalties.... There's now something in the moral agenda which politicians are concerned with rather than priests.'

Femi Otitoju drew attention to the solidarity which had been displayed by other minority communities during the struggle against the Clause.

> For the first time really, people who've been unprepared to accept that being lesbian or gay is to be oppressed, or to get a raw deal, are actually recognising the strength of feeling that exists.

It was generally acknowledged that the fight had brought lesbians and gay men together in an unparalleled display of unity. As Ms Cooper wryly commented: 'It's given us a common enemy – something worse than each other... to fight.' However, Mr Parris was sceptical that these new links were deep enough to be lasting, while author Adam Mars Jones articulated a shared concern that many gay men and lesbians had simply refused to see Clause 28 as a real threat. Asked to suggest the best way forward, Ms Otitoju called for a continuing high profile: 'up with the banners, out with the stout walking shoes'; but Angela Cooper expressed the hope that the gay movement would not have to have marches 'every five minutes to keep moving forward'.

A record attendance on the annual Gay Pride march in London in June 1988, estimated at around 20,000, seemed to prove that the grass-roots bandwagon was still rolling along. Delighted gay activists insisted that the turnout proved that the fight against Section 28 had been 'a huge shot in the arm' for the gay rights cause.[1] OLGA, now enjoying its status as the largest of the campaigning groups with over 600 members, had already publicised its post-clause agenda back in April which included monitoring the effect of the new legislation and supporting organisations financially damaged by its implementation, as well as continuing its broader aim of fighting for gay equality. It was significant that the announcement was accompanied by a strong appeal for financial contributions to carry out this ambitious programme. However, only a meagre 35 members turned up for OLGA's annual conference in September. Despite the disappointing turnout and complaints of a lack of accountability and bad communication they still managed to emanate 'an air of hope and willingness'.[2]

A few weeks earlier more than 50 people out of a more modest membership of around 400 convened in Leicester for CHE's 16th annual conference, but the absence of certain key campaigners was noted. Coverage of the event in the October issue of *Gay Times* was premised by the question 'Whatever happened to CHE?', and revealed that the organisation was still 'quietly chugging along', financially solvent, and encouraged by an influx of more than 120 new members since the advent of Clause 28. But apart from deciding that a return to grass-roots social activities in the regions was essential and voting to support a youth campaign initiative, no coherent long-term strategy to take the organisation into the 1990s was agreed upon. The article gloomily noted that 'visionaries who could set the organisation alight were noticeable by their absence'.

During the following month the annual party conference season saw lesbian and gay rights once again on the political agenda. Following on from the TUC's conference decision calling for the repeal of Section 28 and the establishment of a comprehensive policy to protect lesbian and gay rights, the Labour Conference overwhelmingly backed a motion to remove the Section and re-affirmed the party's existing commitment to 'full equality' for lesbians and gay men. According to Jo Richardson this vote made it clear

'that there will never again be any suggestion of the Labour Party backing off from its support for lesbian and gay rights'.[3]

At the first conference of the newly constituted Social and Liberal Democratic Party (SLD) a motion was passed which committed the party to abolish Section 28, and an amendment to its 'green paper' on civil liberties was accepted which called for

legislation to prohibit discrimination on the grounds of sexual orientation in all fields, both legal and social; creation of a common age of consent regardless of gender or sexual orientation; and the making of 'incitement to hatred on the grounds of sexual orientation' a criminal offence.[4]

Brian Stone, the chairman of the Social and Liberal Democrats for Lesbian and Gay Rights (DELGA), confirmed that the party's leader Paddy Ashdown was 'committed to the rights of lesbian and gay people'. The SLD's former allies, the Social Democratic Party (SDP) did not debate the subject of gay rights during their conference.

Although the Conservative Party Conference also maintained a deafening silence on the issue, the Chancellor of the Exchequer made use of a pre-conference interview on London Weekend

Television to vent some strongly homophobic views. Nigel Lawson not only affirmed his belief that Section 28 was 'right', but made the following comments about homosexuals:

> I think it is unfortunate for them that they are. I don't think it is a happy condition and I think it is unfortunate and I don't think we'd want to have that promoted or proselytized.[5]

At a well attended fringe meeting organised by the Conservative Group for Homosexual Equality (CGHE) those in attendance were encouraged to write to the Chancellor to protest at his comments. A silent torchlight vigil staged by over 100 lesbians and gay men outside the Conference on its wet and stormy first night seemed to have had no significant impact on the assembled delegates. The organisers intended it to express 'the gay spirit rising', as one of them explained in *Capital Gay* on 30 September: 'We are fed up with political campaigning in conventional ways and we wanted to do things in *our* way on *our* ground to make us feel good about ourselves.'

This articulation of the feeling that the existing gay movement was not providing appropriate and positive responses to the new threats highlighted by Section 28 was obviously felt in other sections of the gay and lesbian community and was encouraging the emergence of alternative campaigning initiatives. In January 1989 it was announced that a British version of the American Aids Coalition to Unleash Power (ACT-UP) was to be formed. In the United States ACT-UP was well known for its angry and imaginative public protests to force government agencies and public bodies to take more direct action to counter the spread of Aids and support people with HIV. The first meeting of the group in London attracted nearly 100 people and it was agreed that a non-violent demonstration should be mounted at the annual shareholders meeting of the giant drug company Wellcome to protest at the enormous profits being made from the anti-HIV drug AZT. In the following months the group floated helium-filled condoms over the walls of Pentonville prison to protest against the Government's repeated refusal to distribute condoms in jails and 'zapped' the offices of the *Daily Mail* after its bigoted columnist George Gale had described active homosexuals as 'potential murderers'.

The new Stonewall Group, set up in May 1989, was pledged to adopt a much more conventional approach, despite naming itself after the riot which had heralded the birth of the gay liberation movement. Ian McKellen and Michael Cashman, along with a number of other celebrities previously involved with the Arts Lobby, had joined up with journalist Duncan Campbell, ex-Tory MP Matthew Parris and seasoned lesbian and gay rights campaigners including Peter Ashman, Lisa Power and Jennie Wilson, to establish a professional parliamentary, media and legal lobbying organisation. Its priorities would be to establish an all-party parliamentary working group to liaise with sympathetic politicians and to monitor gay and lesbian issues in legislation. Mr McKellen told *Gay Times*:

> Our aim will be to identify in what way the law should be changed... and to provide people who can function well in the media, people who can argue for the changes that need to happen. We are keen to get people who are gay and lesbian in the mainstream of society, who are not out, to come out. If they know there's an organisation like this that is well respected... they are far more likely to come out and help in raising money and offering expertise.[6]

The group itself was constituted as a non-profit-making limited company with a controlling body of 20 members (ten lesbians and ten gay men) who would elect five directors to oversee its work. The Iris Trust was established as an associated charity raising funds for education and research. Ian McKellen and Michael Cashman mounted a gala performance of Martin Sherman's harrowing play *Bent*, which charted the imprisonment and murder of gay men in Nazi concentration camps in the 1930s, to raise an impressive £25,000. Most of this money was used to fund a full time Director post, ably filled by Tim Barnett, a former councillor in the London boroughs of Greenwich and Lewisham, and founding co-ordinator of the National Association of Volunteer Bureaux. In an interview with *Gay Times*, Britain's first 'professional homosexual' commented:

> Our claim is to develop an expertise on the issues. It isn't to be representative of the entire community... but we clearly have to be sensitive to what other groups want us to do.[7]

He revealed that Stonewall's first task was to draft a homosexual equality bill in consultation with MPs, MEPs and other lesbian and gay campaigning organisations. He also pinned hope on the European Community as a catalyst for possible future progress.

A CHINK OF LIGHT

In respect of its stated aims and priorities Stonewall was treading well-worn campaigning paths. However, its emphasis on the European dimension as a long-term prospect was an interesting one. In the 1950s and 1960s gay law reformers had pointed up the greater freedoms enjoyed by homosexuals in many European countries in relation to Britain, and it is a disgrace that such an argument is as true today as it was then. In 1990 the United Kingdom shares with Bulgaria the dubious honour of having the highest homosexual age of consent in Europe, while Ireland remains the only Western European country where homosexual sex is still totally prohibited. In contrast, seven of the twelve member states of the European Community (EC) have an equal age of consent for heterosexuals, homosexuals and lesbians (varying from 12 to 16 years); four also have anti-discrimination laws to protect their gay and lesbian communities, and in 1989 Denmark gave partnership rights to same-sex couples which placed their relationships on a par with heterosexual marriage. Even in many Eastern European countries the *legal* position of gay men and lesbians is better than in Britain: there is a non-discriminatory age of consent in Poland (15), and the gay male age of consent in Austria, Czechoslovakia and Hungary is 18. Of course, the social situation for the gay and lesbian population in many of those countries has been very repressive until relatively recently.[8]

Gay campaigners had first started to make use of the provisions of the European Convention of Human Rights in the early 1970s to argue their case against legal discrimination, but without success. The European Court did not issue a pro-gay judgment until 1981 when it found in favour of Jeff Dudgeon and forced the British Government to extend the 1967 Act to Northern Ireland two years later. Another six years were to pass before the Government felt it necessary to pressurise both the Isle of Man and Jersey to decriminalise gay sex in line with the ruling – only to meet stiff and intractable opposition. This initiative was doubtless prompted by the European Court's identical ruling in 1988 against the Irish Government after openly gay senator David Norris had initiated a case to force the Republic to revoke its laws outlawing male homosexual behaviour.

In 1978 30 campaigners from 14 different countries met in Coventry to found the International Gay Association (IGA). Three years later they celebrated a very successful lobbying exercise of the Assembly of the Council of Europe where an all-embracing gay rights charter was accepted. This resolution was passed on to the Council of Ministers and disappeared without trace.[9] In 1984 these recommendations formed the basis of the Squarcialupi Report which urged member states to abolish all legal restrictions against consenting adult homosexual relationships; to introduce equal heterosexual and homosexual ages of consent; to outlaw descrimination on the grounds of sexual orientation in the workplace; and to reject the classification of homosexuality as a mental illness. This was passed by a large majority in the European Parliament, but despite an announcement during the debate suggesting that the Community's Commission was intending to prepare a measure protecting the employment rights of lesbians and gay men no concrete proposals emerged.[10] Although the Commission of the European Court of Human Rights considered a case relating to Britain's privacy section of the 1967 Act which Martin Johnson initiated after his private party had been raided by police in 1982, this never reached the Court itself and other applications challenging the law on the armed forces (John Bruce), the age of consent (Richard Desmond), public housing (Mary Simpson) and immigration (anonymous) also all failed. However, in 1986 it was another European Court ruling against the UK over imported inflatable sex dolls which was widely believed to have persuaded the Government to drop the charges over the importation of allegedly obscene books by 'Gays the Word' Bookshop.

New opportunities were recognised by gay rights campaigners in the late 1980s, initially in response to direct elections to the European Parliament in 1989, when Neil Kinnock promised that Labour MEPs would keep up pressure for gay rights in cooperating with other European socialist parties. The election took place against the background of preparations for the unified single market in 1992, and the emergence of a view that the removal of economic barriers to access would have to be accompanied by a 'social charter' to ensure that workers' rights were harmonised throughout member states to allow a free flow of labour. Former Labour candidate Peter Tatchell argued that this would put social issues to the forefront of the European agenda as many European politicians wanted to enhance the power of the Parliament by working towards a more integrated 'community' of member states rather than just a 'common market'. To take advantage of this new trend he proposed a wide range of initiatives which included attempts to get the European Charter of Human Rights incorporated into British law and the preparation of a European Charter for Lesbian and Gay Equality to be submitted to the European Parliament.

In the mean time the International Lesbian and Gay Association (ILGA), now representing gay and lesbian groups in 33 countries, had applied for 'consultative status' with the Council of Europe which would allow it to be automatically sought out for its views on all gay and lesbian matters; but it was recognised that this could take years to achieve. In the mean time, working in tandem with Stonewall, it was lobbying MEPs to put forward alterations to the Social Charter to extend its provisions to cover gay and lesbian rights including employment protection. In November 1989 Labour MEP Stephen Hughes introduced an amendment to the Social Charter which urged member states to give priority to 'the right of all workers to equal protection regardless of their nationality, race, religion, age, sex, sexual preference or legal status'. This was passed by a substantial majority and sent on to be considered by the Council of Ministers, who could simply choose to ignore it. Even if this happened, Colin Kotz, administrator of the European socialist group, confirmed that the Parliament would continue to put forward gay rights amendments to any draft directives and action programmes as appropriate; he described the EC as 'a door waiting to be pushed open'.[11]

There was further cautious optimism when EC President Jacques Delors responded to a question from Stephen Hughes about anti-gay discrimination by acknowledging that 'all forms of discrimination' were contrary to article 100A of the EC treaties and promising that broader measures to tackle the matter would be included in the Social Charter. The MEP felt Delors' reply was rather ambiguous, but described the response as 'a chink of light'.[12] However, on a consultative visit to the Commission in February 1990 a Stonewall delegation was told by a senior official that it was unlikely there would be any specific action relating to sexual orientation arising from the Charter since this required unanimous agreement by all member governments – which would not be forthcoming. The lobbyists were encouraged to provide documented evidence of legal restraints which would prevent the free movement of gay men and lesbians in the Community after 1992. Tim Barnett told *Gay Times*:

> The Commission is softening a bit. They are no longer arguing that they haven't got legal competence to deal with lesbian and gay issues. Now they're arguing they can't act because of politicial opposition from member states like Britain. This, at least clarifies the problem and shows where we need to direct our lobbying methods.[13]

He predicted that there was 'a very real chance' the Commission would take initiatives to combat anti-gay discrimination within the next two to three years. In the mean while the ILGA would be compiling a dossier on the impact of the single market for lesbians and gays to present to the Commission, as requested.

NOTHING TO GAIN BY BEING REASONABLE?

On the domestic front gay rights campaigners at the beginning of the 1990s are faced with a wide range of social and political issues. There is a continuing concern over the effects of the iniquitous Section 28. Looking back over the first year of its operation in the June 1989 edition of *Gay Times* journalist David Smith observed that the predictions that it would severely damage gay life had been proved false and therefore dismissed the Section as a 'toothless law'. Although he admitted that the threat of its application had motivated some 15 cases of anti-gay discrimination, he pointed out that the pressure brought to bear on councils in five of these cases had resulted in an overturning of their original decision. He therefore concluded that since the Section could be subject to successful legal challenge it was time for the debate to move on to other long-standing matters such as employment discrimination and a reduction in the age of consent. His view was roundly attacked in the following month's copy of the magazine: another article described the Section as 'a symbolic thorn in our side' which had made it much easier for self-censorship and overt prejudice to flourish in the way that its proponents had always intended. At the end of that year it was reported that the Scottish Homosexual Action Group (SHAG) had failed in their attempt to raise money to launch a legal challenge to the decision by Edinburgh District Council to refuse funding to their lesbian and gay 'Lark in the Park' festival. Other organisations had refused to help finance a 'judicial review' for fear that the decision would be upheld, thus setting a 'dangerous precedent'.[14]

OLGA, which had set itself the task of monitoring the effects of the Section, had been reduced to campaigning for its own survival, and in March 1990 was sending out desperate pleas for financial support to prevent its collapse. However, when *Capital Gay* reported in May that an emergency meeting had been called with the intention of disbanding OLGA, it also revealed that a new radical group, 'OutRage', had been set up to launch a high profile civil disobedience campaign. According to one of its organisers:

We get bombarded with homophobia in the press, in the streets, in our everyday lives. And we want to focus the anger people feel about that into positive, direct action. It's a matter of gay rights being human rights, and our demanding that we get them.[15]

This tradition of direct action had its roots in the philosophy of GLF, which in turn derived from the American gay liberation movement sparked off by the Stonewall riot. Back in 1987 the Lesbian and Gay Youth Movement (LGYM) had handed a leaflet to delegates at the ill-fated Law Reform Conference arguing that the preparation of draft legislation was pointless, and doomed to failure in the prevailing climate of homophobic prejudice. Instead LGYM welcomed 'all other intiatives which lead to street and propaganda campaigns against bigots, and which start from an understanding that we've nothing to gain by being reasonable'. This same frustration and anger over the Aids crisis had led American gay activists to found ACT-UP, which soon crossed the Atlantic to take root in London. The speed with which British ACT-UP's novel protests gained support, in turn inspiring SHAG to adopt similar high profile public tactics, and doubtless influencing the imaginative initiatives taken by the dare-devil dykes against Clause 28, demonstrated that there was a reservoir of frustration within the gay and lesbian community which required an outlet.

While this type of high-profile public demonstration is well suited to the American political arena, in the more restrained and inhibited British context, it can have a counter-productive effect. The activities of the abseiling lesbians might have been cathartic for those involved, may have provided a valuable morale-booster and certainly succeeded in putting the matter on to the front pages of the tabloids, but it also alienated many of those opposed to the Clause. OLGA's organiser Eric Presland offered the justificiation for such action in a letter to *Gay Times* in March 1988.

> People have always done illegal things in the cause of civil rights. They have killed themselves, they have sat down, they have set fire to things, they have smashed statues, they have defaced money. And they have eventually won their arguments. But we just float down from a public gallery in a mock-Gothic fantasy out of William Morris. What style! What elan! And how very camp. What on earth harm did it do to anyone?

Given the fears being articulated about the aggressive proselytising behaviour of gay activists both within Parliament and amongst the public at large, one could argue that these demonstrations played into the hands of those advocating the restrictions in the Clause. It was certainly not this strategy which brought about the minor but significant changes to the legislation, which were achieved by the traditional methods of mobilising key sectors of Establishment opinion, organising discreet lobbying of influential politicians, backed up by mass public demonstrations and a flood of letters to Peers and MPs. Antony Grey, who used most of those conventional weapons to such effect in the 1960s, made a useful comment on this issue in the aftermath of the Section 28 campaign.

> We do need to beware of the lure of street theatre as a substitute for much duller and more traditional forms of political action. Parliamentary abseiling and chaining oneself to Sue Lawley's legs is doubtless spiffing for those so inclined, and makes a camply spectacular point, but is irrelevant in serious political terms.[16]

As the gay campaigning group with most experience in the political arena CHE decided to celebrate its 21st birthday in 1990 by returning to its historical roots and focusing its efforts once again on fighting for an equal age of consent. At a sparsely attended annual conference in May its members were assured by Labour MP Jo Richardson that her party would not back away from its commitment to lesbian and gay equality in the run-up to the next election. However, she expressed her personal concern over the recent pronouncement by shadow Home Secretary Roy Hattersley that any lowering of the gay age of consent would be left to a free vote under a Labour Government. This strategy was presumably based on the spurious argument that it would render the new-look Labour Party less prone to Conservative attacks over its support for lesbian and gay rights, but in the context of the party's repeated commitment to equal rights for all, such an anomaly was totally illogical. If equal opportunities for women and ethnic minorities were to be protected in Government-sponsored legislation, the exemption of this most fundamental of equal rights for gay men would not only separate this one issue from the others thereby making it an easy target for opposition, but would once again give a signal that in the final analysis the Labour Party considered gay rights as being less important than other human rights.

The very mention of a gay age of consent of 16 by Roy Hattersley had already galvanised the Tory party to the attack, doubtless spurred on by the fact that the Labour Party was enjoying its greatest lead in the opinion polls for more than 50 years and Mrs Thatcher's personal standing was slipping disastrously towards the lowest level ever enjoyed by any Prime Minster. The Conservative Chairman of the Commons home affairs committee warned: 'This is a very vulnerable age. Adults should be free to make their own decisions. But to make it so low it brings in schoolchildren is going too far.'[17] Tory Chairman Kenneth Baker was reported to be 'appalled' by the plan: 'Parents will be shocked to know that this protection for their children could be removed by Labour.'[18] An editorial in *The Times* on 13 February 1990 trotted out all the old dogma about boys needing protection to justify the opinion that the law should be left as it was 'in the light of the threat of Aids. This is not the time to be seen to be relaxing vigilance against such a scourge.' However, the leader article in *Today* praised Labour for bringing this 'excruciating' issue 'out of the closet' for consideration by all parties, and questioned whether youths between 16 and 21 needed any more protection than girls of the same age.

In reply to a parliamentary question from Labour's Gavin Strang, Home Office Minister Chris Patten had recently revealed that in England and Wales in 1988, ten men over the age of 21 had been imprisoned for between two and four years for consensual buggery or attempted buggery with young men between the ages of 16 and 21; a further 13 men over 21 had received prison sentences ranging from six months to three years for consenting acts of 'gross indecency' with men between 16 and 21 years old. Dr

Strang went on to ask if the Government had any intention of introducing legislation to protect lesbians and gay men from legal discrimination, to which the Minister replied: 'We have no plans to change the criminal law insofar as it affects homosexual relations'.[19] The Prime Minster stepped into the fray in person during Question Time in Parliament on 15 February.

> MR DAVID MARTIN: Does my right hon. Friend agree that for various reasons, including the spreading and contracting of AIDS, any proposal to reduce the age of consent to homosexual activities is wholly unacceptable and utterly crackers?

> THE PRIME MINISTER: I agree with my hon. Friend. I think that any such proposal would give totally the wrong signal at this time. It would give offence to many people and worry many more and would give us great problems for the future.[20]

In the aftermath of these skirmishes the Channel Four gay magazine series 'Out on Tuesday' and the *Guardian* newspaper jointly commissioned a poll of MPs which revealed that a free vote in the Commons on a proposal to reduce the gay age of consent to 16 would be heavily defeated. Just over 50 per cent of all MPs wanted no change in the age (this figure was 68 per cent among Tory MPs, but only 23 per cent for Labour); while only 32 per cent opted for a reduction to 18 years (26 per cent of Conservatives and 38 per cent of Labour MPs respectively); and a mere 12 per cent approved of a drop to 16 (only 1.4 per cent of Conservatives agreed, as opposed to nearly 30 per cent on the Labour side). It was small compensation to learn that 90 per cent of all respondents did not want to see homosexuality made illegal, and that over 82 per cent of Labour MPs would support legislation designed to outlaw discrimination against gays in employment, while 75 per cent would back the repeal of Section 28. Former Tory MP Matthew Parris told the *Guardian* that, given these figures, the idea of an equal age of consent being achieved was 'sheer fantasy'. *Gay Times* calculated that even if the Labour Party came to power with a 100 seat majority after the next election the chances of a reduction of the age of consent to 18 on a free vote was far from certain.

THE FACE OF BRITISH SEXUAL POLITICS

In a *Gay Times* editorial, John Marshall described the findings of the poll as 'deeply regrettable' and the opposition of so many Labour MPs to the age of 16 'a disgrace'. He went on to argue cogently that the fight for an equal age of consent was central to the wider issue of equality for both gay men and lesbians on the grounds that harsh restrictions on public displays of homosexuality and the draconian measures designed to prevent young men from adopting a gay lifestyle until they were 21 were rooted in the view that homosexuality was unnatural and therefore fundamentally unacceptable.

> The law assumes that homosexuality is immoral and un-desirable.... By altering the age of consent for gay men we not only break this legal framework but we also challenge the underlying philosophy: we challenge the notion that homosexuality is a second-rate lifestyle and we question the idea that barriers should be placed in the way of people who might choose to adopt such a lifestyle. By reducing the age of consent we go a long way to legitimising homosexuality in our culture as morally equivalent to heterosexuality.... A victory on this issue would be an enormous achievement, both practical and symbolic, which could change the face of British sexual politics.[21]

One month later the Stonewall Group began to circulate copies of a draft Homosexual Equality Bill which had been prepared by veteran gay rights campaigner and lawyer Peter Ashman in consultation with CHE and Liberty (formerly the NCCL). This Bill not only proposed reducing the gay age of consent to 16, but outlawed discrimination against lesbians and gay men, established legal rights for same-sex couples and made it a crime to incite hatred on the grounds of sexual orientation. After a period of consultation with other lesbian and gay groups it was hoped that it would be published before the next election and therefore available to be put before the next Parliament. According to *Capital Gay*, the Bill was intended to serve both 'as a focal point and a rallying cry in the campaign for equality'.[22] Of course, the idea of a gay rights Bill is not a new one: the three national gay rights organisations had produced their own version back in 1975, and had thereby drummed up hitherto unprecedented displays of mass support and a great deal of sympathetic publicity in the media. The fact that Stonewall provided the framework in which this Bill could be produced was an achievement in itself, and in sad contrast to the previous unhappy and unsuccessful attempt in 1987.

At the beginning of the 1990s, with the upheavals in Eastern Europe and the growing concern over global ecological issues bringing the ideals of co-operation and co-ordination to the fore in all political spheres, there is a recognition that Thatcherism's creed of individual greed is increasingly inappropriate and discredited. As the prospect of a Labour Government begins to look like a real possibility it is vital that the gay movement in Britain should begin to take its own political initiatives once again, after a decade of fighting a fierce rearguard action against the twin threats of a killer disease and a moral backlash. The emergence of the Stonewall Group as an uncompromisingly self-selected, polished and tightly knit professional organisation marks a hopeful new start in that direction. Interestingly enough, it has opted for a structure which bears striking similarities to that of the old HLRS, with a charitable arm to raise funds and a separate campaigning section headed by a full time administrator and a small voluntary staff. By rejecting the need for a mass membership and keeping decision-making in the hands of a small elite committee containing essential expertise, Stonewall has built in a safeguard against the debilitating factional in-fighting which has damaged and restrained almost every other gay campaigning organisation. It has also ensured a direct input from all the major political parties by inviting a small but impressive group of public figures to become patrons of the Iris Trust, and thereby guarded against the damaging accusation that it had sold out to any one political creed.

Sadly, and almost inevitably, Stonewall has already found itself under attack from within the lesbian and gay community. In a letter to *Gay Times* John Jackson, a CHE activist, criticised the new organisation for its 'celebrity crusade' which he claimed was 'unaccountable to the community it served', and wondered why the £20,000 it had raised hadn't been offered to fund full time administrators for OLGA and CHE.[23] Another correspondent was concerned that Stonewall did not seem to be 'complementing' existing organisations but 'presiding over them' and wondered if the group considered everyone else to be 'too inarticulate or insufficiently concerned' to get involved in campaigning.[24]

The whole question of the politicisation of the lesbian and gay community is one which lies at the heart of the struggle for their equal rights. Of course, 40 years ago any gay man who expressed his sexuality was a criminal, and it has only been 23 years since homosexual behaviour was decriminalised. It is hardly surprising that it took several years before the emerging gay and lesbian population found the courage to take advantage of the last dregs of liberal tolerance from the 'permissive sixties' to begin fashioning their own unique identity, and thereby unleashed a new era of hope in which the establishment of social, commercial and political organisations by and for themselves became a reality. But within a few brief years those fragile achievements were under threat from a gathering moral backlash which pushed lesbians and gay men on to the defensive, and put them in a very vulnerable position when they found themselves in the front line of the most terrifying public health threat of the post-war era. Given these pressures it was perhaps inevitable that unity within the movement should have remained so elusive.

Although it is unlikely that any sectional interest group has ever enjoyed complete agreement on its aims and methods of operation, the divisiveness and fragmentation within the gay rights movement has seemed stark in comparison to other areas of minority politics. Unlike the women's movement or the racial equality movement which both have a natural constituency to appeal to – after all, the fact that you are black or Asian or a woman is self-evident – the vast majority of gay men and lesbians are not only able to pass as heterosexual, but often refuse to acknowledge their true sexuality, even to themselves, and therefore cannot or will not identify themselves as belonging to an oppressed minority. Futhermore, their essential 'difference' relates to their sexuality, which many of these people quite rightly regard as a uniquely private, personal matter inappropriate for public discussion. These two sets of attitudes are central to the 'Catch 22' situation facing the gay rights movement.

An individual's sexual preference should, of course, be a purely private matter of no concern to the law unless it involves violence or coercion. By enforcing the view that same-sex relationships are undesirable and must therefore be restrained and discouraged by the law, this country has continued to make homosexuality a political issue. One look at the criminal statistics is enough to make the point: in England and Wales in 1989 the police recorded 2,022 offences of 'indecency between males', a figure which almost equals those recorded at the height of the witch-hunt of the mid 1950s and represents the largest increase ever to occur in a single year; convictions for other sexual offences between men increased from 1,051 in 1985 to 1,148 in 1988; and at least 23 men were jailed in 1989 for consensual sex with 16 to 21-year-olds. Until full homosexual equality is achieved there will be a need for a campaign not only to change the laws which prevent this from being possible, but to fight for as long as it takes to remove the prejudice and ignorance surrounding the whole subject of sexuality in this country. At the height of the Clause 28 campaign a correspondent in the *Guardian* had quite rightly, but rather optimistically, claimed: 'There is no such thing as "non-political" involvement in the issues surrounding gay rights and... the gay movement has recognised that the personal *is* political.'[25]

Ironically, as tens of thousands of gay men, lesbians and their heterosexual supporters thronged on to the streets and lobbied politicians in an unprecedented show of solidarity against the iniquitous Clause, the very existence of a gay and lesbian 'community' was being questioned in both the gay and straight press. On closer inspection this preoccupation turned out to be politically motivated, since the line most invariably taken was that the concept of a 'gay community' was a 'silly, trendy left-wing term'[26] which ignored the fact that the millions of homosexuals had no more in common than their sexual orientation – a philosophy which echoed Mrs Thatcher's conviction that there was no such thing as society, only individuals and their families. Behind these attacks was a genuine concern that the gay rights issue had become too closely associated with the 'loony left' of the Labour Party whose extravagent tactics had brought retribution in the shape of the Clause. Paul Davies in *Capital Gay* dubbed it the 'fatal attraction of the left', while Ken Livingstone's plan to 'cobble together' a platform of oppressed minorities to form the electoral base of the new radical Labour Party was dismissed as 'a Somewhere-Over-The-Rainbow Coalition which offers little to the friends of Dorothy because, like the Wizard of Oz, its power is illusory'.[27]

Whilst it is certainly valid to question the wisdom of having the cause of lesbian and gay equality associated exclusively in the public consciousness with any one political party, it seems grossly unfair to denigrate the enormous achievements, both practical and political, which have stemmed from the pro-gay policies of the GLC and other Labour councils. Given that the left of the Labour Party has been the only political grouping prepared to fight for genuine equality and complete social and legal acceptance of sexual minorities, it was inevitable that the gay movement should turn away from the ever more homophobic stance of the Conservative Party and the empty promises of the centre to co-operate with politicians who were literally prepared to put their money where their mouths were. The passing of Section 28 may have placed new restrictions on local authorities, but those with a genuine will to support gay rights have still continued to demonstrate their commitment, while it has largely been Conservative boroughs that have used the legislation as a convenient excuse to withdraw funding and support from lesbian and gay initiatives.

The battle against the Clause also provided a new-found solidarity between lesbians and gay men which had been sadly lacking in the political sphere since the majority of lesbians left the male-dominated GLF in the early 1970s to throw in their lot with the women's movement. Although many women continued to maintain a significant minority presence in CHE and other campaigning organisations throughout the late 1970s and into the 1980s there was every sign that a separatist stance was being maintained despite the growing backlash. Understandably, many women have felt that they had little to gain from campaigns to lower the gay male age of consent, to prevent police from adopting *agent provocateur* tactics in public lavatories, or to fight for money and research on Aids – a disease from which they were least at risk.

Lisa Power, a dedicated activist in both single- and cross-gender organisations, believed passionately that while women, black people, young people and disabled people all needed access to their own specific interest groups, there were still sufficient fundamental issues affecting all members of the gay and lesbian community to unite everybody in a common purpose.

> whatever sex or race or age we are, I promise you that to the rest of the world we're all queers. They don't care for the niceties of what sort of queer we are when they sack us or discriminate against us or beat us up. They will take us for what unites us, whether or not we acknowledge it. Will we keep refusing to work together until we end up dying together?[28]

As Jeffrey Weeks so astutely summed up:

> The lesbian and gay community rarely exists as a geographi-

259

cal entity; it does not necessarily involve any common ideo-
logical, economic, political or social features; it exists more
in the mind than on the ground. It is nevertheless a reality,
for it is based around the idea of positive lesbian and gay
identities that have been forged against so many odds during these past decades.[29]

MASTERS OF PROPAGANDA

As lesbians and gay men face the many challenges of the 1990s there
are some reasons for cautious optimism. The trials and tribulations
of the last decade have left their community stronger, more coherent, more united and more visible than ever. The establishment of
Stonewall as a modern, streamlined, professional, non-partisan
lobbying outfit designed to react quickly and effectively without
being hamstrung by reference to a mass membership and yet
aiming to work within the broad consensus of its constituency,
suggests that the campaigning movement has finally come of age.
However, there is still an enormous amount to be achieved and
major battles still to be fought: Aids has probably set the struggle
for equal rights back by more than a decade, and still remains as a
terrifying personal threat hanging over every individual. It is vital
that gay men continue to set an example to the heterosexual
majority by using the fear of the deadly virus to unite in common
purpose, rather than allowing it to divide them one from another
causing what Frederic Raphael described as 'the amputation of
possibility'.

> The brute murderousness of Aids threatens to change not
> only what people do with and to each other but also – with
> possibly profound results – the way in which we regard each
> other in every respect. The terror and suspicion of others,
> even when naked, may lead to a society in which no one
> trusts anyone any more.[30]

The appearance of Aids was the single most important factor in
allowing the majority of the British press to unleash an unrelenting
torrent of unabashed homophobia which reversed the trend towards greater understanding and sympathy towards gay men and
lesbians among the general public, and paved the way for Section
28. In the early 1970s the principal complaint about the press by
the GLF was that it was ignoring the growth of the new movement,

but by 1978 journalist Roger Baker noted that the term 'gay' was regularly appearing in most newspapers and concluded that 'gay news is not necessarily bad news in our popular press'.[31] How different the picture was a decade later, with terms like 'Poofter', 'Lezzie', 'Pervert' and 'Queer' being used as common currency by the tabloids and vicious columnists such as George Gale, Paul Johnson and Ray Mills.

For more than eight years Terry Sanderson has monitored press coverage of homosexuality in his media-watch column for *Gay Times* and been 'horrified to see it deteriorate from mild disapproval to hysterical condemnation';[32] he firmly believes that this has been a deliberately orchestrated campaign with a specific political purpose:

> The right-wing of the political establishment has realised what a potent force homophobia is, and is exploiting it for its own advantage. With the majority of the press in their pocket, the Tories have become the masters of propaganda. Gays, among others, are prime targets in this campaign.[33]

While women and ethnic minorities have some small protection under the law the tabloids have been free to indulge in extravagant anti-gay abuse without fear of reprisal. According to Mark Hollingsworth, author of *The Press and Political Dissent*:

> For most of Fleet Street, dissidents like the gay community have ventured outside the traditional structures of society... and entered an almost criminal world of disruption and anarchy. Their views are somehow outside the orthodox arena for debate.[34]

It is this mentality which has encouraged the systematic dehumanisation of gay men and lesbians, thereby providing encouragement to those with violently homophobic dispositions to vent their feelings more freely. The significant rise in violence against homosexuals in recent years must surely owe something to such a diet of press denigration. Journalist Jeremy Seabrook saw the whole tone of the tabloids in more sinister terms when taken in the context of their coverage of the Aids crisis. In December 1986 he argued that their deliberate 'creation of ignorance' and continual denigration of individuals to sub-human species such as 'beasts' and 'swine', was 'a sustained attempt to resurrect the mob'.[35]

At the end of the 1980s there were hopeful signs of increasing public intolerance of the excesses of the tabloids, and after threats of parliamentary action to restrain their most blatant abuses, Fleet Street suddenly agreed to adopt a voluntary code of conduct. Although this provided that 'irrelevant references to race, colour and religion' would be avoided there was no mention of the two groups most routinely abused – women and gays. The Press Council, mean while, set to work to prepare a more stringent set of guidelines of its own to replace this voluntary code. However, despite a high pressure lobbying campaign from gay activists the Council refused to include protection on the grounds of sexual orientation in the proposals which were simply intended to consolidate the lessons of previous rulings – the lack of any legislation on gay and lesbian discrimination along the lines of the Race Relations Act was mentioned as being relevant to the decision. The Council's Director advised that the best hope for change was for gay campaigners to work for a successful adjudication on an anti-gay story.

It was therefore with amazement and delight that Terry Sanderson and other gay activists who had initiated numerous complaints about tabloid abuse over the years greeted the Press Council's unexpected ruling against the *Sun* in May 1990, which stated that terms such as 'poof', 'poofter' and 'woofter' which were used 'with evident offence and intended to wound homosexuals' were 'no longer acceptable'. The Council further hinted that although any mention of sexual orientation had presently been excluded from its new code, that could change in the future. The *Sun* was furious, claiming the decision was an attack on its 'freedom of speech', and pouring scorn on the Press Council in a spiteful editorial.

> we know a great deal more about how ordinary people think, act and speak. Readers of the *Sun* KNOW and SPEAK and WRITE words like poof and poofter. What is good enough for them is good enough for us.[36]

This reaction, along with Paul Johnson's jibe in the *Spectator* that Mr Sanderson was a 'liberal fascist', merely proved that the gay journalist had been right in hailing the judgment as 'a bit of a landmark'.[37] It is imperative to the future success of the fight for gay equality that the excesses of the right-wing press are muzzled, otherwise the essential arguments for reform will never reach and persuade the general public. The battle to win over the hearts and minds of the nation to the cause of gay rights which must be one of the main priorities of the 1990s still has a long way to go.

THE ONE THING YOU
ARE NOT SUPPOSED TO DO

There seems a fair amount of unanimity on a strategy for the 1990s which centres around the need to harness effectively the energies unleashed in opposition to Section 28 and turn them into positive support for a broad-based reform Bill. However, there is an urgent need for the lesbian and gay movement to reconsider the philosophical underpinnings of its case. The opposition to gay equality has become focused on the idea that homosexuals are personally inadequate and morally inferior as a result of choosing an unnatural and unhealthy lifestyle and that a relaxation of the law will cause an increase in their number because they actively seek to indoctrinate and corrupt other people, especially the young.

In the past this view has been challenged on two main fronts. Firstly, to counter the 'corruption' theory the supporters of gay law reform have argued that sexual preference is fixed at a very early age, and therefore a young person's predilection towards their own sex or the opposite sex has been firmly established before they reach the age of 16. That being the case, they cannot be at risk of being persuaded or forced into sexual activity which is contrary to their own nature, and the teaching of 'positive images' is simply designed to help them to grow up to enjoy their sexual and emotional life to the full. This argument lay at the heart of the identification of lesbians and gay men as a clearly defined sexual minority. But concern over the spread of Aids from the homosexual population to heterosexuals has forced society to acknowledge that there are a significant number of people who do not conveniently fall into either of these two neat categories, but enjoy sexual relationships with men and women. The existence of bisexuals fatally undermines this picture of two static states of homosexuality and heterosexuality.

As long ago as 1948 Alfred Kinsey had posited the theory that sexuality was a continuum between exclusive homosexuality and exclusive heterosexuality, and his famous Report had shown that 37 per cent of American men had some overt homosexual experience during their lifetime, and that 18 per cent had at least as much homosexual experience as heterosexual experience between the ages of 16 and 55. And even more significantly, the incidence of homosexuality seemed to increase with age. Subsequent research indicates that an individual's relative position on that sexual continuum changes at different points in their life. Other studies have suggested that the expression or suppression of homosexual behaviour is affected by social and cultural factors.

In January 1989, *Gay Times* editor John Marshall drew attention to a number of these points and suggested that the gay movement needed to re-examine this idea of a fixed dichotomy as a basis for campaigning:

> we need to develop a political strategy in the 1990s which fully acknowledges the complex and fluid nature of human sexuality. By insisting too strongly on our fixed 'minority status' we run the risk of failing to confront the arguments put against us... and we also run the serious risk of adopting a new form of sexual conservatism which will ultimately be self-defeating.[38]

In part this new philosophy has already been suggested by the emphasis on gay rights as human rights. In recent debates some MPs have taken that argument a stage further and placed sexual pluralism alongside political, ethnic and cultural diversity as one more factor in our increasingly heterogeneous society. As Jeffrey Weeks pointed out to the CHE conference in May 1990: only by accepting the validity of the variety of sexual expression can we shift the debate away from obsessions with restraint and control to a concern for the value of diversity, the encouragement of sexual choice, and the responsibility for ourselves and others which that entails. Few politicians have yet fully accepted the multi-racial and multi-cultural reality of contemporary British society. It is going to be an even more daunting task to force them to make the fundamental reassessment of their basic attitudes to all forms of sexuality, but until the lesbian and gay movement tackles that problem the achievement of full legal and social equality for everyone, regardless of their sexual preference, will remain a pipe dream.

In the shorter term the initiative for countering the prevailing prejudice and ignorance towards gay and lesbian lifestyles which underpins the entrenched myth of all homosexuals being sad and second-rate lies squarely with each individual. The concept of 'coming out' as the cornerstone of the gay rights movement dates back to the heady days of GLF, when it was believed that if every lesbian and gay man threw off their oppression and declared their own pride in their sexuality, discrimination would inevitably fade away and a new freedom would ensue. Although many lesbian and gay people have taken the difficult and courageous step of revealing themselves to the world at large and risked their reputations, livelihoods and personal relationships in the process, they have been in the minority. The closet has remained a safe and secure haven for the vast majority, undoubtedly influenced by the fact that the growing visibility of the gay community over the last two decades, far from creating greater tolerance and understanding, has alarmed the heterosexual majority and unleashed a homophobic backlash.

In part this reaction must have been influenced by the onset of Aids and the hysterical propaganda campaign around the concept of 'the gay plague' which served to reinforce the old definition of homosexuality as a moral and physical sickness which now had damning consequences not only in the next life, but in this one too. What was worse, it was impossible to identify who might be infected. At the very time when the thawing of the Cold War was making the old model of the homosexual as an automatic traitor outmoded, his role as a sexual fifth columnist was given a nasty new contemporary twist. As early as 1981 Roger Baker had attributed this particular fear to a belief in the 'body-snatcher principle' made popular in the 1950s science fiction film which had been re-made in 1979.[39] The alien 'body-snatchers' looked identical to humans, could recognise and communicate with each other, had appeared from nowhere, and increased their numbers by converting humans into their own kind. As more ordinary homosexuals have emerged into the light of day and thereby undermined the safe and comfortable stereotypes which were easy to laugh at, the old certainties have been eroded and it is now possible that anyone might be that way: the friendly stranger in the bus queue, work colleagues, your best friend, possibly even your husband or wife!!

The gay movement has to face up to these fears and find ways to allay them. It also has to be accepted that, while openly gay men and lesbians are now pursuing successful careers in many areas of public and political life (although still mainly in the media and the arts where they have always enjoyed a considerable degree of acceptance), there are important sections of the Establishment where the merest hint of homosexuality leads to disgrace and dismissal. This was illustrated very graphically in January 1990 when unsubstantiated allegations in the press of a 'gay scandal' among the Scottish judiciary were sufficient to bring about the resignation of one Judge, Lord Dervaird, despite the fact that no disciplinary or criminal charges were being laid against him. There was a tragic irony in the fact that the news of his departure was accompanied by assurances that homosexuality was not in itself a bar to an appointment as a judge. The recent American obsession with 'outing' – the deliberate exposure of an individual's homosexuality by the gay press – has so far been rejected in Britain, largely because of our more stringent libel laws. Forcing public figures out of the closet does nothing to further the cause of gay rights and reduces those involved to the level of the tabloid press who have mercilessly pursued such a vicious policy for the last decade.

At the height of the Clause 28 struggle a barrister had written to *Gay Times* citing details of his 43 year relationship with his partner (described as 'one of the country's best cancer specialists') which he claimed was just as morally acceptable as any Christian marriage, but he defended their need to remain anonymous in order to avoid 'unfortunate consequences'. Two correspondents subsequently attacked his decision to remain closeted as 'cowardice', arguing that by coming out he and his partner could disprove the view that homosexuals were incapable of stable relationships and undermine the bigots who he complained were perpetrating these myths. In reply the anonymous writer made a perfectly valid point.

> One method of winning a war is storming the battlements, the other is by way of infiltration.... We have friends who were magistrates and were required to stand down from the bench, friends who came out and were removed from the boards of prisons, schools and hospitals. What on earth has been achieved by this other than their own self-respect? Important as that has been it has hardly achieved anything for the gay movement.[40]

In the final analysis the lesbian and gay movement will only prosper if it capitalises on the diversity of the many individuals who make up its 'community' – whatever their sex, colour, creed or political persuasion. While the struggle for equality must be pursued, it must not distract us from our most important role: living and loving as gay men and lesbians. One of the characters makes this point very eloquently in Noel Greig's play *The Dear Love of Comrades* about the life and work of one of the earliest gay activists, Edward Carpenter.

Sit and write your books; about a world where there's no such thing as a couple, where there's no jealousy and no guilt; where it isn't a crime to love your own sex. Write till there's not a scrap of paper left and the ink's run dry. One day it might all come true, but there's people living here and now who'll thank you much more for doing the one thing that you're not supposed to do. Which is to be homosexual. Not to think and write and talk about it, but be it. In whatever way you can. And something else, you won't be thanked for it and you won't be remembered for it. But, you might be loved for it.[41]

NOTES

INTRODUCTION: MEDIEVAL AND MONSTROUSLY CRUEL LAWS

1 DRIBERG Tom, *Ruling Passions* (Jonathan Cape, London 1977)
2 3/9/43

CHAPTER ONE – A FIT SUBJECT FOR MUSIC HALL HUMOUR: 1950-6

1 H.C. Debs. Vol. 300, Cols 1397–8
2 11 August 1885
3 WESTWOOD Gordon, *Society and the Homosexual* (Gollancz, London 1952)
4 CUDLIPP Hugh, *At Your Peril* (Weidenfeld & Nicholson, London 1962)
5 *Sunday Pictorial* 25/5/52
6 *Sunday Pictorial* 8/6/52
7 WESTWOOD, op. cit.
8 *Sunday Times* 1/11/53
9 H.C. Debs. Vol. 521, Cols 1294–9
10 WILDEBLOOD Peter, *Against the Law* (Weidenfeld & Nicholson, London 1955)
11 28/3/54
12 BOOTHBY Sir Robert, *My Yesterday, Your Tomorrow* (Hutchinson, London 1962)
13 H.C. Debs. Vol. 526, Cols 1745–56
14 H.L. Debs. Vol. 187, Cols 737–67
15 WOLFENDEN Sir John, *Turning Points* (The Bodley Head, London 1976)
16 Ibid.
17 *New Statesman* 21/1/55
18 HALL CARPENTER ARCHIVES. GAY MEN'S ORAL HISTORY GROUP, *Walking after Midnight*, 'John Alcock' (Routledge, London 1989)

19 Ibid., 'David Ruffel'
20 RENAULT Mary, *The Charioteer* (Longman Green & Co, London 1953)
21 GARLAND Rodney, *The Heart in Exile* (W. H. Allen, London 1953)
22 WILDEBLOOD, op. cit.

CHAPTER TWO – TALKING METAPHYSICS TO A GOLDFISH: 1957–8

1 Command Paper No. 247
2 WOLFENDEN, Sir John, *Turning Points* (The Bodley Head, London 1976)
3 4/9/57
4 4/9/57
5 5/9/57
6 8/9/57
7 10/9/57
8 11/9/57
9 Rev. Dr Joseph Moffett in the *Scotsman* 6/9/57
10 *The Times* 9/10/57
11 Canterbury Diocesan Notes, October 1957
12 6/9/57
13 4/9/57
14 H. L. Debs. Vol. 206, Cols 733–832
15 *Gay News* No. 124 'Ten Years After'
16 Ibid.
17 31/10/58
18 15/11/58
19 3/11/58
20 December 1958
21 H. C. Debs. Vol. 596, Cols 365–507
22 27/11/58
23 27/11/58
24 30/11/58
25 27/11/58
26 28/11/58
27 30/11/58
28 WALKER Kenneth, *Sexual Behaviour, Creative and Destructive* (Kimber, London 1966)

CHAPTER THREE – KEEPING WOLFENDEN FROM THE WESTMINSTER DOOR: 1959–63

1 24/3/59
2 23/6/59
3 HALL CARPENTER ARCHIVES. GAY MEN'S ORAL HISTORY

GROUP, *Walking after Midnight* – Bernard Dobson (Routledge, London 1989)

4 29/6/60
5 28/6/60
6 H. C. Debs. Vol. 625, Cols 1453–514
7 3/7/60
8 30/6/60
9 30/6/60
10 30/6/60
11 3/7/60
12 18/5/60
13 ABSE Leo, *Private Member* (Macdonald & Co, London 1973)
14 H. C. Debs. Vol. 655, Cols 843–60
15 10/3/62
16 Albany Trust Pamphlets – Winter Talks 1962/3
17 21/10/64
18 21/10/61
19 CANT Bob and HEMMINGS Susan (Eds) *RADICAL RECORDS: Thirty Years of Lesbian and Gay History*, Chapter 2 – 'Battling for Wolfenden' by Allan Horsfall
20 20/5/60
21 *Guardian* 10/11/58
22 *News of the World* 24/7/60
23 30/4/63
24 25/10/62
25 3/9/61
26 HAUSER Richard, *The Homosexual Society* (The Bodley Head, London 1962); WESTWOOD Gordon, *A Minority* (Longmans, London 1960)
27 HERON Alastair (Ed.) *Towards a Quaker View of Sex* (Society of Friends 1963)
28 22/7/60
29 2/11/59

CHAPTER FOUR – BURBLING ON ABOUT BUGGERY: 1964–7

1 Home Office Statement 16/7/64
2 17/7/64
3 20/7/64
4 11/5/65
5 H.L. Debs. Vol. 266, Cols 71–172
6 H.L. Debs. Vol. 266, Cols 631–711
7 *Gay News* No. 124 'Ten Years After'
8 H. C. Debs. Vol. 713, Cols 611–20
9 4/6/65
10 28/5/65
11 N. O. P. 19–25 October 1965
12 H.L. Debs. Vol. 269, Cols 677–730

13 H.C. Debs. Vol. 724, Cols 782–874
14 13/2/66
15 5/2/66
16 19/2/66
17 10/2/66
18 3/6/65
19 8/6/65
20 10/6/65
21 11/2/66
22 H.L. Debs. Vol. 274, Cols 605–52
23 H.L. Debs. Vol. 275, Cols 146–77
24 H. C. Debs. Vol. 731, Cols 259–68
25 CROSSMAN Richard, *Diaries of a Cabinet Minister*, Vols 1–3 (Hamish Hamilton & Jonathan Cape, London 1975–7)
26 H. C. Debs. Vol. 738, Cols 1068–148
27 H. C. Debs. Vol. 748, Cols 2115–200
28 H. C. Debs. Vol. 749, Cols 1403–525
29 CROSSMAN, op. cit.
30 ABSE Leo, *Private Member* (Macdonald & Co, London 1973)
31 HALL CARPENTER ARCHIVES. GAY MEN'S ORAL HISTORY GROUP, *Walking after Midnight* – 'John Alcock' (Routledge, London 1989)
32 12/7/67
33 27/7/67
34 H. L. Debs. Vol. 285, Cols 522–6
35 *Guardian* 22/7/67; *Daily Telegraph* 22/7/67
36 FROST Brian (Ed.) *The Tactics of Pressure* (Galliard, London 1975)
37 RICHARDS, Professor Peter G., *Parliament and Conscience* (Allen & Unwin, London 1970)
38 *Encounter*, July 1972
39 ABSE, op. cit.
40 *Encounter*, op. cit.
41 *Gay News* No. 124 op. cit.
42 ABSE, op. cit.
43 *Gay News* No. 124 op. cit.

CHAPTER FIVE – GETTING RADICAL ABOUT THE WHOLE THING: 1967–73

1 WOLFENDEN Sir John, *Turning Points* (The Bodley Head, London 1976)
2 15/7/67
3 *Mister* Vol. 5, No. 2 Summer 1978 / *Gay News* No. 157 Dec. 1978: 'Ten Years Ago' by Roger Baker
4 *Gay Times* June 1987
5 16/9/67
6 24/3/68
7 *Titbits* 2/11/68

8 *Out* No. 5 (June/July 1977) 'Allan Horsfall: The Unsung Hero' by Jeff Grace
9 4/9/68
10 5/9/68
11 *New Statesman* 12/9/68
12 9/9/68
13 21/1/68
14 *Wolverhampton Express and Star* 12/1/68
15 'Gay power comes to Sheridan Square' by Lucien Truscot IV 3/7/69
16 HALL CARPENTER ARCHIVE. GAY MEN'S ORAL HISTORY GROUP, *Walking after Midnight* – 'John Fraser' (Routledge, London 1989)
17 Ibid. – 'Bernard Dobson'
18 2/1/71
19 17/1/71
20 8/1/71
21 Jan. 1971
22 *Watford Evening Echo* 14/1/71
23 9/4/71
24 WEEKS Jeffrey, *Coming Out: Homosexual Politics in Britain, from the Nineteenth Century to the Present* (Quartet, London 1977)
25 WALTER Aubrey (Ed.) *Come Together: the years of Gay Liberation 1970–73* (Gay Men's Press, London 1980)
26 *Western Daily Press* 15/6/72
27 *Gay News* No. 32 September 1973
28 WEEKS, op. cit.

CHAPTER SIX – STANDS ENGLAND WHERE IT DID?: 1973-7

1 10/4/73
2 *Hereford Evening News* 10/5/74
3 *Gay News* No. 163 March 1979 'CHE x 10'
4 *Malvern Gazette* 30/5/74
5 *Gay News* No. 47 June 1974
6 *Gay News* No. 43 March 1974
7 *Gay News* No. 41 March 1974
8 *Gay News* No. 4 August 1972
9 *Gay News* No. 58 November 1974
10 H. C. Debs. Vol. 885, Cols 1552–3
11 *Gay News* No. 64 February 1975
12 2/7/75
13 *Gay News* No. 76 July 1975
14 STURGESS Bob, *No Offence: The case for homosexual equality at law* (CHE, SMG, & USFI, London 1975)
15 *Gay News* No. 84 December 1975
16 Ibid.
17 *The Times* 10/3/76

18 *Scottish Daily Express*, Glasgow 16/3/76
19 H. C. Debs. Vol. 907, Cols 615–16
20 H. C. Debs. Vol. 907, Col. 258
21 *Gay News* No. 94 May 1976
22 29/1/76
23 11/7/76
24 16/5/76
25 11/5/76
26 *Gay News* No. 98 July 1976
27 H. C. Debs. Vol. 918, Col. 136
28 H. C. Debs. Vol. 917, Col. 264
29 H. C. Debs. Vol. 918, Cols 136–56
30 H. C. Debs. Vol. 918, Cols 1570–84
31 *Gay News* No. 111 January 1977
32 H. L. Debs. Vol. 383, Cols 164–96
33 *Gay News* No. 119 May 1977
34 H. L. Debs. Vol. 384, Cols 10–73
35 *Gay News* No. 122 June 1977
36 *Spectator* 16/7/77

CHAPTER SEVEN – TELLING THE CAT IT WAS DECLARED AN OFFICIAL VEGETARIAN: 1977–82

1 *Gay News* No. 128 October 1977
2 H. C. Debs. Vol. 935, Cols 645–65
3 H. C. Debs. Vol. 948, Col. 959 (21/4/78); Col. 1934 (28/4/78)
4 WHEEN Francis, 'Homosexuals Unite against Anglo-Saxon Attitudes', *New Statesman*.
5 8/3/79
6 22/2/79
7 *Gay News* No. 128 October 1977
8 *Gay News* No. 167 May 1979
9 Standing Committee F Official Report, Session 1979–80. Vol. IX, Cols 967–8
10 29/6/79
11 *The Times* 24/4/80
12 *Gay News* No. 193 June 1980
13 13/12/71
14 *Gay News* No. 183 November 1979
15 H. C. Debs. Vol. 989, Cols 284–322
16 28/7/80
17 23/7/80
18 The *Glasgow Herald* and the *Scotsman*, 27/8/80
19 *Gay News* No. 197 August 1980
20 *Gay News* No. 202 October 1980
21 H. L. Debs. Vol. 413, Cols 1810–69
22 H. C. Debs. Vol. 989, Col. 704 W

23 30/6/76
24 19/7/77; Northern Ireland Standing Advisory Commission on Human
   Rights, *Report on the Law Relating to Divorce and Homosexuality* (HMSO,
   London 1986)
25 18/7/77; H. C. Debs. Vol. 935, Cols 471–2
26 *Dublin Evening Press* 20/7/77
27 3/3/79
28 H. C. Debs. Vol. 963, Col. 1486
29 *Gay News* No. 163 March 1979
30 *Guardian* 8/5/79
31 H. C. Debs. Vol. 969, Col. 466 W
32 *Belfast Telegraph* 19/9/80
33 *Belfast News Letter* 20/9/80
34 H. L. Debs. Vol. 412, Col. 1581
35 *Gay News* No. 227 October 1981
36 *Gay News* No. 238 April 1982
37 *Belfast Telegraph* 15/3/82
38 H. C. Debs. Vol. 29, Cols 833–53
39 H. L. Debs. Vol. 435, Cols 412–25

CHAPTER EIGHT – THE LESSONS WE SO TEDIOUSLY UNLEARNED: 1982–4

1 *Gay News* No. 117 April 1977
2 *Gay News* No. 119 May 1977
3 *Gay News* No. 187 March 1980
4 *Report on the Age of Consent in Relation to Sexual Offences: Policy Advisory
   Committee on Sexual Offences.* April 1981 Cmnd. 8216
5 7/4/81
6 10/4/81
7 *The Times* 10/4/81
8 19/4/81
9 10/4/81
10 10/4/81
11 28/4/81
12 H. C. Debs. Vol. 5, Cols 244–55
13 *Gay News* No. 209 February 1981
14 *Gay News* No. 225 October 1981
15 *Gay News* No. 230 December 1981
16 H. C. Debs. Vol. 28, Cols 21–2
17 TATCHELL Peter, *The Battle for Bermondsey* (Heretic Books, London
   1983)
18 *Gay News* No. 260 March 1982
19 H. C. Debs. Vol. 50, Cols 580–644
20 H. C. Debs. Vol. 60, Cols 61–91
21 14/5/84
22 20/5/84
23 *Gay Times* No. 71 July 1984: 'Mediawatch' by Terry Sanderson

24 All press comments quoted in ibid.
25 *Capital Gay* 25/5/84
26 Report: H. L. Debs. Vol. 455, Cols 1093–186; 1199–252
27 H. C. Debs. Vol. 65, Cols 1111–21 (29/10/84)
28 Reported in the *Islington Gazette* 23/11/84

CHAPTER NINE – BEING DEFINED
BY OUR COCKS: 1984–6

1 17/12/81
2 11/12/81, 18/12/81
3 26/11/82
4 *Gay News* No. 258 January 1982
5 11/5/83
6 H. L. Debs. Vol. 443, Cols 894–6
7 21/11/84
8 21/12/84
9 *Daily Mail* 17/1/85
10 Ibid.
11 11/1/85
12 20/1/85
13 1/2/85
14 7/2/85
15 H. C. Debs. Vol. 73, Col. 14
16 13/2/85
17 19/2/85
18 18/2/85
19 24/2/85
20 22/2/85
21 H. C. Debs. Vol. 73, Cols 498–500 W
22 *Capital Gay* 29/3/85
23 *Capital Gay* 26/9/86
24 Dr Tony Pinching in *Sunday Times* 24/2/85
25 H. L. Debs. Vol. 461, Cols 358–87
26 SHILTS Randy, *And the Band Played On* (Penguin, Harmondsworth 1987)
27 30/8/85
28 15/9/85
29 27/9/85
30 2/10/85
31 *Capital Gay* 4/10/85
32 29/11/85
33 H. C. Debs. Vol. 88, Cols 1–2 W
34 6/12/85
35 13/12/85
36 26/9/85
37 30/3/86
38 25/4/86

39 KRAMER Larry, *The Normal Heart* (Methuen/Royal Court, London 1986)
40 21/2/85
41 *Capital Gay* 9/1/87
42 9/11/86
43 H. C. Debs. Vol. 105, Cols 801–66
44 8/1/87
45 12/11/86
46 Dr David Miller of the Middlesex Hospital; *Observer* 9/11/86
47 21/11/86
48 *Guardian* 12/12/86
49 12/12/86
50 12/12/86
51 14/12/86
52 *Guardian* 16/12/86
53 *Guardian* 13/12/86
54 Dr Runcie's comments as reported in the *Daily Mail* 22/11/86
55 FITZPATRICK Dr Michael and MILLIGAN Don, 'The Truth about the Aids Panic' (Junius, London 1987)

CHAPTER TEN – LIKE A TURKEY VOTING FOR CHRISTMAS: 1986–7

1 H. C. Debs. Vol. 61, Col. 86 W
2 H. C. Debs. Vol. 65, Cols 941–2 W
3 Reported in the *Guardian* 25–29 June 1985
4 12/11/85
5 9/4/86
6 10/4/86
7 *City Limits* 19/1/85: 'The Moral Majority Comes Out'
8 Comment by Councillor Andy Harris. Ibid.
9 *Capital Gay* 13/9/85
10 GLC (October 1985)
11 11/4/86
12 *Gay Times* No. 91 April 1986
13 18/10/85
14 18/10/85
15 2/5/86
16 3/5/86
17 6/5/86
18 16/5/86
19 H. L. Debs. Vol. 474, Cols 701–72
20 *Daily Telegraph* 3/6/86; *Daily Express* 4/6/86
21 Reported in the *Daily Mail* 1/7/86
22 27/7/86
23 H. L. Debs. Vol. 479, Col. 552
24 H. C. Debs. Vol. 106, Col. 759
25 H. C. Debs. Vol. 106, Cols 1176–246

26 H. L. Debs. Vol. 483, Cols 310–38
27 H. L. Debs. Vol. 484, Cols 179–83
28 H. L. Debs. Vol. 484, Cols 706–9
29 Second Reading Debate on 8 May: H. C. Debs. Vol. 115, Cols 997–1014
30 *Capital Gay* 31/1/86
31 Quoted in *Capital Gay* 13/3/87
32 During the programme Geoffrey Dickens also made the following comments about recriminalising homosexual behaviour: 'Sometimes we have to interfere with individual liberties to do what is right and I think you would find the general public would think that this was quite acceptable.... Certainly it would mean that we would have to close down gay and lesbian clubs and this sort of thing, and certainly publications would be limited.'
33 *Capital Gay* 5/6/87
34 *Capital Gay* 9/5/86
35 *Capital Gay* 29/5/87
36 26/5/87
37 26/5/87
38 *Capital Gay* 19/6/87
39 *Gay Times* July 1987
40 Ibid.

CHAPTER ELEVEN – A SMELL OF WEIMAR: 1987–8

1 *Guardian* 8/4/88
2 Standing Committees A and B Official Report Session 1987–8. Vol. II, Cols 1165–231
3 9/12/87
4 13/12/87
5 18/12/87
6 15/12/87
7 H. C. Debs. Vol. 124, Cols 987–1038
8 21/12/87
9 *Sun* 17/12/87
10 *Gay Times* January 1988
11 *The Times* 28/12/87
12 *Gay Times* January 1988
13 10/1/88
14 H. L. Debs. Vol. 491, Cols 947–1033
15 15/1/88
16 27/1/88
17 Reported in the *Independent* 25/1/88
18 25/1/88
19 Reported in the *Sun* 30/1/88
20 H. L. Debs. Vol. 492, Cols 846–99, 928–74, 993–1022
21 5/2/88
22 2/2/88

23 3/2/88
24 13/2/88
25 H. L. Debs. Vol. 493, Cols 585–643
26 *Gay Times* March 1988
27 22/2/88
28 H. L. Debs. Vol. 494, Cols 67–84
29 H. C. Debs. Vol. 129, Cols 370–432
30 24/5/88
31 26/5/88
32 *Observer* 22/5/88
33 29/5/88
34 18/3/88
35 Ibid.
36 *Gay Times* April 1988
37 14/1/88
38 18/1/88
39 10/2/88
40 23/1/88

CHAPTER TWELVE – AN AIR OF HOPE AND WILLINGNESS: INTO THE 1990s

1 *Gay Times* July 1988
2 *Gay Times* October 1988
3 *Gay Times* November 1988
4 Ibid.
5 *Capital Gay* 14/10/88
6 *Gay Times* June 1989
7 *Gay Times* December 1989
8 TATCHELL Peter, *Out in Europe* (Channel Four Television and Rouge Magazine 1990)
9 *Gay News* No. 226 October 1981
10 *Capital Gay* 10/2/84; 23/3/84
11 *Capital Gay* 1/12/89
12 *Capital Gay* 26/1/90
13 *Gay Times* March 1990
14 *Gay Times* December 1989
15 *Capital Gay* 18/5/90
16 *Open Mind* No. 4 (Conservative Group for Homosexual Equality [CGHE] Summer 1988)
17 *Daily Express* 12/2/90
18 Ibid.
19 H. C. Debs. Vol. 166, Cols 304–6 W
20 H. C. Debs. Vol. 167, Cols 390–1
21 *Gay Times* April 1990
22 11/5/90
23 *Gay Times* March 1990
24 *Gay Times* December 1989

25 *Guardian* 18/1/88
26 *Capital Gay* 27/2/87 (Letter)
27 12/2/88
28 *Capital Gay* 25/4/86
29 *Gay Times* December 1989
30 *Listener* 19/2/87
31 *Mister* Vol. 5, No. 2 Summer 1978/*Gay News* No. 157 Dec. 1978: 'Ten Years Ago' by Roger Baker
32 *Guardian* 28/5/90
33 SHEPHERD Simon and WALLIS Mick (Eds), *Coming on Strong: Gay Politics and Culture*, 'Gays and the Press' by Terry Sanderson (Unwin Hyman, London 1989)
34 *Gay Times* October 1986
35 *Guardian* 22/12/86
36 14/5/90
37 *Capital Gay* 18/5/90
38 *Gay Times* January 1989
39 *Gay News* No. 221 August 1981
40 *Gay Times* April 1988
41 GREIG Noel, *Two Gay Sweatshop Plays – Dear Love of Comrades* (Gay Men's Press, London 1981)

CHRONOLOGY

28 April 1954	Setting up of a Committee to study the law relating to homosexuality (later to become the Wolfenden Committee) announced in the House of Commons
19 May 1954	First Debate on Homosexuality in the House of Lords
4 September 1957	Wolfenden Report published
4 December 1957	Wolfenden Report debated by the House of Lords
May 1958	Homosexual Law Reform Society formed
26 November 1958	Wolfenden Report debated by the House of Commons
29 June 1960	Kenneth Robinson's motion asking the Government to 'take early action' to implement the Wolfenden Report defeated by 213 votes to 99
9 March 1962	Leo Abse's Bill to implement some of the Wolfenden proposals talked out in the House of Commons
15 July 1964	Director of Public Prosecutions asks for all cases of homosexual behaviour to be reported to him by Chief Constables
7 October 1964	The North Western Homosexual Law Reform Committee holds its inaugural meeting in Manchester with Allan Horsfall as its Secretary and Rev. Bernard Dodd as its Chairman
22 May 1965	The House of Lords debate homosexual law reform: the majority of speakers favour decriminalisation
24 May 1965	The House of Lords votes in favour of Lord Arran's Sexual Offences Bill to decriminalise homosexuality between consenting adults over the age of 21 by a majority of 94 to 49 votes
26 May 1965	Leo Abse's attempt to introduce the Sexual Offences Bill in the House of Commons under the Ten Minute Rule defeated by 178 votes to 159
28 October 1965	Sexual Offences Bill passes its Third Reading in the House of Lords by 116 votes to 46

8 December 1965	Humphrey Berkeley introduces the Sexual Offences Bill into the House of Commons
11 February 1966	Sexual Offences Bill passes its Second Reading in the Commons by 164 votes to 107
31 March 1966	Parliament dissolved for a general election: the Sexual Offences Bill automatically lapses
10 May 1966	Lord Arran re-introduces the Sexual Offences Bill into the Lords; it receives a Second Reading by 70 votes to 29
16 June 1966	Sexual Offences Bill passes its Third Reading in the Lords
5 July 1966	Leo Abse introduces the Sexual Offences Bill in the Commons under the Ten Minute Rule procedure and it is approved by 264 votes to 102
19 December 1966	Sexual Offences Bill passes its Second Reading in the Commons on a technicality
23 June 1967	Report Stage of the Sexual Offences Bill not completed due to filibuster by opponents
4 July 1967	Sexual Offences Bill passes its Third Reading in the Commons by 101 votes to 16
21 July 1967	Sexual Offences Bill passes its Third Reading in the House of Lords
27 July 1967	Sexual Offences Bill receives Royal Assent and passes into law
1969	The North Western Homosexual Law Reform Committee changes its name to the Committee for Homosexual Equality (CHE)
9 May 1969	Scottish Minorities Group (SMG) formed
28 June 1969	A police raid on the Stonewall Inn in New York's Greenwich Village sparks off a three day riot and the American Gay Liberation Movement is born
13 November 1970	First meeting of the British Gay Liberation Front at the London School of Economics
October 1971	GLF Manifesto published
January 1972	SMG launches its campaign to reform the law in Scotland and begins work on a draft Bill
June 1972	Law Lords find *International Times* guilty of a 'conspiracy to corrupt public morals' for publishing contact adverts for gay men
1 July 1972	First Gay Pride March takes place in London
8 April 1973	CHE holds its first National Conference in Morecambe
January 1974	Northern Ireland Campaign for Homosexual Law Reform (CHLR) set up
April 1974	At its second National Conference at Malvern CHE decides to launch a law reform campaign
June 1974	CHLR decides to prepare a case to present to the European Court of Human Rights arguing that the refusal of the UK Government to extend the 1967

	Act to Northern Ireland is an infringement of the European Convention of Human Rights
3 July 1975	A draft law reform Bill for the whole UK is launched by CHE, SMG and USFI
14 July 1975	Roy Jenkins asks the Criminal Law Revision Committee to investigate all sexual offences laws; it would first consider the law relating to the age of consent
10 March 1976	Merlyn Rees promises that the Northern Ireland Office will re-examine proposals to extend the 1967 Act to the province
3 November 1976	The attempt to have the clause consolidating the anti-gay laws in Scotland removed from a Scottish Consolidation Bill is defeated by 37 votes to 27
10 May 1977	Lord Boothby's Bill to extend the Sexual Offences Act to Scotland receives its Second Reading in the Lords by 125 votes to 27
14 June 1977	Lord Arran's Bill to reduce the homosexual age of consent to 18 is defeated in the Lords by 146 votes to 25
7 July 1977	Lord Boothby's Bill passes its Third Reading in the Lords and passes to the Commons
18 July 1977	Roy Mason promises to issue draft proposals to extend the Sexual Offences Act to Northern Ireland
19 October 1977	Ian Paisley launches 'Save Ulster from Sodomy' campaign
March 1978	The European Commission agrees to consider the case presented to it by Jeff Dudgeon who argues that he is being unfairly discriminated against as a gay man in Northern Ireland because of the British Government's refusal to extend the Sexual Offences Act to the province
28 April 1978	Robin Cook fails in his second attempt to get Lord Boothby's Scotland Bill introduced in the Commons
26 July 1978	The Order in Council to extend the Sexual Offences Act to Northern Ireland is published
March 1979	The Liberal Party produces a special mini-manifesto on gay rights
2 July 1979	Mrs Thatcher's Government announces that the Northern Ireland Order in Council will be dropped
22 July 1980	Robin Cook's amendment to the Criminal Justice (Scotland) Bill which extends the Sexual Offences Act to Scotland is passed by 203 votes to 80
August 1980	CHE Annual Conference votes to split the organisation into two parts: one for campaigning (CHE), and one for social needs and counselling (GCO)
19 September 1980	The European Commission of Human Rights decides that Jeff Dudgeon's case is admissible and passes it on to the European Court of Human Rights for judgment

21 October 1980	House of Lords pass Robin Cook's amendment to the Criminal Justice Bill by 59 votes to 48
10 April 1981	The Criminal Law Revision Committee recommends that the homosexual age of consent be reduced to 18
17 August 1981	Ken Livingstone gives strong backing to gay rights and promises that the GLC will introduce anti-discrimination policies to help to counter prejudice against the gay community
22 October 1981	European Court of Human Rights finds in favour of Jeff Dudgeon
18 March 1982	The Government publishes a draft Order in Council to extend the Sexual Offences Act to Northern Ireland
25 October 1982	The Order in Council extending the Sexual Offences Act to Northern Ireland is passed in the Commons by 168 votes to 21
February 1983	Peter Tatchell is defeated in the Bermondsey by-election after an unprecedented smear campaign by the tabloid press
31 January 1984	An attempt to remove the clause of the Police and Criminal Evidence Bill allowing arrest to be made for 'an affront to public decency' is defeated during the Committee stage by 11 votes to 7
14 May 1984	Jim Wallace's amendment to the Police and Criminal Evidence Bill proposing that arrests for soliciting should only be made by uniformed police officers in order to stop the police using *agent provocateur* tactics against gay men is defeated
16 May 1984	A new amendment to the Police Bill defining indecent assault as a 'serious arrestable offence' is passed by the House of Lords
29 October 1984	The final attempt to remove indecent assault for the list of serious arrestable offences is defeated in the Commons
10 November 1984	At a demonstration in Rugby, Labour MP Chris Smith publicly states that he is gay
14 February 1985	Health Minister announces in the Commons that Aids will not be made a notifiable disease, but that Health Authorities would have 'reserve powers' to detain highly infectious Aids patients
18 March 1985	First debate on Aids takes place in the House of Lords
4 October 1985	The Labour Party Annual Conference passes a motion calling for full legal equality for gay men and lesbians
12 November 1985	Conservative Party Chairman Norman Tebbit uses the Disraeli Memorial Lecture to launch an attack on the 'valueless values of the permissive society'
9 April 1986	Norman Tebbit makes another attack on the 'poisoned legacy of the permissive society'

2 June 1986	The Government introduces an amendment into the Education Bill to make local authorities ensure that sex education gives due emphasis to 'moral considerations' and the 'value of family life'
September 1986	The Labour Party Annual Conference passes a gay rights motion committing the next Labour Government to introduce legislation to outlaw discrimination against gay men and lesbians
21 November 1986	The House of Commons debates Aids for the first time
5 December 1986	Conservative MPs use a Commons debate on local government to attack the gay rights policies of London boroughs run by Labour councils
18 December 1986	Lord Halsbury's Bill to prevent local authorities promoting homosexuality passes its Second Reading in the Lords
3 February 1987	The Halsbury Bill passes its Committee Stage in the Lords
11 February 1987	The Halsbury Bill passes its Third Reading in the Lords
8 May 1987	Dame Jill Knight introduces the Halsbury Bill for its Second Reading in the Commons, but the debate is suspended as the Chamber is not quorate
24 May 1987	A law reform conference organised by the Campaign for Legislation for Lesbian and Gay Rights to draw up a new Bill of Lesbian and Gay Rights to be presented to the next Parliament is wrecked by factional disputes
11 June 1987	Chris Smith is re-elected to the House of Commons with a substantially increased majority
October 1987	Margaret Thatcher, at the Conservative Party Conference attacks the 'positive images' policies of Labour councils with her comment that 'Children... are being taught that they have an inalienable right to be gay'
8 December 1987	David Wilshire introduces a new amendment into the Committee Stage of the Local Government Bill which forbids local authorities from 'promoting homosexuality' or teaching the acceptability of homosexuality as a 'pretended family relationship'. This is accepted without a vote as Clause 28 of the Bill
15 December 1987	An Opposition attempt to amend Clause 28 during the Third Reading Debate is defeated
9 January 1988	Ten thousand gay men and lesbians march through London to protest against Clause 28
11 January 1988	Clause 28 discussed by the House of Lords in the Second Reading Debate on the Local Government Bill

1–2 February 1988	All opposition amendments to the Clause are defeated during its Committee stage in the House of Lords, although the Government offers several minor re-wordings. Angry lesbians abseil down from the public gallery at the end of the debate
16 February 1988	The Clause passes its Report Stage in the Lords
20th February 1988	A crowd of lesbians and gay men (estimated at 13,000–20,000) march through Manchester to protest against the Clause
29 February 1988	The Clause passes its Third Reading in the Lords
9 March 1988	An Opposition amendment to Clause 28 is defeated by 254 to 201 votes during its Third Reading in the Commons and becomes Section 28 of the Local Government Act
24 May 1988	Section 28 comes into force
October 1988	The Labour Party Conference and the SLD Party Conference both back gay rights legislation and pledge that they will scrap Section 28. Chancellor Nigel Lawson affirms his belief that Section 28 was 'right' and makes homophobic comments in a pre-conference TV interview
January 1989	First meeting of British ACT-UP
May 1989	The Stonewall Group is set up
13 February 1990	Shadow Home Secretary Roy Hattersley announces that a Labour Government would permit a free vote on reducing the gay male age of consent to 16
15 February 1990	Prime Minister Margaret Thatcher tells the Commons that any reduction in the gay male age of consent would be 'wholly unacceptable'
5–6 May 1990	CHE celebrates its 21st birthday with an annual conference decision to concentrate its campaign on the reduction of the gay male age of consent to 16
10 May 1990	Direct action group OutRage is established
11 May 1990	The Stonewall Group begin to circulate a draft Homosexual Equality Bill for discussion in the lesbian and gay movement

GAY CAMPAIGNING GROUPS

Campaign for Homosexual Equality
PO Box 342, London WC1X 0DU
Tel: (071) 833 3912

Conservative Group for Homosexual Equality (CGHE)
Box BM/CGHE, London WC1N 3XX

International Lesbian and Gay Association: UK Group,
c/o: Nigel Warner,
141, Cloudsley Road,
London N1 0EN

Tel: (071) 278 1496

Labour Campaign for Lesbian and Gay Rights
PO Box 306,
London N5 2SY

Social and Liberal Democrats for Lesbian and Gay Action (DELGA)
SLD HQ,
4, Cowley Street,
London SW1P 3NB

Tel: (0734) 588785

Stonewall Group and Iris Trust,
2, Greycoat Place,
London SW1P 1SB

Tel: (071) 222 9007

Scottish Homosexual Rights Group (SHRG)
58A, Broughton Street,
Edinburgh EH1 3SA

Tel: (031) 557 2625

Northern Ireland Gay Rights Association (NIGRA)
PO Box 44, Belfast BT1 1SH

Tel: (0232) 664111

Up to date information on these contacts and any other gay or lesbian-related matters can be obtained from:

London Lesbian and Gay Switchboard,
BM Switchboard,
London WC1N 3XX

Tel: (071) 837 7324 [24hrs]

NAME INDEX

SUBJECT INDEX